Navigating Athletic Identity, Retirement Transitions, and Self-Discovery

Navigating Athletic Identity, Retirement Transitions, and Self-Discovery

Exiting the Arena

Gary Senecal and Christian Williams

LEXINGTON BOOKS
Lanham • Boulder • New York • London

Published by Lexington Books
An imprint of The Rowman & Littlefield Publishing Group, Inc.
4501 Forbes Boulevard, Suite 200, Lanham, Maryland 20706
www.rowman.com

86-90 Paul Street, London EC2A 4NE

British Library Cataloguing in Publication Information Available

Library of Congress Cataloging-in-Publication Data

Names: Senecal, Gary, author. | Williams, Christian (College teacher), author.
Title: Navigating athletic identity, retirement transitions, and self-discovery : exiting the arena / Gary Senecal and Christian Williams.
Description: Lanham, Maryland : Lexington Books, [2024] | Includes bibliographical references and index. | Summary: "Athletes might face a myriad of psychosocial difficulties when they retire from professional or elite level competition. This book explores the nuances of those struggles, focusing on identity reconstruction and the processing of grief related to the loss of self and sport"-- Provided by publisher.
Identifiers: LCCN 2023057935 (print) | LCCN 2023057936 (ebook) | ISBN 9781666929812 (cloth) | ISBN 9781666929829 (epub)
Subjects: LCSH: Athletes--Psychology. | Athletes--Retirement. | Adjustment (Psychology)
Classification: LCC GV706.4 .S458 2024 (print) | LCC GV706.4 (ebook) | DDC 796.092--dc23/eng/20240212
LC record available at https://lccn.loc.gov/2023057935
LC ebook record available at https://lccn.loc.gov/2023057936

Contents

Introduction

Elite athletes dedicate a significant portion of their lives to their respective sports, honing their skills, pushing their limits, and achieving at the highest levels of competition. Their journeys, filled with dedication, sacrifices, and countless hours of training, often start in the quiet corners of playgrounds, gymnasiums, and training fields. However, every athletic career, no matter how illustrious, ultimately comes to an end. The transition from the pinnacle of competition to retirement is not just a culmination of physical endeavors, but a pivotal moment in an athlete's narrative, encompassing a unique blend of challenges, reflections, and adaptations. For some athletes, the decision to retire is a deliberate decision, a poised exit at the peak of their capabilities. For others, it's an abrupt conclusion dictated by an unforeseen injury. And there are those who grapple with the disheartening reality of deselection, a deviation from the narrative they had envisioned for their careers.

A vast body of research has been devoted to understanding this transition, with a particular focus on the retirement and deselection experiences of elite athletes. This collective body of research has made strides in revealing nuances of the complex mosaic of athletic retirement. Research in gerontology and thanatology have drawn parallels between the journey of athletic retirement and the aging and end-of-life journey in the broader population. While the time frame may be condensed for athletes, the psychological and emotional challenges they encounter in retirement closely mirror those observed in the aging and end-of-life phases of the general population.

In addition to these valuable contributions, another substantial body of research has been dedicated to understanding the transformation of one's identity during the transition to athletic retirement (Brewer et al., 1993; Petitpas et al., 2013). At the core of these discussions had been the importance of identity reconstruction and reconceptualization in the post-sport phase. Athletes who manage to diversify their self-identity often find their post-sport transition smoother, allowing them to anchor themselves in new endeavors. Yet, it's not uncommon for athletes to grapple with what's termed "identity foreclosure" during their careers—an unwavering attachment to their athletic persona (Brewer et al., 1993; Marcia, 1966; Petitpas & France, 2010). This constricted self-view often extends into their post-athletic lives, binding them to a singular, often stifling athletic persona, which can impede their capacity to adapt, evolve, or even relinquish their athletic identity.

Despite the wealth of research available, there remains a noticeable gap, particularly in the exploration of the complex emotions of elite performance and transition to athletic retirement, including the experiences of grief and loss, which often intertwine with an athlete's process of identity transformation after retiring from their sport (Manthley & Smith, 2023). In the current project, we explored the well-established concept of athletic identity by considering transitioning identity as a potential dimension of loss. Ultimately, we posit that identity transition can manifest as two distinct forms of loss. For some individuals, it represents a loss of their athletic identity, while for others, it signifies the cessation of performance at an elite level. By understanding the emotional and psychological impact of the retirement transition in athletes, we can gain valuable insights to better support and facilitate their successful navigation through career transitions and life after sports.

This book delves deeply into the multifaceted journeys of these transitions, providing a close-up view of the emotional, psychological, and physical landscapes that elite athletes navigate as they depart from the competitive arena. It shares accounts of the diverse experience of athletes including triumphant farewells and painful goodbyes, tales of personal reinvention, battles with identity loss, the quest for new passions, the weight of public and private expectations, and the resilience and adaptability required to find new purpose outside the spotlight. It includes stories of athletes who faced their vulnerabilities head-on, of those who rediscovered themselves beyond the field, and of those who grappled with the weight of unfulfilled dreams. From vulnerable accounts of transformation to the poignant moments of reflection, this book captures the raw, unfiltered essence of what it truly means to exit the arena.

Chapter 1

Setting the Stage

EXPLORING ATHLETIC TRANSITION THROUGH THE LENS OF IDENTITY THEORY

An athlete's journey is a dynamic and multidimensional compilation of experiences, self-discovery, and personal growth. At the heart of this journey lies the complex and intricate concept of athlete identity, a facet of one's overall identity that is uniquely shaped by participation in sports and athletic endeavors. According to Brewer and colleagues (1993), athletic identity is the "degree to which an individual identifies with the athlete role" (p. 237) and incorporates this role into their self-concept. This identity represents the value and significance individuals associate with being an athlete and reflects how individuals perceive themselves in relation to their athletic performance (Brewer et al. 1993).

Seminal research by Brewer and colleagues (1993) operationalized the concept of athletic identity and provided a systematic approach to understanding just how profound an effect this psychosocial construct can have on athletes during competition and in the midst of retirement or deselection. In particular they recognized that athletes often have a unidimensional self-concept, identifying themselves primarily as athletes to the exclusion of other roles (Brewer et al., 1993). From this research, the original 10-item version of the Athletic Identity Measurement Scale (AIMS) was developed (Brewer et al., 1993). The AIMS was originally designed to encapsulate "both strength and exclusivity of identification with the athlete role," as well as to encompass the "social, cognitive, and affective aspects of athletic identity" (Brewer et al., 1993, p. 242). In essence, the AIMS sought to measure the degree to which an individual identifies with the athlete role (Brewer & Cornelius, 2001).

The AIMS offers a quick, reliable, and valid method for screening these important aspects of athletes' personalities. It functions as a resource to assist in identifying athletes who may be more susceptible to facing the challenges associated with having a strong and exclusive athletic identity (Brewer et al., 1993; Brewer et al., 2022). The AIMS has been revalidated and updated over the years, shaping the understanding of athletic identity as a complex structure that involves personal and social identity around the sport, which may lead to positive outcomes, but can also have negative effects on an individual (Brewer et al., 2022). The 7-item version of the Athletic Identity Measurement Scale (AIMS) was created as a result of a refinement process to reduce redundancy of construct. Brewer and Cornelius (2001) found that this shortened version increased efficiency without sacrificing its effectiveness. Both the original 10-item AIMS and the 7-item AIMS (AIMS-7) are used today. The choice between the two often depends on the specific needs of the research or clinical setting. We have chosen to utilize the original 10-item version with our participants in this study.

Athletic identity is often deeply intertwined with an individual's self-concept and self-worth (Brewer et al. 1993), especially if they have invested a significant amount of time and effort into their sport, forming a crucial aspect of their overall self-identity. Excelling in their sport can significantly enhance an athlete's self-esteem and self-worth, providing them with a sense of accomplishment and pride (Brewer et al., 1993). This positive reinforcement can be a powerful motivator and contribute to a robust and healthy self-image. However, athletes often face challenges that can threaten this self-perception, such as injuries, deselection, or unexpected transitions into retirement. These obstacles can have a profound and often negative impact on an athlete's self-worth and self-concept, leading to feelings of loss, frustration, or inadequacy. The dichotomy between the highs of success and the lows of facing hurdles is a common thread in many athletes' careers, illustrating the double-edged nature of athletic identity. To fully appreciate the complexities of athletic retirement, we posit that it is important to consider the development and subsequent deconstruction of athletic identity through the lens of identity theory.

EXPLORING THE LAYERS OF SELF: THE ROLE OF IDENTITY THEORY IN ATHLETIC IDENTITY FORMATION

Identity can be described as a multifaceted and evolving self-perception that encompasses various aspects of an individual's personality, beliefs, and values, and is influenced by their experiences and social interactions (Ellemers et al., 2002; Vignoles, 2017). The formation of athletic identity can be understood through the lens of identity theory, which offers a framework for understanding the ways in which individuals come to adopt and embody their roles.

In the context of athletic identity, this theory helps to conceptualize how individuals integrate the role of being an athlete into their overall self-concept, a self-perception that is influenced both by their personal perceptions and the external social and cultural forces at play. On a personal level, individuals must develop the skills, discipline, and commitment required to succeed in their sport. This involves countless hours of practice, as well as a dedication to maintaining a healthy lifestyle and staying in peak physical condition. In addition to personal factors, social factors also play a crucial role in the formation of an athletic identity. Relationships with coaches, teammates, and competitors provide a support system that helps individuals navigate the challenges of their sport. These relationships also contribute to a sense of belonging and a shared identity with others who understand the demands of being an athlete.

Identity theory, rooted in symbolic interactionism (SI), provides a framework for understanding the complex and nuanced interplay between individuals and the broader social structures that surround them. In SI, the emphasis is on how individuals derive meaning and construct their identities through interactions with others and the society at large (Stryker, 2002). Identity theory builds on this by focusing specifically on the role-based identities that people develop as part of their social interactions. According to Stryker (2002), individuals occupy multiple roles, such as parent, teacher, or friend, each with associated expectations and norms, contributing to their overall self-concept. Stryker emphasized the traditional and standard aspects of role identities, which are ingrained in social networks. In these networks, each role comes with its own associated identity (Stryker & Burke, 2000). Identity emerges as a result of the internalization of the expectations and norms associated with the particular social positions, or role the individual occupies, weaving itself into the very fabric of an individual's self-concept and acting as a compass that guides behavior.

These roles contribute to the formation of multiple identities, which are organized hierarchically in terms of salience, with some identities being more salient or important to the individual and central to an individual's self-concept than others (McCall & Simmons, 1978; Stets & Burke, 2014). This term, identity salience, coined by Stryker (1968), refers to the prominence of a particular identity within an individual's self-concept which can be directly influenced by support, commitment, and rewards (McCall & Simmons, 1978). The salience of an identity is influenced by the commitment individuals have to their roles and the support they receive from their social networks. This theory emphasizes the importance of role commitment, which is the degree to which an individual identifies with a specific role and is willing to invest time and resources into fulfilling the role's expectations. The more salient an identity is, the more likely it is to be invoked in a given situation, guiding the individual's behavior and interactions (Stryker, 1968).

Athletic identity, then, can be seen as one of the many identities that an individual may possess, and its salience will depend on factors such as the individual's level of involvement in the sport, the significance of the sport to the individual, and the social support and recognition that the individual receives from others in relation to their athletic pursuits. The first step in the formation of athletic identity is exposure and initiation into the world of sports. This step can be understood through the concept of "role-taking," where individuals internalize the expectations and behaviors associated with a particular role (Stryker & Burke, 2000); in this case, the role of athlete. As individuals engage in sports, they begin to incorporate the norms, values, and behaviors associated with being an athlete into their self-concept. As the individual continues to invest time and effort into developing their athletic skills, they experience identity salience. The more an individual invests in the athlete role, the more salient this identity becomes, and the more likely the individual is to engage in behavior and choices that align with this identity. This commitment to specific roles is what shapes an individual's social behavior.

Socialization and group membership also play a crucial role in the formation of athletic identity assisting in defining boundaries of behavior, presenting opportunities, fueling motivations, and shaping objectives. Through interactions with coaches, teammates, and other individuals in the athletic community, individuals further internalize the norms and expectations associated with the athlete role. These social interactions contribute to the development of a "role-identity," where the individual's behavior and self-concept are shaped by the expectations associated with the athlete role (Stryker, 2000). In this view, athletic identity and the structures associated with sports serve as enduring frameworks that shape the opportunities and constraints athletes encounter throughout their athletic journeys, profoundly affecting the trajectory of their athletic identities and social behaviors.

Performance and achievement in sport also contribute to the formation of athletic identity. Success in competition can lead to positive feedback from significant others, such as coaches, teammates, and family, further reinforcing the athlete identity. This positive feedback can lead to an increase in "commitment," where the individual becomes more invested in the athlete role and is more likely to engage in behavior consistent with this identity (Stryker & Burke, 2000). Over time, the athlete role becomes integrated into the individual's self-concept, and they begin to see themselves as an athlete. This process of role integration and internalization is influenced by the individual's personal values, beliefs, and experiences, as well as the social and cultural context in which they are embedded. The athletic identity is not static and may evolve over time as the individual's life circumstances, interests, and priorities change. This perspective highlights the active role athletes play in constructing and adapting their athletic environment, emphasizing the reciprocal influence between their athletic self and the sports community.

In the realm of sports, athletes often undergo significant changes and transitions, from active competition to retirement. How these individuals navigate these transitions can be profoundly influenced by their athletic identity. As we delve into this topic, we will examine the ways in which identity theory can provide insights into the challenges and opportunities that athletes face as they move through different stages of their careers.

EXPLORING THE DYNAMICS OF IDENTITY FORECLOSURE

While we have seen that an individual typically possesses multiple identities arranged in a hierarchy of salience, it is important to note that one identity can emerge as the predominant or preferred one. This dominant identity then becomes the principal filter through which individuals perceive themselves and their various other identities (Lally, 2007). When an individual overly focuses on a singular identity, it often benefits that primary role at the expense of exploring and investing in other relevant or age-appropriate roles (Lally, 2007; Lavallee & Robinson, 2007; Murphy et al., 1996). This typically occurs when an individual's identity becomes so salient that other potential identities or roles are disregarded or undervalued. At times the individual's commitment is based on the ideas and values of others, such as parental or societal expectations, rather than being a result of their own self-exploration and discovery. This neglect of diverse roles, due to the dominance of one, can lead to potential identity challenges later on (Brewer et al., 1993; Lally, 2007; Stryker, 2000). Individuals may at times lack the understanding or examination of their own desires, visions, or values (Brewer & Pepitas, 2017). Consequently, they can struggle when exposed to new perspectives or experiences that challenge their unexamined identity roles.

Petitpas (1978) was one of the first psychologists to bring light to identity research as it related specifically to athletes. He coined the term "athletic identity foreclosure" to describe the tendency of elite athletes to construct narrow forms of identity, centered primarily or solely on their athletic self, and to the foreclosure of other forms of self. This phenomenon is often seen in young athletes who fully commit to the role of being an athlete at an early age without exploring other potential facets of their identity (Borak et al., 2022; Brewer & Peptitpas, 2017). This athletic identity becomes so consuming that it limits the exploration of other identities, causing identity foreclosure. While this can lead to success in their athletic careers, it may lead to difficulties later in life when their sports career ends, as they have defined their identity so narrowly and haven't developed other aspects of self (Grove et al. 1997). High levels of athletic identity have also been correlated with increased mood disturbances after sustaining an injury (Brewer et al., 1993). It is important to note that athletic identity and identity foreclosure should be seen as separate constructs as not every athlete with high athletic identity engages in identity foreclosure (Good et al., 1993) and despite the multitude of risks, athletic identity is correlated with many positive attributes that increase athletic performance (Borak et al., 2022). However, the concept of identity foreclosure helps us understand the dynamics of identity formation and the potential issues that can arise when one misses a critical exploration phase in their personal development.

NAVIGATING THE TRANSITION: THE EXPERIENCE OF ATHLETIC RETIREMENT

The transition from elite athletic performance to retirement is a complex journey encountered by all athletes at some stage in their careers. It signifies a shift from a lifestyle characterized by rigorous training schedules, intense competition, and the physical demands of sports, propelling athletes into a new chapter filled with different challenges and opportunities. The range of emotions that accompany this transition can be extensive, including grief and loss, as athletes grapple with leaving behind their athletic identities, structured routines, social networks, and the adrenaline-fueled world of competitive sports. Additionally, athletes may experience feelings of relief, excitement, fear, anxiety, or even depression as they navigate this pivotal life change. This transition has been found to increase the risk of psychosocial challenges, including mental health symptoms (Miller & Buttell, 2017; Wilkinson, 2021), as athletes navigate a myriad of challenges that can significantly reshape their self-concept and overall identity. This underscores the importance of comprehensively understanding the intricate emotional landscape and complexities that retiring athletes navigate. As we explore the complexities and emotional terrain experienced by athletes during this significant life shift, we gain insights into the profound effects it can have on their self-concept and overall sense of self.

Unlike other forms of career retirement or deselection from the workforce, one of the most unique aspects of athletic retirement is just how early in life it happens and just how short of a professional career most athletes have. The average age of professional retirement from most sports occurs at some point in the athletes' twenties, after roughly three to seven years of professional competition (de Subijana, et al., 2020). Furthermore, leaving sport has also been conceptualized as a form of "social death" as it may lead to unemployment, psychological crisis, depression, confusion, and loss of identity (Houlston, 1982; Lally, 2007; Weiss, 2001). According to Alfermann's (2000) findings, approximately 15–20 percent of retired elite athletes encounter transition distress, necessitating mental health support to adapt to this considerable life shift.

Athletic identity and its accompanying social status, once considered a protective factor for mental health and overall well-being, now prove to have a negative impact on elite athletes' emotional well-being (Fortunato & Marchant, 1999; Sothern & O'Gorman, 2021). This negative impact is influenced by various factors such as the pressures of elite competition, the need to preserve their identity, and the constant demand to stay relevant and be selected (Sothern & O'Gorman, 2021). For elite athletes, winning, results, and achievements hold paramount significance and are intimately linked to their mental well-being, identity, and self-worth (Buckley et al., 2019; Douglas & Carless, 2009).

In studies focusing on elite-level athletes, researchers identified a negative correlation between strong athletic identity, identify foreclosure, and adaptive coping strategies during the transition to retirement (Grove et al., 2013; Park et al., 2013). Athletes with higher levels of identity foreclosure experienced more significant challenges during the transition process in regards to mental and behavioral disengagement, denial, poor coping strategies, and emotional dysregulation, often requiring lengthier adjustment periods (Douglas & Carless, 2009; Lavallee et al., 1997; Parkes, 1988; Torregrosa et al., 2015). Similar to other significant life transitions that demand psychosocial adaptation, retiring from elite performance necessitates athletes to reevaluate their self-concept, constructed worldview, and self-assumptions (Alfermann et al., 2004; Den Elzen et al., 2022). They must strive to reconcile the life they are moving toward with the life they once had as elite athletes, a journey that is even more complex when the transition is unexpected, sudden, or outside of their control (Alfermann et al., 2004; Fortunato & Marchant, 1999). Athletes who encounter an unforeseen termination of their careers or face deselection are more prone to experiencing distress during retirement compared to those who voluntarily choose to retire on their own terms (Blakelock et al., 2016; Fortunato & Marchant, 1999; McGlinchey et al., 2022; Wippert & Wippert, 2010). These athletes are more likely to have unfinished business via unmet career goals or aspirations and to feel cheated (Barcza-Renner et al. 2020). This holds especially true for athletes who experience a career-ending injury, as it has consistently been linked to increased distress, lower scores in mental health assessments, and the adoption of maladaptive behaviors, including disordered eating and substance abuse (Furie et al., 2023; Mannes et al., 2019).

As elite athletes transition into retirement, they often encounter various consequences, such as experiencing feelings of loss and sadness (Menke & Germany, 2019), anger and resentment (Kaul, 2017), diminished self-esteem and confidence (Schmid et al., 2023), symptoms of anxiety (Wilkinson, 2021), depression (Menke & Germany, 2019), sleep challenges, and difficulties in social functioning (Blakelock et al., 2016). A meta-analysis conducted by Gouttebarge and colleagues (2019) found that the occurrence of mental health symptoms varied among elite athletes with prevalence rates ranging from 16 percent for psychological distress and 26 percent for anxiety and depression. When athletes' careers are terminated involuntarily these experiences can be exceptionally intense and involve thoughts of suicide, suicide attempts, and traumatic experiences (Miller & Buttell, 2017). Moreover, athletes may encounter various secondary losses, not all of which are sport-related (Menke & Germany, 2019). These losses include the loss of self (Manthey & Smith, 2023; Papa & Maitoza, 2013; Wilkinson, 2021), the loss of purpose and meaning, the loss of structure and routine in their daily lives (Menke & Germany, 2019; Papa & Maitoza, 2013), the loss of social support and camaraderie (Manthley & Smith, 2023), the loss of community, and for many, the loss of a body that performed at peak physicality (Buckley et al., 2019; Manthey & Smith, 2023). Menke and Germany's study (2019) suggests that athletes may encounter more significant emotional challenges related to the loss of identity compared to unfulfilled sports goals or careers.

In athletic retirement, feelings of grief and loss are common (Fortunato & Marchant, 1999) as athletes experience a loss of identity as elite athletes and the status associated with it, loss of opportunities to perform as athletes, and loss of athletic dreams (Fortunato & Marchant, 1999). These losses are often not recognized by others (Menke & Germany, 2019). The lack of recognition of athletic retirement as a loss means that it is more likely to be disenfranchised, which undermines individuals' resilience and their ability to move on with their lives. For elite athletes, grief can take many forms and requires that they leave behind a significant part of themselves, and for some, their athletic identity, in order to move forward with the next chapter of their lives. While not all athletes will encounter substantial psychological distress during the retirement transition, the majority do acknowledge it as a profoundly challenging period in their lives. For some, the experience is comparable to losing a good friend, further highlighting its emotional significance (Menke & Germany, 2019). Numerous athletes have expressed being unprepared to handle the emotional symptoms that arise during this transition (Menke & Germany, 2019) and the many layers of unexpected losses (Manthey & Smith, 2023).

Many athletes report experiencing what is often referred to as "body grief," a process of mourning and lamenting the loss of the athletic ideal and grappling with the changes or limitations of their physical body (Broadwater, 2022). This phenomenon is particularly common among elite athletes who have dedicated much of their lives to achieving peak physical performance and identifying with their athletic prowess (Silver, 2021). The transition away from the athletic lifestyle can evoke a myriad of complex emotions as athletes adapt to a new reality. In this new phase, their bodies may no longer perform at the same high level, undergo changes in appearance and sensations, and be susceptible to the lingering effects of sports-related injuries, resulting in a mixture of feelings and challenges to navigate (Silver, 2021; Stephen & Bilard, 2003). Athletes frequently grapple with emotions related to body dissatisfaction, difficulties in adjusting to changes in weight or muscle mass, and challenges in accepting their natural body composition when confronted with deeply ingrained body ideals (Buckley et al., 2019; Papathomas et al., 2017; Stephen & Bilard, 2003). The experience of body grief can be a significant element in an athlete's transition to retirement, adding complexity to the adaptation process as they mourn the loss of their former athletic physique or the idealized body they had envisioned. As a result, athletes may resort to maladaptive and compensatory coping mechanisms, such as restricting food intake or engaging in excessive exercise, in an attempt to regain control over their body changes (Buckley et al., 2019; Papathomas et al, 2017). Adapting to retirement necessitates that elite athletes cultivate fresh perspectives, establish new routines, and build different relationships with food, exercise, and their bodies, aligning with a post-sport lifestyle. Often, this process involves undoing years of maladaptive beliefs and relearning the true capacity of their bodies and what constitutes a healthy fitness regimen in their new phase of life.

Elite athletes have consistently oriented their decisions toward performance outcomes throughout their careers, prioritizing a lifestyle that often restricted engagement in various activities and social interactions, favoring those that would optimize performance over simply enjoying them (Manthey & Smith, 2023). During their athletic careers, they were part of teams that provided them with continuous companionship, connected them with like-minded individuals who shared a competitive drive, and acted as a community and support system for several years (Manthey & Smith, 2023; Wippert & Wippert, 2008). In high-level professional careers such as professional sports, individuals frequently identify as much with the people they work with as they do with the work itself (Fowlkes, 1990). The relationships formed in the workplace have been compared to the level of commitment found in marriages (Fowlkes, 1990). Upon retirement, many athletes experience a rapid loss of this valuable resource and connection point as they are no longer part of the team, and daily interactions with teammates are no longer part of their routine and experience. Their lifestyles, which were once centered solely around athletic performance, now contain a significant void where their team and coaches once were. Athletes may struggle to find similar connections and support systems in their post-athletic lives. Moreover, due to society's failure to fully recognize the depth of these relationships, the loss of teammates is often not validated, leading to an additional layer of disenfranchisement in the athlete's grief experience, as they mourn the absence of those relationships in their lives.

The presence of social support, both during the career transition and in the postretirement phase, can be highly influential. It acts as a protective factor, helping to mitigate the negative consequences and feelings of loss that often accompany this life-changing event (Brown et al., 2018; Lavallee et al., 2007; Parkes et al., 2013). However, despite the positive influence of support for athletes the type and quality of social support that athletes have access to varies significantly (Park et al., 2013). Athletes who lack access to strong social support systems or perceive them as lacking understanding and empathy often encounter greater challenges during the transition and may experience increased feelings of isolation (Brown et al., 2018). Furthermore, the findings from a study by Brown and colleagues' (2018) identified that athletes frequently experience struggles and are hesitant to seek support, particularly concerning mental health issues. These emotions may be connected to the perceived social costs associated with losing their "elite" identity in the sports world (Brown et al., 2018) as well as the stigma associated with help seeking and expressions of vulnerability within this population (Gouttebarge et al., 2019; Manthey & Smith, 2023). Despite the recognized value of professional support and mental health counseling during this transition and into retirement (Wilkinson, 2021), widespread disengagement with such services has been observed (Mannes et al., 2019).

The way deselection is managed within elite sports culture has been identified as a significant contributing factor to the challenges athletes face during retirement. McGlinchey et al. (2022) and Wilkinson (2021) highlight that many athletes find this process stressful, embarrassing, and traumatic, often neglecting the human behind the performance metrics. This is especially true when release conversations occur publicly, in front of teammates, when athletes learn about it from external sources before being informed by the coach, or when deselection comes as a complete surprise (McGlinchey et al., 2022). The handling of such scenarios varies widely, with some individuals caught completely off guard, experiencing a period of shock, while others have the opportunity to prepare themselves for the upcoming changes. This confirms previous research that indicates that athletes who perceive a higher level of control over their lives tend to experience more positive transitions (Park et al., 2013). The findings of Wippert and Wippert's (2008) research indicate that the manner in which the retirement process is handled and the level of support received can have a substantial impact on athletes' well-being, influencing factors such as sleep patterns, alcohol consumption, and how they perceive negative events during the transition period. This suggests that having a sense of agency and influence in their postretirement endeavors can contribute to a smoother and more fulfilling transition for athletes leaving their competitive careers.

Cultural expectations surrounding retirement can create misconceptions about how to approach this life transition and the grief that often accompanies it. For instance, expecting athletes to immediately transition into the next phase of their lives may hinder their capacity to process grief effectively and utilize adaptive coping mechanisms (Manthey & Smith, 2023). As a result, athletes who face challenges during the retirement transition or experience mental health struggles may encounter stigma, especially if they haven't yet determined their next steps or future plans. The transition into retirement for elite athletes is influenced by numerous psychosocial factors, making each individual's experience unique. These factors include the level of identity foreclosure, individual self-concept, the reasons behind their retirement, their perception of control over the process, the level of social support they receive, their financial stability, and the resources available to them (Brown et al., 2018; Fortunato & Marchant, 1999; Lavallee et al., 1997; Mannes et al., 2019; Menke & Germany, 2019). Therefore, gaining insights into the transition through the perspectives of elite athletes becomes essential. By acknowledging that this process poses challenges for most elite athletes, our examination of these obstacles can serve as a means to offer support and motivation, rather than focusing solely on the negative aspects of the transition. The purpose of this research was to explore the lived experience of athletic retirement for elite athletes, understanding their subjective encounters, the significance they attach to these experiences, and how they have transformed their perspectives on sport and retirement.

GRIEF, LOSS, AND DISENFRANCHISED GRIEF

Grief, while a painful experience, has long been understood as a normative response to loss, one that influences an individual's emotions, thoughts, and behaviors (Aoun et al., 2015; Arizmendi & O'Connor, 2015; Corr, 1999; Hall, 2014; Howarth, 2011; Zioosk & Shear, 2009), a reaction that encompasses both psychological and physiological responses (Averill, 1968; Penman et al., 2014). Grief is typically understood in relation to tangible loss, such as the death of a loved one, and the experience of bereavement (Knight & Gitterman, 2019; Zioosk & Shear, 2009). Despite being a universal phenomenon, grief experiences are often misunderstood due to significant variations in how grieving and mourning rituals are expressed. These differences are influenced by societal and cultural expectations and norms that shape individuals' perceptions of what constitutes appropriate forms and expressions of grief (Averill, 1968; Corr, 1999; Doka, 1989). Although it is widely acknowledged that every grief experience is unique and influenced by various factors, there persist societal assumptions that impose limitations and exert influence on this process (Costa et al., 2007). These assumptions may include expectations about how long grief should last, how it should be expressed, or what is considered an acceptable way to grieve.

In addition to societal expectations regarding grief, there exist social norms that govern our thought processes and define the acceptable range of responses and emotions individuals are expected to display publicly in specific circumstances (Doka, 2008). This extends not only to how individuals should grieve but also includes whether social confirmation is provided (Fowlkes, 1990), what type of support should be offered, and by whom (Doka, 2008). Moreover, studies have revealed that individuals who are grieving encounter a conflict between societal perspectives on time-limited and selective social support for those deemed less resilient, and their own perceived advantages of receiving support throughout the grieving process (Kirby et al., 2018). Such societal pressures can lead individuals to suppress or alter their grief to fit within perceived norms, potentially hindering their ability to process their emotions in a healthy and authentic manner.

Social support has been found to buffer the negative effects of loss (Cacciatore et al., 2021) and has been found to serve as a protective factor for those who are grieving (Aoun et al., 2020). Research suggests that having access to empathy, support, and understanding during the grieving process has been linked to decreased feelings of loneliness and isolation (Cacciatore et al., 2021), reduced levels of depression, and symptoms of complicated grief (Costa et al., 2007). It also enhances a sense of validation and contributes to more positive outcomes when faced with loss. Despite substantial evidence demonstrating the potential of social support to alleviate adverse consequences, a significant number of individuals who experience grief resulting from loss express dissatisfaction with the support that they receive (Aoun et al., 2015).

Grief is not just about the death of a loved one but all of the ways in which their loss is felt in one's life, creating a cascade of secondary losses (Penman et al., 2014; Ratcliffe et al., 2022) such as the role that a spouse played as coparent, partner, mentor, companion, etc and the loss of future experiences, plans, and opportunities (Gitterman & Knight, 2019; Fowlkes, 1990; Ratcliffe et al., 2022). While grief is often explored in relation to bereavement, it can also occur in response to non-death losses and major life transitions (Den Elzen et al., 2023; Doka, 2016; Papa et al., 2014) such as loss of relationships

(Cesur-Soysal & Ari, 2022; Doka, 2008; Fowlkes, 1990), injury and functional limitations (Peña-Vargas et al., 2021; Yehene et al., 2021; Zisook & Shear, 2009), loss of employment (Papa & Maitoza, 2013; Smith & Delgado, 2020), infertility (Den Elzen et al., 2023; Ratcliffe & Richardson, 2023), and many others. The grieving process can lead individuals to encounter a loss of roles that have defined their identities, such as the loss of a specific career or meaningful engagements they once had (Papa et al., 2014). These losses elicit grief reactions in a similar fashion to losses caused by death and require a similar process of meaning making, healing, and recovery (Gitterman & Knight, 2019; Harris & Winokuer, 2019; Smith & Delgago, 2020).

Non-death losses, while distressing, are often not regarded as losses that are expected to invoke a grief reaction and therefore do not receive the same attention and acceptance by society as bereavement (Gitterman & Knight, 2019). Responses to non-death loss are often perceived more as signs of stress or depression rather than expressions of grief (Gitterman & Knight, 2019), which emphasizes society's failure to acknowledge non-death losses as legitimate forms of grief (Corr, 1999). In such circumstances, there is greater potential for the grief to be undervalued and unrecognized by others and in many cases the individual themselves (Knight & Gitterman, 2019), leading to the potential for either outright suppression of symptoms or a lack of self-awareness of one's own emotional experiences. This is particularly true when an individual internalizes societal messages about appropriate grief reactions, thereby creating self-imposed expectations regarding how transitions and adverse situations should be managed, and suppression of self-awareness of their personal grief experiences (Corr, 1999).

Disenfranchised grief, as developed by Kenneth Doka (1989), describes the grief process that occurs when a loss is not socially recognized, supported, or validated. The individual experiences loss and its resulting grief response, but that grief may not be acknowledged by those around them or society as a whole. Disenfranchised grief was initially applied to situations in which the relationship was not recognized, the loss was not recognized, or the individual was not expected to have a grief reaction to the situation and perceives exclusion from the right of grieving (Doka, 1989; Doka, 2008). This is further reinforced by social support networks that do not recognize these grief experiences or the need for social support to validate the pain of loss (Attig, 2004; Doka, 2008). The experience of disenfranchisement has been found to complicate the grief process while simultaneously creating barriers to receiving much needed social support (Doka, 1989). When grief occurs in contexts that are not socially understood and sanctioned, such as often occurs with non-death losses, individuals often experience intense feelings of grief while also feeling isolated from social supports and those who may have otherwise served to buffer the effects of loss (Coker & Riforgiate, 2023). This disenfranchisement of grief experiences has been acknowledged as an empathetic failure, reflecting a lack of understanding and awareness of the challenges encountered by individuals who have suffered loss and the emotional responses that accompany such losses (Neimeyer & Jordan, 2002). Failures of empathy are common in response to non-death losses, primarily due to the lack of recognition of the significance of these losses and the impact on an individual's sense of self and identity (Packman et al., 2014).The experience of failures of empathy can hinder the grieving process and exacerbate feelings of loneliness, isolation, and distress (Attiq, 2004).

For many individuals who experience loss, they have often long since internalized the norms of grieving, the measurement by which their own grief experience is assessed (Costa et al., 2007; Doka, 2008). This process can lead to self-initiation of disenfranchisement, which occurs when individuals invalidate or judge their own grief responses as inappropriate, exceeding what is socially acceptable (Kirby et al., 2018; Robson & Walter, 2012), or the loss as insignificant (Cesur-Soysal & Ari, 2022; Doka, 2008). Kirby and colleagues (2018) found that when individuals perceived that their grief experience was outside of socially acceptable timelines for grieving or that their symptoms were not within societal norms, they were more reluctant to share these experiences with others or seek out formal social support. The experience of non-death losses often triggers a profound feeling of disconnection as it disrupts an individual's fundamental beliefs about themselves and the world, ultimately causing the fragmentation and estrangement of their identity. While not all elite athletes will experience grief during the transition to retirement, they are more likely to have that grief experience disenfranchised by others.

THE LINEUP: INTRODUCING THE ATHLETES AND THE ENGAGEMENT PROCESS

For this project, we conducted 30 semi-structured interviews with male and female former team sport athletes. Each athlete had competed at an elite level as defined by our research team, with a minimum involvement at the Division-1 scholarship level of NCAA competition. Over half of these athletes proceeded to engage in some form of professional sports following their collegiate careers. The final makeup of the participants consisted of 12 female and 18 male athletes.

We asked participants to complete a brief demographic survey before being selected for the study. We used a general demographic questionnaire to gather information on age, gender, contact information, current occupation, and highest level of athletic competition. To delve into the depths of athletic identity and its impact on retirement transitions, we utilized the AIMS, described earlier in this chapter, to screen for the strength of the individual's connection to their athletic identity. Each participant was asked to complete the AIMS, reflecting on their peak athletic career period. We then filtered our participant pool, selecting only those who scored above 50 out of the possible 70 points on the AIMS, as this range is indicative of a strong athletic identity according to the scale's creators.

Our intention here was to interview athletes who had what the designers of the scale considered high athletic identity. The threshold of 50 was strategically chosen based on the hypothesis that participants who identified as having high athletic identity would likely experience the most difficult transitions from sport. Research over the last thirty years has confirmed that a score of 50 is indeed a marker of strong athletic identity and correlated with difficulties participants experience in retirement from sport (Brewer et al., 1993; Lochbaum et al., 2022).

However, it's important to note that reaching an elite level in sports doesn't inherently equate to a singular athletic identity. While numerous athletes exhibit the talent and determination necessary to excel in elite sports, they might not necessarily fully immerse their identities into their athletic pursuits. Our study, therefore, specifically focused on those athletes who had fostered a more singular athletic identity, aiming to understand the impact of such identity loss after retirement.

Additionally the timing of this study likely impacted the data collected, as all interviews were conducted virtually via Zoom, primarily during the COVID-19 pandemic. Some of the participants in this study were deselected from professional athletics during the pandemic. While it was challenging to ascertain the pandemic's exact role in their deselection, these individuals strongly believed that public health measures made it significantly more difficult for them to sustain their professional careers. This was evident in one participant's recounting of how the NFL reduced its rosters from 90 to 75 players, resulting in him not being invited to a 2020 training camp. The COVID-19 pandemic was also a time of deep introspection for many people, not just retired athletes. The global crisis prompted individuals to engage in significant self-reflection about various aspects of their lives, including their careers, families, relationships, and most pertinently for this study, their identity. This heightened introspection during the pandemic might have influenced the participants' reflections and responses during the interviews, ultimately shaping the dataset collected for this project.

The following chapters represent the key themes that emerged from our study and share the voices and experiences of our participants as they recount their exits from the arena. These sections delve deep into the athletes' personal narratives, chronicling their transition experiences, adaptations, and reformations. We aim to offer an authentic and comprehensive insight into the unique journeys undertaken by these individuals as they stepped away from their professional athletic careers.

Chapter 2

Original Formation of Identity

Though we began this project with the goal of exploring identity loss, we recognized that to fully grasp this concept, we first had to comprehend how an athletic identity is formed. We began our interviews by inquiring into the nature of identity formation for all participants, asking when their earliest recollection was of identifying as an athlete. Several common themes emerged from most of the participant responses.

MIDDLE CHILDHOOD/PREADOLESCENCE

It was evident that a significant number of participants developed a robust athletic identity at an early stage in life. Temporally, it's worth noting that the majority of participants committed to this strong athletic identity during middle to late childhood, often prior to entering adolescence.

Anna had an incredibly unique and profoundly impactful experience shifting her commitment to athletic identity. She described how her family, especially her father, influenced her to move to a hockey academy at 11 years old: "I have played hockey since I was 11 years old, and I went to [hockey academy] up in [American city/state] because there wasn't any opportunity for women's ice hockey in [American city]. So, I moved up to [American city] and right from there I went to [college]. There, my whole identity was being a hockey player." Anna was one of the participants in this study who struggled significantly with athletic retirement, making her narrative a focal point that will be frequently revisited throughout this analysis. Throughout the project, her narrative stands out as nearly archetypal, representing the common struggles athletes encounter when retiring from their sport. Undeniably, her profound and unwavering dedication to sports from such an early age is a significant aspect to be taken into account as we delve further into her story.

In contrast, Steve's experience differs from Anna's in that his parents didn't actively push him to compete in sports. However, his exposure to sports was early and frequent due to his father's career. Steve described how he was infatuated with sports from as early as he can remember.

> As far back as I remember having memories as a child, sports had always been a huge part of my life. I was attracted at a very early age. My dad was the team doctor for a couple of high school teams. He played football at [college] so he had that background and I would just tag along with him on the sidelines every weekend during the football season. As far back as three, four years old. I was the type of kid that if I wasn't out with my friends, I would be out by myself in the yard trying to work on a skill, playing some kind of sport. Whatever was in season, I wanted to play it. If I could have played six sports a year I would have played six. I think as I look back now that I have three young boys, I'm glad that they've branched out a little bit more than I did. I was so centered on sports and what I needed to do to get where I wanted to go. I knew I wanted to play in the NFL at probably seven, eight, nine years old.

Like so many athletes in this study, the commitment to athletic identity was not only early for Steve but also largely driven by one's parents, usually one's father. Different from Anna, this was less of a case of a parent intentionally and explicitly moving a child into strong identity commitments in sport; Steve grew up in an environment saturated with sports. This environment likely, albeit subconsciously, played a significant role in molding his strong and nearly exclusive commitment to his athletic identity. However, this seems to be more of a case of the child almost autonomously achieving industriousness in sport when welcomed into that arena. A commitment to sport at 7 to 9 years old is undoubtedly young, even for participants in this study. However, unlike other participants in this study, the commitment to athletic identity was not pressed by one's parents. Steve's parents showed him a door, and at a very young age, he walked through it briskly.

Jermaine recounted how his parents—specifically, his father—worked to press him toward sports in early childhood. However, it wasn't until he reached middle to late childhood that he truly engaged in playing sports and fully embraced his athletic identity.

> I was a crazy kid, I definitely had ADD. I was playing with different toys every second, I didn't have the patience. I tried rollerblading when I was 5 and I hated it because I wasn't good at it right away. My dad just kept pushing me into things though. I was the biggest kid in my family and neighborhood. I played basketball when I was 7 or 8, and my parents signed me up for the recreational public league. I was tall and I was a decent athlete, so it came easier to me. I was good at it, so I liked it. I was that kind of kid. I was impatient and if I wasn't good at something, I was going to put it down. Basketball just came easier to me, same thing with football. I tried flag football and I was good at it, and I just loved it. It came easier to me so I really liked it. Around late elementary school

> and in middle school I started to take it more seriously, but I just enjoyed it because I was good at it.

In Jermaine's case, his journey toward forming a personal athletic identity occurred at a stage in life that aligned with the majority of participants in this study. Like several other participants, a recurring theme we will explore further in this analysis is the significant role his father played in his commitment to and pursuit of athletic success. However, what set Jermaine apart was that his drive to establish an athletic identity wasn't primarily motivated by the need to succeed and satisfy his father's expectations. Similarly, it wasn't an innate fascination with sports, as seen in Steve's case, that drew him into the world of athletics. Instead, it was the sense of achievement and competence that initially fueled his attachment to sports.

Joe shared that while his athletic identity was solidified at an early age, there was a defining moment when he realized that he was performing at an elite level and had potential to go all the way to the NHL. "I got a call when I was in high school to move away to play in the USHL with the top 200 players in the country ages 16–20, if you can get to that league you are pretty much guaranteed a D1 scholarship. It is the top league in the country before college. I think getting to the USHL, which is that junior hockey league right before college, was the moment I knew that I was in the top 1 percent of the country at this." Much like Jermaine, Joe's commitment to athletic identity was fostered once he began to experience a significant level of success in hockey. However, in contrast to Jermaine, this transition happened later in adolescence rather than during childhood or early adolescence.

The experiences of these three participants indeed have a common thread: their commitment to an athletic identity was shaped by unique experiential and motivational factors, especially in the context of their involvement in sports and the influence of their fathers. However, not all participants in this study were molded into a sports-centric identity during their childhood. For some participants, they had parents, caregivers, teachers, and even some coaches who were intentional about introducing them to a wide array of experiences and, consequently, establishing a more multifaceted sense of identity beyond just athletics.

While Kurt's parents strongly encouraged his involvement in sports during his childhood, they were also purposeful in nurturing him into a well-rounded individual with a diverse set of skills and a more comprehensive sense of identity.

> My parents got me into piano when I was young. I got into it again by playing in college and, who knows, I'll probably get into it again in the future. My parents also signed me up for Boy Scouts. I didn't get into it as much just because a lot

> of it had to do with the weekends and I was playing sports on the weekends and once I got to high school I wasn't able to do that. But I always thought it was cool to know how to do things in general. Whenever there is something with the car that was broken, my dad would be the one to fix it so I thought that was cool, being able to learn how to do that. Or mow the lawn, do things around the house, tie knots like you do in Boy Scouts. Just knowing practical life skills I thought was cool. It really helped me realize that there's things out there that are cool outside of being a football player. . . . Another thing I'd like to say, I feel like I had, and I still do, have a sense of responsibility. In football it was always to be the best football player I could be because my brother who has Down syndrome, couldn't do that. For me, being his older brother, I was always the one that would be taking care of him all the time and he was probably the biggest part of my life.

Similar to nearly all the participants in this study, Kurt's parents were strongly dedicated to introducing him to the world of sports and fostering his success. However, what sets Kurt apart from other participants in this study is that his parents also demonstrated a parallel commitment to exposing him to a broader range of experiences and helping him develop a more diverse sense of identity beyond just sports.

As mentioned in the earlier passage, Kurt's role as the older brother of a child with Down syndrome significantly enriched his social and emotional awareness, leading to a broader and more multifaceted sense of identity. Even though Kurt dedicated himself to a sports identity from a young age, he credits the way his parents raised him, emphasizing qualities like compassion, empathy, and perspective, as a crucial factor that made him more at ease with his transition from the NFL as an adult.

> That's probably the most crucial thing that has allowed me to be who I am. To be empathetic, to be compassionate, to put yourself in other people's shoes, to realize there's more out there than just yourself. Although my brother brought a lot of beauty to our family, there's also a lot of very difficult things that came (from his diagnosis). Always having to be selfless and be there for someone else kind of puts things in perspective. That, without a doubt, was super impactful in my life in general and probably had to do with facilitating my transition. . . . Growing up, a trip to the grocery store wasn't really a trip to the grocery store.

He shared that the exposure to the importance of empathy and being emotionally wholesome coupled with his parents' consistent messaging on the need to develop as a whole person helped him to develop immense gratitude for what hard work looks like and the sacrifices his parents made to lay a path for the family.

> Without a doubt that was extremely impactful for who I was in high school. That, in tandem with the messaging I was getting from my parents when I was younger about being all around and not being so single minded, had a big impact on me. Also, I think I always had a subconscious gratitude and obligation. My dad was born in Cuba and his family had to come over here because when Fidel Castro took over in 1960. My dad came over in [date], so yeah, they left because of that and coming here to a free country and being able to experience what they wanted to experience and achieve what they wanted to achieve without communism is something that, maybe more so imbedded in his life, but because he was my dad I kind of picked up on that through osmosis. I never feel bad for myself. I mean I probably should sometimes because of the way it ended [in the NFL]. But I was always thinking, "No, man. You have it made. No matter what it is there's always someone who has it worse so keep going forward."

Though there is a lot to unpack in this passage, we offer it as a juxtaposition to a more univocal introduction into sport by some participant's parents, specifically, compared to Anna. Anna and Kurt had relatively similar athletic identity scores in the prescreening process for this study. However, Anna developed a strong identity while being sent away to a boarding school whose primary mission was athletic development. When Anna retired from hockey, she described a sense of isolation and even estrangement from her siblings and family. She missed out on the opportunity to cultivate intimacy, solidarity, and empathy with them during her youth, which became a source of lamentation as an adult navigating life beyond sports. Similar to Anna, Kurt had an incredibly high athletic identity, but his parents were intentional about balancing his commitments from an early age. This resulted in a more diverse sense of self, interests, and close relationships, which facilitated a smoother and even enjoyable transition into life after he was cut from the NFL.

Arianna shared her experience of being recognized for displaying what her peers and adult mentors considered as more traditionally masculine traits and abilities. As early as the age of 5 to 6, she mentioned her strong inclination and determination to compete with and against boys in sports. From a very young age, Arianna found herself drawn to these activities, and she began to shape a distinct sense of identity by distancing herself from what were conventionally regarded as more traditional female pursuits and hobbies.

> [Sport] was one of the first things I found success in as an elementary school student. So, I was always the female that played with the boys. The girls were playing Barbies at recess and I was in the soccer game. I think early on I was being identified by others as being athletic. I think I bought into the idea of myself being athletic and it all snowballed from there. . . . It seemed like I was always a little different than the norm at that time. . . . I liked to constantly be outside playing basketball in the street or running around playing a form of

> tag or street hockey or whatever it might be. I tended to always move in that direction.

Finally, Henry described just how ubiquitous youth hockey was growing up in Western Canada. It was right around middle school where his serious identification as an athlete began to solidify. "I grew up in Western Canada where hockey is huge, obviously. I would say to my buddies down here that I don't have one friend from growing up back home that didn't play hockey in some avenue. So, when things started to get more serious, honestly around eighth grade, that's when the trajectory started taking off a little bit where the pyramid got a little tighter. I was lucky to be in that spot and then the guys you're hanging around all the time are those hockey guys." Henry's strong commitment to his athletic identity was primarily influenced by the culture and environment in which he was raised. Unlike some previous participants, it wasn't a case of his parents pushing him into hockey or sending him away to immerse him in sports. Instead, Henry was born into a world where hockey was an integral and ever-present part of the culture. It was the natural backdrop of his upbringing, which had a profound impact on his athletic identity development. It became the atmosphere in which his passions and commitments were forged. Much like several other participants in this study, this pervasive hockey culture played a pivotal role in shaping a profound commitment to sports within his identity.

MENTORSHIP IN ATHLETIC IDENTITY

Anna's account highlights the significant influence her coaches had on her athletic identity, which sometimes came at the expense of cultivating a broader sense of self outside of sports. She explained that her coaches would often push her to prioritize hockey, even to the extent of missing classes and limiting her academic involvement. This emphasis on sports over academics was pervasive in her adolescent educational environment, where athletic success was explicitly favored and valued more than intellectual engagement and pursuits.

> When I got to college, my coach looked at me like, "You know you've got all this money to play hockey, right? Not to take a Bio class." And I thought of that because he was like, "We do power plays on Thursdays at 5 p.m. You have to be here." And I was like, "You're right. I have to be here!" So, I put hockey first, always. I think it was because at my school, [high school sports academy], we didn't even go to school. I don't know who developed that program, but our lives were hockey came first, school was later. It was just a school for training

> Olympic winter athletes. We had an alpine skiing team, and they would go to Chile for four months, and just ski all day for four months. And they would just ski all day and wouldn't go to class. And we would be like, "Oh, we're going to leave Wednesday night to drive to Minnesota, and we'll be back on Tuesday." And we wouldn't go to school. I just never put as much time and focus and energy into school, because I had that identity of, "I'm a hockey player; this is what I'm going to be." And it doesn't set you up for anything else. *I came from a high school where hockey was all you did, and it was the only thing that made you important.*

As a teenager, there were few options when it came to self-worth and identity and for Anna. Though she showed some level of intellectual curiosity in college, any commitments she might have wanted to make to an identity outside of sport were dismissed by her coaches and mentors. The message was unmistakable when her parents enrolled her in a youth sports academy for high school: athletic identity and athletic success would always take precedence over any pursuit of self-complexity, balance, or academic achievement. Throughout the most formative years of her identity development, she was consistently encouraged to be nothing more or less than an elite hockey player.

Steve's perspective takes a different approach, emphasizing the importance of mentorship that goes beyond solely shaping an athlete's identity. While he himself had a strong and singular athletic identity throughout his youth and NFL career, he recognized the value of imparting a message of self-complexity to his own sons and the players he coaches. This suggests a broader view of mentorship that aims to nurture a more multifaceted sense of self in young athletes, acknowledging the importance of identity beyond sports.

> I'm also way more forgiving of younger people than I would be of myself. It's the mental health piece that I don't think I ever thought about when I was an athlete. When I do things, I know that there's ramifications of how I talk to a kid. I don't know everything about that kid. Maybe he is driven, but maybe he's really vulnerable. Maybe he's a fragile kid in some ways that I don't ever see. Maybe his home life isn't great. So I always try to strip it back and say, "Talk to me first about you. I'll talk to you about the football piece after." My players will tell you that I always ask, "I don't want to hear about football, I want to hear how your day is going. How is school going? How is your family?" That type of stuff. With my boys, I'm the same way. They're not super competitive and they're not super athletic. This is weird, but part of that is a relief for me. In some ways, I wish they would be more competitive. However, there's a piece of me that's like, I hope they are never as critical of themselves as I was or as solely focused on one thing. It's dangerous sometimes. You can be on that line. Whenever it ends, that outcome can be really negative.

Steve's experience as a former NFL quarterback, spanning approximately a decade, underscores the significant development of his athletic identity, even though he was not pushed into sports by his parents. His struggles upon retiring from the NFL are a testament to the profound impact of his athletic identity. Nonetheless, as a high school coach now, he is aware of just how damaging the promotion of univocal identity in sport can be for his players or his sons.

He further described how it is difficult to convince parents to support their children in developing self-complexity. Instead, too many are opting for singular identity and specialization.

> I can't stand specialization. The piece I can't do anything about, no matter how hard I try, is the parent piece. And I wish I could get through to the parents the way I can get through to the kids sometimes. Because they're doing irreparable damage to their kid. . . . They're trying to do what's best for them, for the most part. But I often think, how much of this is about you and not your son or your daughter. AAU culture . . . football has somewhat been immune to it, but that's going to change. You don't have a proper perspective when you're in that world. When you're 13 years old and you're basically told, "Don't worry about your friends. We'll take care of school. Don't worry about other things you might have that you love. Your path is football, or baseball. We're going to play all summer. We're going to go to every invite. We gotta get you exposure." The kid is 13. He can't even spell exposure. And then the pressure . . . and I see it all of the time. I'll talk to my parents about it and they'll nod their head like, "Yeah, I totally agree with you." And everything I tell them not to do, they do the following summer.

As a coach committed to nurturing self-complexity in his players, Steve described the ongoing challenges posed by parents who share a mindset similar to what Anna experienced during her adolescence. The incessant desire to have one's child achieve elite status in sport continues to be ubiquitous in American youth and high school sport. Despite recognizing the issues associated with this singular focus, the unintended consequences persist and impact the nation's young athletes. Even the guidance of coaches working with presumed elite athletes often falls short in dissuading the mentors and adults who are steering children toward a one-dimensional sense of self centered around sports. This underscores the complex and persistent nature of the issue.

Praise: Positive Reinforcement Conditioning

Tim's struggle to cultivate a robust sense of self beyond football highlights the significance of the sport in his life. He candidly acknowledged that sports were the only context in which he felt genuine love and respect, and he quickly recognized the direct link between his performance and the attention and validation he received from it.

> Well, there's a lot that's wrapped up in into that and for me it's where I found my, the love, the respect, the wantedness was all tied into sport and I hadn't explored other areas where I felt that, for example, you know, I grew up in a single-parent household. So, when I would come home, my mother would praise me and gosh, you know, very much focused on my talent, very much focused on my results. So, when I got good results. I got love, I got "let's go get some ice cream," you know, at a young age, to hey you know you are up for all conference and all this and all that. And so there was a lot of when I was in sport, I felt wanted. I felt respected. I felt love, especially when I was getting results. And when I stopped playing, all those things seemed to go away.

From a very young age, this participant learned to associate his talent with his sense of worth, a perspective reinforced by his mother's praise and admiration for his athletic abilities. This quickly became how he sought love, attention, and respect in his life, linking his self-esteem and confidence to his athletic performance throughout his career and into retirement. A connection that caused a great deal of pain as he tried to find non-sport success after an injury left him without viable options to achieve his dream of playing in the NFL.

Anna described how her talent in college outweighed some of her otherwise detrimental behavior to the team. Nonetheless, she was continually praised by her coaches for her talent and ability.

> He was never going to bench me, he was never going to make me miss a shift. Everyone else had to be there an hour and a half early, and I would show up 30 minutes before eating a sandwich. I was always late. I was always just doing whatever I wanted to do. . . . So, when the whole team was warming up, I was sitting there, just jumping around listening to music. But if someone was like, "What are you doing?" I would just say "This is how I prepare." But everyone else had to do it or they got in trouble for it.

Anna received almost unconditional positive reinforcement for her talent and performance, while also eschewing any form of punishment from her coaches for behavior that she recognized as detrimental to her team. This level of unconditional praise for her talent and turning a blind eye to her poor behavior shaped a disposition of entitlement toward both hockey and her obligations as a teammate. Regarding identity formation, a deeper sense of entitlement and lack of accountability in her athletic career likely deepened the attraction to sport. Why pursue curiosity or self-exploration when one is offered a space to behave without consequences and with unbridled praise in the world of sport? Such a psychosocial atmosphere is more likely to deepen one's identity commitments in sport, as was the case with Anna who struggled deeply when faced with a life without hockey.

Hayden described just how profound an effect the praise and adulation of being a professional athlete was for shaping his identity and solidifying his motivational and emotional commitments to sport. "I struggle with it. I just struggle. It is corporate America and I'm in medical sales. You know, you struggle with being a man. You struggle because the bus isn't parked at the stadium and you're not getting out of the bus at the stadium and being asked for twenty autographs—you aren't a part of that, and they don't want your autographs anymore." He discussed just how difficult it is to develop a nuanced and diverse sense of identity or be honest about the actual challenges of being a professional athlete. Instead, as a professional baseball player, he felt compelled to hide this complexity in face of adulation from fans.

> When people love you, you are duped to the fact that it is associated with something they love-like baseball or sports. They are putting themselves in this fantasy of what it would be like to be you. So, they want a small piece of you. When you are in pro sports, and you are walking down a tunnel or something, and everybody is just reaching out for a piece of you. You feel like an animal, there is a piece of you that doesn't feel human. It is a really weird experience. It would almost baffle people if you explain to them that the job sucks right now, baseball is horrific, and you are so down about it. They would be absolutely baffled to hear that because you have this "dream job." You feel almost pressured to act in a certain way. There is this fantasy that they have about it. You feel in a way to give them what they want. It is almost not their fault. There is an expectation from them because they just got it; they have been seen as superman their whole life.

Hayden articulated a similar sense of entitlement and power to Anna. The success cultivated in his career led to a tremendous amount of adulation from fans, but also from family, peers, and coworkers. He has spent a lot of his life being praised, and that praise has made it difficult to sever his identity from sport. However, different from Anna, Hayden described the challenges that can come from receiving so much unbridled praise. Despite the power felt from such praise, Hayden also felt trapped by not feeling supported to demonstrate a more complex sense of self while competing. He undoubtedly enjoyed the praise but longed for an opportunity to express more of himself to fans, peers, and loved ones. Instead, the admiration from fans diminished his sense of identity and confined him within a singular, one-dimensional self.

Hayden described the experience of having his peers and coworkers remain enamored by his past as a professional athlete. In this final passage, he provides valuable insight into how the adulation received from athletic success can be profoundly limiting, constraining an individual's identity and opportunities for growth and fulfillment beyond the realm of sports.

> When I got out of baseball, one of the hardest things for me was to not mention baseball to anybody. It is almost like a strategy I say to myself when I meet people, when I talk to people, I never mention baseball. I want to really see if the person is receptive to me as a person without baseball. The minute you say professional sports, you're simply looked at and treated differently. They more or less treat you in the identity of the professional sports player as opposed to you as an individual. Your job title might not be as exciting to them and they might actually stereotype you as a certain person and they don't really care.

Despite having felt a sense of pride in his career and accomplishments as a professional baseball player, Hayden shared being intentional about avoiding the topic altogether when introducing himself to novel peers or coworkers.

Parental Reinforcement Techniques

Anna recounted how her father played a significant role in encouraging her to engage in hockey from a very young age. Interestingly, at the age of eight, she was even financially incentivized by her father to begin her hockey journey. "I started playing when I was in third grade. . . . My brother played hockey, so I was always talking about hockey. Then my dad actually bribed me with money to start playing." She continued to describe how one of the great fears she had in retirement from hockey was the lack of connection she would have with her father after her hockey career ended.

> My family life was a lot of, "Everything's about (Anna). She is the golden child." So, while that always, my brother and sister would feel a little left out, it gave me the feeling of, "Wow, my dad loves me. My dad is so proud of me." And another thing that I really struggled with, and I remember crying about it one night was, "What is my dad going to talk to me about? Is he not going to like me? I provide nothing to him once I am done with hockey." I think it put a lot of pressure on me, because our conversations and the way that he treated me and the way that he followed up with me, the interest in my life faded when I stopped playing ice hockey. That's probably why I started really getting into roller derby again and doing well with it. We started talking more again and it gave me that reassurance of that father-daughter connection.

Anna's experience serves as a vivid illustration of transactional affection being closely tied to her success in a sport that her father introduced her to at an exceptionally young age. She lamented how even when she had to retire from hockey, her relationship with her father began to fray. It likely drove her, subconsciously, into another athletic endeavor—Women's competitive roller derby—in her mid-twenties so that she could rekindle his affection. Such transactional affection for one's child is clearly psychologically and emotionally damaging. However, for the sake of this study it makes it far more likely that one will restrict identity commitments only to that source of affection, in this case a restricted sense of identity in hockey.

Finally, she explained how her siblings have reacted to the skewed relationship that her father had toward her and her hockey career.

> Something I'm trying to do is reflect back and have conversations with (my siblings), such as, "Hey, I know that must have been really hard for you, if Dad's coming to my ice hockey game and he's been to every single ice hockey game that [I've] ever had, and he didn't go to your speech pathology speech," or whatever. I think it's been harder on my siblings just feeling like my dad doesn't necessarily care about them to the extent that he does for me. But I think my siblings also acknowledge that they feel like he benefits off of me more than them.

Anna's relationship with her father indeed appears unique and, in certain aspects, supportive and enriching, especially in the context of her hockey career. However, it's notable that his devotion to her seems to have been primarily linked to her success in hockey, resulting in direct and unwavering affirmation from him. This dynamic likely played a significant role in shaping her identity around sports and may have influenced her to be less exploratory in other aspects of her identity later in life. The strong connection between her success in hockey and her father's approval may have contributed to her reluctance to venture into other areas of identity exploration. Though this project is not focused on understanding the psychological damage this form of devotion to one athletic child over one's others, it seems that a sense of resentment has developed between Anna and her siblings. The unintended consequence of singling out and continuously reinforcing one child, particularly due to their athletic prowess, can result in the cultivation of a deep yet restricted sense of identity. Moreover, it may contribute to the distancing of relationships between the child and their siblings. This underscores the complex dynamics that can emerge within families when one child's athletic success is prioritized to such an extent.

Juan, likewise, described how his parents, uncles, and family were a massive influence in him falling in love with sport early in life. "I have been playing competitively since I was 4 or 5. My dad was an athlete, and my mom was an athlete growing up. And all my cousins and my pretty much entire family are athletes as well so that was always a motivating factor to me. My dad just loved it and went everywhere with me for it." Despite his incredibly successful collegiate football career and the fact that he had several tryouts with NFL teams in his early twenties, Juan is one of the few participants in this study who was stimulated by and excited for his immediate career after retirement and deselection. Although he would have eagerly pursued an NFL opportunity if it had materialized, he quickly discovered that his role as a scout was deeply satisfying and intellectually engaging. Nevertheless, he was one of the participants who mentioned throughout the interview that his father likely struggled more with his football retirement than he did. Specifically, throughout the interview, he described how much sports meant to his father and how his father felt more of a void in Juan's retirement. The profound dedication of his father to his athletic career resonated throughout his life and undeniably played a role in reinforcing his identity formation and his unwavering commitment to sports.

Hayden also described how his parents and family were a tremendous influence in his developing a deep passion for success and achievement in sport, even at a young age.

> It was probably since I was eleven or twelve years old. That is when the locals and my family really started to talk. I started to get headlines in all the local newspapers with my performance since I was a little boy. That is when you start to date yourself and think, "Man, I am good." You just run with it and then all of a sudden all that stuff is happening. Then my personality starts kicking in. I was the guy who was going to lift weights all the time, I was going to do a million practice swings, run a million sprints. Now you got your older uncles, your grandfather saying if you want to be the best you have got to outwork people, you have to get there early, you have to stay late. And I didn't rebel against that! I was one of the rare kids that actually listened and sped into it. I always say to myself and other people when we talk sports about baseball, they would always say "I really struggle because my son doesn't want to put the work in." I kind of laugh inside because I was the absolute opposite. . . . It honestly is when I felt most close to who I know I am. I absolutely loved it. I loved the workouts. I loved training until almost absolute exhaustion. I loved hitting a million baseballs. You got blisters that are killing you. I don't know man, I just absolutely loved it.

Similar to previous participants, parental and familial influences played a serious role in influencing the initial inculcation to sport and, thus, athletic identity for Hayden. However, despite his parents being deeply invested in his athletic success early, Hayden was thrilled by the early success he was experiencing, even at a relatively young age. Local headlines and press coverage generated a sense of excitement and further solidified his commitments to the identity associated with sports. Yet, it is impossible to consider this fact without considering the role of parental reinforcement. For a child, it is challenging to imagine parents not playing a role in showing a child their own press clippings and headlines. Just as Hayden was becoming captivated by the headlines, his parents were actively providing them to him and reinforcing success in sports as a meaningful and worthwhile pursuit.

Kurt detailed how his father, specifically, was a massive influence in his life when it came to being introduced to sport as young as two years old. What's intriguing about this passage is how Kurt also described his father's role in shaping a well-rounded sense of identity as a person outside of sports.

> My dad started pitching to me when I was two. Like actual small baseballs and apparently, I was hitting them when I was two in my basement, not even on the T. I think he liked sports and he kind of just did it with me. He never pressured me to do sports but I just really liked it. . . . He laid some concrete down in our backyard and we made a basketball court. So, then I just played a ton of basketball outside. . . . Part of the identity thing, I was always told from the very beginning. Ever since I can remember my dad would always teach me, kind of ingrained into me to be all around, be all around, you're all around. like you can be really good at football, but you can also be really smart. That doesn't mean you don't have to be good in school. That doesn't mean you don't have to be nice to girls. You can be super aggressive and quote unquote violent on the football field, but when it comes to real life, you can be a real respectful, stand-up person. It's not like you must be that all the time, you need to know when to be one and when to be the other. I think it helped me transition out of the NFL too, because I took pride in being good at other things.

Though Kurt had parents who were similarly committed to and invested in his athletic career as the previous participants, they also were intentional about diversifying his sense of identity throughout his childhood. The focus was on being well-rounded, of which sport was one form of commitment but no more or less valuable than academics, music, or being a loving brother to his siblings. Kurt was raised in a unique atmosphere in which his parents valued all of these aspects of his identity and pursuits equally. They managed to foster his athletic achievements while simultaneously respecting and upholding every other dimension of his life and self. As will be demonstrated later in this analysis, despite Kurt having a difficult deselection experience at the end of his NFL career, he was incredibly resilient in moving into life after professional sports. This resilience was derived through a sense that his relationships and work outside of football had meaning and were worth investing in.

Ironically, Chris had a notably different reinforcement process when entering sport. As opposed to the overwhelming majority of participants in this study, he was not praised or upheld differently from his peers, siblings, or teammates, even when he reached the NFL.

> My dad never really had an opinion about anything regarding athletics. Just didn't know what he was talking about. So, this quality, I guess I'd be described as tough, mentally tough, physically tough. I dealt with pain well, so I don't have an ego. I'm quiet. Maybe all these qualities that I had personally just fit what I needed to do and just play it out that way. Certainly, no matter what level I played at, if you talked to everybody, everybody thought I sucked. In high school it was like, "Oh he's not even that good, I don't get it." College was the same way, but at some point, I must have been decent and obviously I must have been okay. But when I was playing in college professionally, I had my buddies from home telling me all the time, just waiting for me, like, "He sucked, I just don't get it."

Chris's youth development in sport was almost the exact opposite of several previous participants, specifically, Anna and Hayden. His motivation for engaging in sports wasn't driven by applause or parental encouragement; he simply derived enough pleasure from the game to continue advancing through its ranks. Consequently, his personality became rooted in a kind of identity adaptability, humility, and thankfulness, even as he competed at the highest level in the NFL for more than ten years.

Tess had an incredibly difficult end to her volleyball career. She suffered a career-ending leg injury that was close to becoming an amputation. Nonetheless, years after she fully recovered, she then moved into elite cycling and had a second career as a national champion in American cycling. Her career as an elite cyclist grew out of an intrinsic desire to simply keep competing and exercising. Her previous experience with cycling was merely a form of exercise and nothing more. When asked about how she was able to have such a healthy connection to sport, she described the way her parents introduced her to sport as a child.

> I think some of what my parents did made it so I had a really healthy relationship with sports. They never pushed me, I don't think my mom fully understood the game of volleyball, she got the gist of it but she was never evaluating my stats after the game like "You could have done better." I think because of that I have a really healthy relationship with sports. Whereas, I had one friend in high school whose mom was a coach and when she got done with high school she was like "I'm so done" because her mom would make her do all these things, whereas I feel like I keep going because I see it as a positive outlet. My mom would run when we were growing up, and it would just be three to four miles, but just seeing that politely healthy relationship happen. . . . I feel like with cycling I just signed up for this 50-mile race to begin with and got second and was like "oh this isn't just fun I'm good at it." So having no expectations and then surprising myself, it was like "Okay, yeah, let's see what we can do." I feel like that definitely helped.

Similar to Tess, Tim had a challenging end to his football career after a broken leg and torn ankle ligaments left him watching his window of opportunity for the NFL closing.

> And even then, the whole goal was to get to the NFL, like this was since I was a small school kid. I had to go this unique route to the NFL and it was through Europe at the time. A team out of Frankfurt, Germany had signed my rights, I was hell-bent on going to Germany. I was getting better, I was growing as an athlete. I was my absolute best when I break my leg. So I get the pins and screws taken out and rehabbing takes a lot longer, and my window is closing. I'm now at 27 years old and my opportunity to go to NFL, Europe, left, it was gone. So now I'm without opportunity and coming off injury, I'm approaching my late 20s, my window is gone.

Similar to Tess, he grappled with a sense of loss due to the absence of closure from his football career. Although he wasn't prepared to come to terms with its conclusion, he started to recognize the financial instability it brought, forcing him to balance his responsibilities with his lifelong goal. "There wasn't closure, like, all right, I'm ready to close it. It was just oh shit, I got to get a job. So, I went to a job and moved to Seattle to take a job, and it's putting a Band-Aid on a certain situation which was, I need some money to pay some bills. . . . Once I was healed up, I would feel better. While I am doing it, it was quite a shock for me, to even think of it being over, not having closure, and that lack of closure didn't serve me well in the long term."

Like Tess, Tim turned to other elite athletic competition, however, his motivation came from the "heartbreak" of not going as far as he wanted to and to fill the void where he had once experienced love, respect, and fulfillment. While recovering from an ankle injury, Tim suffered a meniscal tear, and the prospect of undergoing another surgery was the turning point that led him to the realization of "all right, this is done." He found himself without the positive reinforcement and external validation he had once depended on for self-worth, his sense of identity briefly faltered until he made a comeback to elite competition, marking a brief pause in his identity reformation.

> It was almost a two-year process of training for this, and I had been struggling in my career and outside of sports and I just kind of threw myself into this. So, Team USA. We wore the Team USA logo, and it was an experience that was completely different from professional football in that I'm representing not a team, a city, and this is like my country, and I was selected by Team USA to represent us on a relay. We went to the medal, and they did the whole podium and national anthem and the flag coming down. It was just, it was the real deal. And I'm going, I'd always dreamed of being an Olympian and this was the closest I would ever come to experiencing that. . . . It was really exhilarating.

Chapter 3

Identity Foreclosure and Role Confusion in Athletic Retirement

A prevalent, recurring, and pervasive theme in this study was the experience of identity foreclosure for participants. As previously highlighted, identity foreclosure refers to the mental process where individuals limit exploration and diversification of their self-identity. This study confirms that this tendency can be detrimental and maladaptive for former athletes. Athletes who described a strong sense of foreclosure were those that also had the most social, emotional, and psychological challenges in retirement. In the context of this study, they were also more prone to adopting maladaptive grieving methods when grappling with the loss of their athletic career.

IDENTITY FORECLOSURE

Anna and Erica each offered insightful and detailed accounts of the restricted and confined nature of their self-perception during their time in elite-level hockey competition. Anna described how her identity as a hockey player extended to all aspects of her life. "So, I never did anything besides hockey, I never had any social life besides hockey. When I started working out of college, I had work friends, but I was always so busy. I was always the hottest commodity, but I was always busy, and you could never get in touch with me. My whole life has been that or practice. . . . My free time, how I identified, all my friends, my entire life was being a hockey player."

Similarly Erica recognized that even in retirement, she continues to be invested in her identity as an athlete.

> I would say that one of my biggest identifiers is an athlete, probably honestly still now. If I get introduced to a random person not having anything to do with sports, it's always like, "Oh, she played division one hockey." It's always

> a tagline with my name. I'd be lying if I said that I'm not extremely proud of it, because I am. It is the recognition, even when I'm getting courted to coach these teams or whatever, it makes me reflect and look and say well I really did accomplish something that people want to get to know me because of it or have me have my hands in something because of it. That's a good feeling.

These descriptions by Anna and Erica may be the most vivid and accurate representations of identity foreclosure within the entirety of this project. Anna went on to detail the extent to which hockey dominated her life. Despite her professional status, the income from playing hockey wasn't sufficient, necessitating a second job. She outlined her daily routine during this period, revealing a remarkable dedication to her sport. "So, it was an hour to work and then 30–45 minutes to whatever rink, and then I would drive home. So, most days I would work 7:00 a.m.–7:00 p.m., drive to hockey, sleep in my car, and then start practice at 10:00 p.m., get done at 11:30 p.m., get back at 1:30–2:00 a.m., and then I'd be so energized from hockey or needing to get a coffee at 8:00 p.m. before to get through, so it was just really tough." Anna's journey in professional hockey was remarkably distinctive. In many respects, her experiences mirrored the old-school era of professional sports that athletes encountered in past decades. The glaringly inadequate financial support in women's professional hockey necessitated that Anna maintain a full-time job outside of her athletic commitments to support herself. Nevertheless, her determination to remain in the league and continue competing at the professional level remained unshaken. Despite how unhealthy and exhausting her days and habits had become, her identity and passion was so deeply tied to hockey that leaving was not an option. One would think such a schedule would cause exhaustion, fatigue, and chosen retirement for the athlete. However, that was not the case for Anna. She persevered through the rigors of balancing work and hockey, only to be released from the league in her mid-twenties in favor of a younger and more cost-effective player.

Hayden described how his initial intentions upon retirement were to distance himself from his athletic identity and professional identity as a retired Major League baseball player. However, both the reactions of his coworkers and his desire to still hold on to aspects of life as a professional athlete made it difficult for him to fully embrace a shift of identity.

> The minute you say professional sports, you're simply looked at and treated differently. They more or less treat you in the identity of the professional sports player as opposed to you as an individual. Your job title might not be as exciting to them and they might actually stereotype you as a certain person and they don't really care. I struggle with it. I just struggle. It is corporate America and I'm in medical sales. You know you struggle with being a man, you struggle with the bus not being parked at the stadium and you're not getting out of the

> bus at the stadium and being asked for twenty autographs—you aren't a part of that they don't want your autographs anymore.

While Hayden attributed much of the challenge in relinquishing his athletic identity to the perceptions and reactions of his peers and coworkers, there is a discernible sense of personal gratification that he derives from others recognizing his baseball career. His internal struggle between venturing into new territories and remaining in the familiar realm of his career induces a noticeable cognitive dissonance. Hayden explained that ultimately he felt a sense of pride in attempting to develop a multifaceted identity, striving to be recognized as more than just an athlete.

> I have always had a grounded sense of identity anyways. I get it, when people love you, it is more so due to the fact that it is associated with something they love—like baseball or sports. They are putting themselves in this fantasy of what it would be like to be you. So, they want a small piece of you. When you are in pro sports, and you are walking down a tunnel or something, and everybody is just reaching out for a piece of you. You feel like an animal, there is a piece of you that doesn't feel human. It is a really weird experience. I have always enjoyed helping people. Even when I was a pro player, I was always involved in the community. I would always be the guy who signed up to go to the elementary school to read to the kids. I was MVP of the community pro player of the year. I always win those. I just realized this is for a window of time, it is not forever. I had a good grip on the fact that I'm a man in a uniform and I'm 27 and can hit a baseball just as good as everybody in the world. This isn't really who I am, it is just what I do right now.

Hayden was deliberate in his efforts to cultivate an identity separate from sports. His engagement in community service and his framing of professional baseball as "just a job" are testament to this deliberate approach. Nevertheless, having identified as a professional athlete for a significant portion of his life, Hayden found it challenging to wholly adopt a new identity post-sports. This internal conflict even resulted in interpersonal tensions with coworkers whom he felt lacked the credibility he associated with being a former athlete.

> It is hard because sometimes you want to puff your chest out and say to people in regular America, "Do you know who you are talking to? I am in the hall of fame for professional sports. You couldn't hit a 50-mph baseball fast as I could hit one blind folded right-handed." If you want to just absolutely obliterate somebody that is trying to put themselves above you in the regular world. I never did that because first of all it is completely rude. Second of all, get off your high horse. I don't want to practice an ego like that because that is all it really is. You are just being a jerk, but so many people do it that I don't ever want to be that guy. I want to be known as a dude who is just a really humble

> good dude that had a great career and lived with respect for himself, his career and others. . . . My uncle tells me that all the time. He says, "Dude, if I had your job and my manager came down on me. . . . You are one humble dude because I would go tell him to fuck off. And tell him that he is closer to being less of an athlete than he will ever be in his life."

This passage is a succinct demonstration of the cognitive and social tension for Hayden in retirement. In one passage, he artfully discussed the need to move on from baseball, acknowledge its futility, and desire a life that is not defined by his athletic feats. Then, after articulating those sentiments, he described an experience at work where one of his managers or coworkers criticizes his approach, knowledge, or execution. While describing this incident, Hayden quickly reverted to a defensive stance, taking refuge in his past athletic glories. He is fully aware that his ability to hit a fastball is irrelevant to his success in medical sales, yet when faced with adversity or criticism, he finds comfort and validation in his past accomplishments.

Tim described recognizing the marked foreclosure of his athletic identity in retirement and how it significantly impacted his life. "I went to college, not for education, I was there for sports. And so my decision-making was based on my athletic ability, even my future was based on that. I graduated from college but it wasn't what internships am I taking, what recruiters am I talking to? It was what team can I attract to go play professionally. So, it was a constant and consistent decision-making process based around my athletic identity. I didn't realize it then, that I had foreclosed on that identity and not adapted and explored any others." Over time, Tim grew to understand how the messages he received during his childhood had shaped his journey and the challenges he faced. Not only did he have to develop self-awareness regarding his identity foreclosure, but he also needed to put forth a deliberate effort to explore and embrace other potential aspects of his identity.

> So my son goes into sixth grade and middle school, and he comes home with his yearbook, and you know the yearbooks are signed by all the friends and he says, "Dad, do you still have your middle school yearbook?" So, we went through and dug it out and sure enough I opened it up. I have not seen this thing in 25 years, whatever it is. And I look in there at all of us. This is my eighth grade going into high school and almost on every page there was someone who said, "Hey, can't wait to see you in the pros." "Hey [participant], save me tickets." Even teachers. "I can't wait to say that I knew you way back when." I mean, I was shocked to see this. I can imagine what a 13-year old's head would have looked like reading this stuff back then. But reading it now, no wonder why, I was consistently fed this messaging back then. So now I've had to go through this process of breaking up with that identity, identifying what else gives me a

> similar high, similar feeling, and sensation experience outside of sports to go forward in my life post career.

Even though he achieved his college degree, he was never there for anything more than the athletic opportunities that it might provide. This identity foreclosure was apparent in Tim's life from an early stage and continued to shape his self-perception well into retirement. Among the participants, it was those like Tim, with a severely restricted sense of self, who experienced the greatest degree of grief and confusion in their post-sport lives.

WHO AM I NOW?: EMBRACING A FUTURE BEYOND ATHLETICS

The most consistent theme expressed by participants in the immediate aftermath of retirement or even leading up to retirement was a sense of personal confusion. Participants who felt such uncertainty over their identity had little insight into what identity investments might be worthwhile after sport. There was frequently a notable lack of self-assurance regarding their ability to adopt any identity other than that of an athlete. Moreover, there was a pervasive worry that no other identity could be as fulfilling or significant as their athletic identity.

Chris shared that, after bouncing around to a few careers following his retirement from the NFL, he was engulfed by a feeling of restlessness. "I would like just enough, to make enough to pay the mortgage and call it a day. But I also like having that purpose, I didn't like doing radio and TV, it felt very purposeless. But coaching these kids, beating teams and losing teams, teaching lessons, I would imagine in the development part of it, helping these coaches out, being a part of something. I guess it would be more just to have purpose." Similar to other participants, Chris initially experienced anxiety due to a sense of purposelessness postretirement. This experience was terrifying and even debilitating for some of the athletes. While Chris had some knowledge that coaching youth would bring meaning and purpose to his life, he resisted the tendency to dive into that world because of the poor compensation. Ultimately, Chris had come to terms with this anxiety in his own unique way, but this process took time. He had to weigh the benefits of a well-compensated job against the potential for finding renewed purpose and meaning in a mentoring role.

Anna was a participant whose drive and determination were tied deeply to her athletic accomplishments. Anna consistently described the sense of meaning and fulfillment she derived from her distinct and exclusive identity as a professional hockey player. In the following excerpt, Anna reflected on her initial reactions to the end of her college hockey career. "I remember a lot of my teammates at the time were like, 'Oh, I'm excited, I'm ready to move on to the next chapter of my life.' I was in an absolute tailspin, because I was like, 'What am I going to do?' I was feeling that a little bit, just wondering how I was going to fill my time." While several of her teammates were looking forward to and curious about life after college hockey, Anna found the prospect of moving on to be a significant source of anxiety. Fortunately, Anna was able to maintain her athletic identity by securing a professional contract that extended into her mid-twenties. Nonetheless, even a few successful years in a professional league did little to curb the fear of what life would be like without hockey. When she was eventually deselected from professional hockey, she was once again confronted with the same existential crisis regarding her identity without hockey.

Steve found difficulty in conceptualizing his sense of self after he initially left sport. While he took immense pride in his role as a father and cherished the time spent with his children, he faced challenges in cultivating an identity that was distinct and separate from his athletic background.

> I went right into full-time, 100% stay-at-home dad for two years. Talk about a new appreciation for what women go through as mothers. Talk about rewarding, and then you talk about the most fucking hard thing I've ever done in my life. It was all wrapped in one. I was so grateful for the time I had with my two young boys. I've had time with all of my boys, but the two young guys when they were first born, I had them in my arms out of the hospital all throughout. I'm so thankful for that, but it was hard. I had days where my wife and I were just looking at each other with two babies and I'm not working, she obviously can't work, and I'm just like, "What am I doing? Where am I going with my life?"

During his interview, Steve expressed deep gratitude for his current role as a high school football coach, as well as for the joys of fatherhood and his supportive family. He shared an acute awareness of the numerous sacrifices his wife had made to facilitate his lengthy and prosperous NFL career, and he relished the opportunity to give back to her in his retirement. Despite his deep love for his children and the gratitude he felt for the chance to be a full-time father, there remained a palpable emptiness and lack of clear identity and meaning following his departure from the NFL. As will be discussed later, this sense of ambiguity and uncertainty began to dissipate only once he had fully embraced his coaching career.

Henry described how difficult it was to conceptualize a sense of identity that was not intertwined with elite hockey. After concussions ended his professional hockey career, he describes searching for a new sense of self.

> Honestly, I didn't do a good job with that. I would read and listen to podcasts and stuff like that and I dove into the health and wellness side. I read books about coaching and internalized a lot of that competitive angst that you're missing because that part just never leaves you. Whether I'm playing sports against [girlfriend] or golfing with friends, that part will never leave me. But not being able to do that on the level it was before, that part was the hardest thing. That part externalizes as mood changes and being bitter for a good amount of time where a big part of your identity just isn't there anymore and what you connected yourself to just wasn't there. I think that was the biggest part I struggled with—just what's next, and who am I next? I'm learning from the ground floor, where you have to build it all the way back up and you've just been doing hockey for the past 18 years. I have to start at zero again and figure it out.

Many athletes have little immediate insight into struggles with identity foreclosure as they are happening. It is not until years later that they may have profound insights into the struggles they faced. Acknowledging these challenges in real time, while they are unfolding, can be an arduous task. Henry stood out from many retired athletes in that he was acutely aware of the challenges he was facing early on in his retirement. He was proactive and intentional about addressing the loss of his athletic identity. However, despite his efforts, it took him several years to firmly establish a new sense of self. According to Henry, he had to undergo an extensive and deep exploration of his identity, almost like a psychological excavation, in order to lay the new groundwork for his sense of self. This was a long and enduring process, despite his awareness and intentionality to do the work.

Jess echoed the same sentiments, wondering who she truly was after her elite volleyball career was completed.

> It's hard because you can say you've been an athlete for ten years, but you're not really playing anymore unless you're still playing. And there's not a lot of adult volleyball leagues. There are co-ed leagues, but you are playing on a men's net and that's not who I was. That net was way higher than it should be! There's outdoor volleyball, sand volleyball. All of these different things. But even doing those seemed more like a recreational or fun thing. They don't feel like you have to be an athlete to do this. So, it has been hard because it is such a big part of your identity for so long and then it's not really a part of your identity anymore.

Jess competed in a sport that allowed for recreational outlets after she retired. Some athletes, especially contact sport athletes, simply do not experience this possibility. Nevertheless, this attempt to hold on to athletic identity through recreational endeavors could not fill the void she experienced in retirement. She explained that, from her viewpoint, she didn't need to identify as an athlete in order to enjoy recreational sports. In her mind, being an athlete implied engaging in activities that had higher stakes and required a more intense level of commitment. This perception had shaped her understanding of her identity within the realm of sports.

Tim opened up about the numerous challenges he faced in discovering fulfillment during retirement, realizing that he lacked the self-awareness to understand his own preferences and identity beyond the world of sports. Tim ventured into various activities and followed numerous suggestions from others in his quest for fulfillment, but the satisfaction and contentment he sought remained just out of reach. "It was just an incredible amount of confusion and then having to do things that I didn't want to do. I took a job running parking operations and I didn't like the work. It didn't excite me. There was no thrill, no fulfillment. It was just a career. And so, three years into that, I'm going mad thinking this sucks. . . . So I began to chase money." Professional football provided a deep sense of identity, meaning, and purpose for Tim. He was one of the participants in this study who displayed and expressed an incredibly strong sense of athletic identity during his career. Because nothing could fill this void or provide a foundation of identity quite like football, he found himself looking for direction from others as to what he should pursue next. This tendency to take direction was likely derived from his desire to be coached as an athlete. Nonetheless, the suggested directions did not provide any tangible sense of identity, meaning, or purpose. Consequently, he found himself caught up in the mundane pursuit of financial gain, likely as a means to distract himself from the emptiness he felt in terms of his identity.

UNDERSTANDING THE ROLE OF DIETING; EATING TO PERFORM

Several participants shared that the relationship they formed with food and dieting from a young age was directly linked to their athletic performance. For many, this created a disconnect between an understanding of how food fueled their bodies and what constitutes healthy eating and dietary balance. Participants shared that the messaging they received was predominantly related to eating to support peak performance, often centered around restriction and avoidance, and lacked the educational component to foster a healthy relationship with food. For many this dynamic was reinforced by messages that they received from parents and coaches that influenced their beliefs about food choices as good or bad which for some became internalized as a reflection of their own decision-making, leading to a difficult and maladaptive relationship with food, struggles with body image, and engaging in unhealthy compensatory patterns such as binge eating. As they transitioned into retirement, some participants' behaviors and mindsets related to nutrition, body composition, and physical activity shifted significantly. Previous tendencies that were directly linked to performance and athletic identity required realignment as participants learned to adjust expectations regarding exercise and dietary patterns into life after sport. For these participants, retirement brought about difficulties in establishing a balanced approach to eating and forming a positive relationship with food and their bodies. After spending years focusing on eating to perform, many participants recognized that they had not actually developed an understanding of what health looked like outside of sport. Ultimately, they had developed concepts around eating that were directly connected to their athletic identity and were surprised to find themselves unsure and in many cases unwell when they tried to continue these habits into retirement.

Arianna shared that she had "worried every time I ate something, what it was that I was eating. How would it affect my performance?" This was echoed by Issa, who also recognized the significant connection that had been built between sports culture and decisions such as dietary choices "every decision you make is to be a better hockey player." Often these decisions were influenced by outside messaging from coaches and parents, a shock to many in retirement who like Arianna were used to "being told what to do when." Some participants recognized that this was directly linked to the transitional task of moving from a lifestyle that was externally managed in almost every way by coaches and trainers, to one that they were now responsible for planning and implementing. This included planning meals, understanding what would make them feel good, and identifying and incorporating physical activity into their post retirement selves. Erica articulated these exact sentiments "You always have someone telling you what to do. This is what you should be eating, this is when you should be going to bed and then it was kind of like, figure it out."

Yet, for some, this process was coupled with the challenges of having to unlearn unhealthy and maladaptive patterns, as well as to recognize the detrimental impact that they had on their relationship with food. Issa highlighted having to come to terms with the unhealthy nature of her relationship with food. She acknowledged this maladaptive tendency developed from a desire to be a better athlete, as well as how she was conditioned to relate to food and dietary choices. "As far as body image, it was you know, I was always trying to eat towards being a good hockey player. My dad was really hard on me, on what I would eat, and that definitely fucked with my head a lot, especially being a woman. You know, saying are you sure you wanna eat that? I don't think you should do that. You know just like little shit, I just wanted a slice of pizza or whatever." The restriction that resulted from these messages increased maladaptive eating patterns and feelings of guilt and shame for Issa. "Late at night when everyone would go to bed, I would go to the cabinet and eat. I would binge almost anything, I wouldn't purge, but I would just eat junk food because nobody was around. Which was obviously not a healthy mindset or healthy eating habits or relationship with food by any means. It was hard for me to live that way." This created an additional layer to the transition process, having to heal the dysfunctional relationship with food and her body, which highlighted for this participant an aspect of her self-awareness that was underdeveloped.

RESTLESSNESS AND THE SEARCH FOR PURPOSE

Many participants expressed a sense of unease at the onset of their transition from sport into retirement. There was an almost pervasive sense of uncertainty regarding what to do next or, in some cases, how to take up tasks, set up goals, and accomplish them. However, in some cases, the goals that were set served more as random diversions, leaving participants questioning whether those objectives truly aligned with their genuine desires.

Anna detailed how she simply buried herself in obligations after it was clear that her career in professional hockey was ending. "My life was always just go-go-go. So, when ice hockey stopped, I immediately filled that void with getting a new job." She went on to explain how she experienced an urgent need to fill the existential void left by her retirement from hockey by immersing herself in a different sport.

> So, another thing I did to fill that void was all that time and energy that I spent on ice hockey. I chose the next best thing, which was roller hockey. I often reflect on why I made these choices, what drove me to not being satisfied. I think that's a big thing, because I just had to fill the void and I did whatever I needed to do, whether that was sacrificing my relationships with my family, with my partner. . . . I just attributed my feelings of sadness of hockey ending to, "I have nothing here. I have nothing to do. I have no friends, and if I take all of my time and my energy and I switch it to roller hockey. . . . I have games to play. I can do tournaments." So that was just filling the void or desperately trying to grasp onto my identity and all that I knew. . . . My work has been a huge distraction, and in a lot of ways, I feel like it has benefited me personally. And it has not benefited my life with my family or my friends or relationship, but it fills the void for me because it keeps me busy.

She candidly recognized in this section of her narrative that her post-hockey decisions led to a chaotic lifestyle that hindered her capacity for intimacy and time investment in her relationships. Nonetheless, a slower pace of life would have compelled her to confront the emptiness she felt in the absence of hockey. Engaging in constant work and weekly derby competitions served as a coping mechanism from having to face any deep existential question about who she might be without hockey. Staying busy was a safety net against falling into the void.

Jermaine spoke about how difficult it can be to redirect one's motivation and energy following a departure from a high-level athletic career.

> Being an athlete in college is basically like a full-time job. So when you lose that, you try to harness all of that time and energy into something else. And right now it's becoming staying in touch with my family and friends, still having that athletic prowess and the workout mentality as a part of my life and fitting within that image that I want, by keeping fit and keeping some identity there. And the rest of it goes to work, school, furthering my career, and stuff like that. Certain people struggle with that. If you played sports your whole life, when it's gone it's like, where does the rest of my time, identity and energy go? I'm not as passionate about what my next chapter is going to be as I was when I was playing. I'm trying my best and handling it the best I can because it was in the middle of a pandemic, but just trying to keep as busy as possible.

Although Jermaine didn't experience the same level of restlessness in confronting the loss of identity post-football as Anna did after hockey, there was still a real and acknowledged sense of angst after being deselected from the NFL. The very framework of his day-to-day life, which was once dictated by training schedules and game routines, now left him pondering questions like when to exercise, if he even should, and how intensely. There was a tangible level of energy that was displaced after sport. Though he had places to put the energy, none of these alternatives seemed as fulfilling or engrossing as his sporting career once was.

BEYOND THE SPOTLIGHT: POSTRETIREMENT QUEST FOR FULFILLMENT

In essence, many participants in this study faced significant challenges in discovering joy, fulfillment, or meaning in activities or pursuits outside of sport. Like Jermaine, they made an effort to channel their competitive energy into other behaviors, habits, and activities, but none of these endeavors provided a comparable sense of purpose and satisfaction that sports had provided so consistently throughout their lives.

Chris described how, initially, he was looking forward to life after the NFL. He anticipated the freedom from intense physical strain and the rigorous schedule that comes with a professional football career. "I was very intense about it. And then when you're done, I was just ready to go. I didn't have a lot of bad feelings. As well as you can end in terms. So, I left fine, I enjoyed a break from it." However, the reality of retirement was much different than he had imagined.

> And then you get bored, think you want to do something, and then it's a hard transition of, "What do I want to do?" I did a lot of different things. Coaching would have been, because I love football, but it had to be on the high school level. I didn't want to have the professional commitment because of family. I love coaching high school, but financially it's just not the same. . . . I got into radio and TV, so it was relatively easy to do that. I always kind of had that. It was good and bad. I felt like if I didn't have that I would have gone into a lot of different directions, which I regret now, because I'm [age] and don't quite know what to do. I love being busy all the time, but now I'm looking for something else. . . . It was fine for a while, not doing anything, and then the radio and TV was just enough, and then I didn't like that as much anymore, being a talking head. A lot of it is entertainment, a lot of the guys don't know what they're talking about. But I still did it. So far, coaching is the only thing that has obviously been pretty fulfilling for me. . . . I just think the radio and TV thing gave me a crutch to lean on and basically not do anything. I regret that now, and I would have been much more fulfilled coaching than I ever was with radio and TV.

Though he did acknowledge that some occupations, specifically coaching, would have brought him fulfillment, those were not financially suitable to the goals he still had, even after roughly a decade in the NFL. Adopting the role of what he described as a "talking head" in local radio and media felt insincere to him. Naturally, he possessed the intelligence and experience in sports to pursue this option, but he believed his nuanced understanding of professional sports didn't conform to the exaggerated style often prioritized in sports media and talk radio.

Nonetheless, one opportunity that kept him busy for some time after retirement was fatherhood. "I was around my kids all the time. But then also too, it's like, 'All right,' you know [laughs]. . . . It's kind of a mixed bag for me. It's not horrible, but it's not great." Ironically, he believed that transitioning after his football career would have been smoother if it had been shorter. The amount of money he made gave him the freedom and time to try new things after football, but it never forced him to fully commit to a career. Now, he finds himself wandering from opportunity to opportunity, only to discover that none of them offer the same level of fulfillment as being actively involved in the game or coaching.

> In my neighborhood I have a friend of mine who played in the NHL for ten years. We talk all the time about it. He's just hitting it now. My youngest is eight, and he's younger than me, so his youngest is in diapers, he's in that transition. We reminisce about the good old days, and joke around. But just like anything,

> I got into the league at 21, 22, and it lets you stay at that age for however long you play. So, it's like, I was playing football and then all of a sudden, I'm done, and I'm like "I'm 33 and married with two kids, what the fuck happened?"

In contrast to Chris, Hayden did have to settle into a full-time career almost immediately after his professional baseball career ended. He played professionally for roughly a decade, but much of it was in the minor leagues where his salary was limited. He described how he struggles to feel fulfilled in his medical sales job compared to how he felt as a professional baseball player.

> Your job is to just tell the customers you work for how wonderful they are and then just don't tell them anything about your personal life and then go about your business. . . . I hate it. I hate that part of it. I hate being fake. I hate having to cut back on the information and fear that you are going to use that information against me. I don't care! I am who I am. My dad had health problems and my mom is a bitch sometimes. . . . I played ball and I played hard and it is because of those reasons I don't care. In the culture of sports, nobody cares if you have personal problems. You are either good or you are not good. But in the corporate setting, these types of things matter because they are judging you. It is like this whole secretive world of being fake when you are online doing all these zoom calls.

Sales, in some ways, bears similarities to sports. Several participants in this study went into the sales world and found a sense of fulfillment, meaning, and competitive purpose in those careers. However, like Chris, Hayden attributed at least some of this sense of fulfillment to the belief that there exists a substantial degree of inauthenticity within the world of sales. He perceived the sales world as fundamentally transactional, a realm where relationships held significance solely when one could offer something of tangible value to a client, coworker, or manager. Undoubtedly, sport can have a similar level of transactional relationality. It would be valuable to know whether Hayden experienced less of this in sport or if he simply tolerated it more in sports because of his genuine passion and fulfillment as a professional baseball player.

BEYOND THE "HIGHS": THE POST-SPORTS EXPERIENCE

Another void experienced by participants who felt identity foreclosure was centered around a loss of opportunity to feel the strong and intense emotions experienced in sport. They made many attempts to replicate the exhilarating "highs" often encountered in elite competition. However, other activities outside of sport failed to provide the same consistent rush of adrenaline that was often expected and predictable in sport.

Chris explained how the stress and pressure of playing in the NFL provided an incredible adrenaline rush for him. One that, more often than not, sparked his focus, energy, and commitment. However, as he approached the end of his career, he shared feeling exhausted from the rush. "After 11 years I took everything I had to take personally and expressed it out. I feel like, I guess that maybe got me there so long, but it probably shredded me emotionally." Upon retirement, he described initially feeling a sense of relief at the onset of life after sport. "That period of time was very intense for me, so when I was done. . . . I just had to get away from it. I invested so much of my time and energy and I think I needed to get away from that. I needed to step back, but after time, I kind of lost my mojo." After a few years of reprieve, he found himself unnerved by the lack of emotional stimulation in his quiet life after sport. "I enjoy the process of it, the stress of it, and I love being devastated when we lose, and I certainly love when we win. It's meant a lot to me the past couple of years, it's made me a better person. So there's something there, a little taste again, I'm getting back into it. But for the better part of the last seven years, I was just toast. I didn't have a lot to give. At least to stick my neck out there and really be held accountable." In this passage, he acknowledged that he had been burned out by the torrent and intensity of competition, particularly in terms of his own competitive demeanor in sports. After spending over a decade in the NFL, he was exhausted and wanted respite from the relentless competition. However, after that period of respite, he felt a strong desire to go back into the world of competition, despite its all consuming nature. His life with it was exhausting, but his life without it felt dull. Even in retirement, he still craved a taste of it, fully cognizant of the sacrifices it entailed.

Hayden explained how he both experienced and observed numerous professional athletes grappling with the loss of excitement in their lives after their sporting careers. "If you are in really high professional sports, what is the only activity that is going to replicate the bottom of the ninth, drilling a home run or a touch down? Whatever it may be, it is all addictive behaviors. Gambling, drinking behaviors, whatever. Two guys I played baseball with got their pilots license after they retired. They crashed them into a beach and a building. . . . They are so used to that feeling, dude. It is like you live in that feeling. The only thing that replicates it are the ridiculously high thrill activities. That could be catastrophic." Hayden offered a nuanced description of how high-risk or even self-injurious tendencies can be appealing to former professional athletes who enjoyed the adrenaline rush of high-stakes circumstances in sport. He is not the only participant who drew parallels between this allure and addiction or substance use. While such a comparison might seem extreme, one should exercise caution before dismissing it as hyperbole. The essence of the argument lies in the ongoing, widespread, and at times, all-encompassing void that individuals experience when the adrenaline rush of sports is no longer present. Although various forms of work and career provide opportunities at adrenaline rush and high-stakes endeavors, these tend to be infrequent and sporadic. What sets sports apart, and perhaps justifies the comparison to addiction, is the remarkable consistency of these experiences, occurring almost daily in elite-level sports.

Arianna also confirmed that one of the most difficult aspects of leaving elite-level competition was the emotional void she experienced in relation to high-stakes moments in sport. "I would say missing the high of big moments in sport is the hardest part. If I craved anything about playing at that level again it would be to, you know, win the big game. Even to lose one. Just to have that feeling where something is on the line. I miss experiencing the emotion that goes along with that level of sport." For Arianna, it wasn't necessarily the feeling of success or accomplishment when the game is in balance that she mourned the loss of. Rather it was the mere ability to have something exist in the balance, to have the stakes be raised, that she yearned for in retirement. Whether it resulted in victory or defeat, these situations demanded a heightened emotional investment. The absence of regular opportunities to elevate her emotions to this level has created a void in her life after sport.

Tim also recognized that he spent a great deal of time "chasing the high" and striving to replicate the same feelings of love and respect that accompanied his achievements in athletics. "I retired from professional sports in (year). I struggled for 6 years on where I can get that same high. Where do I get that same love and respect and the feeling of high performance? I just couldn't find it and I struggled with jobs and developing my career. . . . The best part about sport was being able to explore my limits or lack thereof. Physically and mentally, being able to push myself past my boundaries. . . . It was always extremely exhilarating for me to try to knock down those boundaries." The allure of sport to Tim was a journey of self-transcendence, one where he pushed and tested his physical limitations in competition. In some respects, this was a different expression of "the high" compared to other participants. In a somewhat unique way, Tim was deeply drawn into this process, losing himself while pushing his body's ability to its competitive limits. Finding oneself on the other side of perceived limitations can indeed be an exhausting and even dangerous endeavor. Nevertheless, the thrill of confronting these fears and boundaries can become addictive and challenging to replace in life after retiring from sports.

THE CHALLENGE OF RELATING: ATHLETE SKEPTICISM FOR NONATHLETES

One of the unique psychosocial aspects observed in participants who exhibited a high level of identity foreclosure was their tendency to harbor skepticism toward nonathletes in their retirement. This skepticism was primarily manifest in the workplace, affecting interactions with coworkers and supervisors, but at times, it also extended beyond the professional sphere to include friends and family members.

Juan explained how he harbored skepticism toward coworkers or colleagues who were not former athletes. His skepticism was most pronounced when it came to what he perceived as disparities in work ethic between athletes and nonathletes.

> You just can see the differences between athletes and nonathletes, just from a value standpoint. And, I'm not saying it's everybody, but you definitely can tell who are athletes just by the way that they carry themselves and what they value. . . . Time management standpoint, meeting deadlines, being on time with meetings, discipline, self-discipline. Not having someone have to micromanage you and hover over you to do the right thing or get your work done. Being able to work well with others in the team. It's just something that you can notice if someone were to tell you that they were an athlete and you're like, "Oh, okay. Makes sense."

Certainly, these are strong opinions articulated by Juan, particularly when it came to his coworkers and colleagues who do not have an athletic background. He openly criticized their work ethic, their sense of solidarity, and their ability to manage day-to-day tasks and responsibilities. It is challenging to determine whether these perceptions of coworkers constituted an accurate assessment of work ethic and demeanor or were merely influenced by his background. Nevertheless, for the purposes of this study, such distinctions do not matter. What does matter is that a former athlete who has experienced some degree of identity foreclosure toward sports may encounter difficulties in establishing trust and cohesion with coworkers and colleagues during retirement.

Hayden articulated how it was difficult for him to take management or direction from his bosses when he left the world of professional baseball. In his role as a medical salesman, his boss directed him to implement specific strategies during sales meetings. He described his feelings when receiving criticism and instructions from his boss. "You want to puff out your chest and say to people in regular America, 'Do you know who you're talking to? I am in the hall of fame for professional sports. You couldn't hit a 50-mile-per-hour fastball. I could hit one blindfolded.' You just want to absolutely obliterate somebody that is trying to put themselves above you in the regular world. . . . I want to say to my manager, 'Dude, I was signing autographs for your kids. Now you are telling me that my organization skills are bad?'" He went on to explain how he often resisted these inclinations. However, his perspective on coworkers and bosses whom he perceives as nonathletes is quite revealing. It's important to note here that this is solely Hayden's perception of these individuals. It is entirely possible that some of the coworkers he has developed a significant level of cynicism toward were athletes at some point in their lives, and perhaps even highly accomplished ones. The key distinction lies in the fact that they did not play his sport at his level and, thus, there is a gap in his respect for their skill and acumen.

The obvious question that arises here is: What does the ability to hit a fastball have to do with achieving success in the field of sales? On the surface, presumably very little. However, many athletes echoed this sentiment in their lives after retiring from sports. There is a nearly unanimous inclination to hold on to a sense of their past identity and the skills that constituted that identity. Skills exhibited in other domains can be easily dismissed or seen as inferior. It appears that this could be a mechanism for safeguarding one's self-esteem in a new environment where one's abilities may not shine as brightly as they did in professional sports. In essence, it's a way of saying, "Even if I'm not excelling in sales, it doesn't really matter because none of these individuals can achieve what I once did in sports." In other words, this subconscious and immediate skepticism serves as a form of protection for the retired athlete who may be experiencing professional mediocrity for the first time.

Hayden concluded this section of the interview with a particularly insightful observation that supports the notion that this skepticism and isolation may serve as a means of shielding oneself from vulnerability in the face of new insecurities in a professional world beyond the realm of sports. "That is a lot of the reason why a lot of them stay in [sport] culture. They do not feel any other value than in what they did as a player. Now they have to just coach because they do not see themselves as anything else."

Joe shared that his identity as an athlete and a hockey player, while opening many doors in his retirement career as a financial advisor, limited his opportunities for truly connecting with peers and coworkers.

> All my friends are still athletes. They are former college hockey players, really most of them. The only other friends that I have that aren't college hockey players were other [alma mater] athletes. I'm friends with all the golfers and wrestlers from [alma mater], guys like that. I would like to be able to be friends with more people. I don't know how to do it yet. I don't know what social platforms can allow me to meet people and relate to people. What do I do if I'm not

> working or hanging out with [girlfriend]? I'm golfing, working out, doing yoga, and I'm doing a spin class. I'm only doing athletic things right? So it's still my identity as far as the shape I keep my body in and my ability to relate to people. I need to get better at branching out further but it's still who I am.

Joe expressed a desire to "branch out" of his athletic circle in life after sport. Unlike some other participants who were dismissive of colleagues and coworkers without elite-level sports experience, he was not nearly as critical in his expressions. Yet, he did struggle to trust that colleagues who were not former athletes would share his interests or demeanor in these activities. While he acknowledged that people who were not elite athletes also participated in activities like golf, yoga, and spin classes, he struggled to find common ground and initiate connections. While he wanted to find other connection points, he remained skeptical about his ability to genuinely relate to individuals who did not identify as athletes. Although he was cognizant of the potential consequences of reduced identity, he continued to grapple with the challenge of bridging the gap between himself and peers who were not former athletes in life after sports.

ANTISOCIAL TENDENCIES AND ENTITLEMENT: POSTRETIREMENT IMPLICATIONS

For several participants, what appeared to be a possible consequence of being solely invested in their identity as athletes was a feeling of entitlement and a disregard for one's peers in life outside of sport. This sense of entitlement may be connected to the skepticism they held toward nonathletes. In this study, some athletes also mentioned observing antisocial behaviors among their peers while they were in elite competitive environments. A significant portion of these behaviors were linked to participants experiencing a culture of antisocial tendencies on the teams they competed on or against.

Hayden recounted how he had observed his teammates and peers behaving with a sense of careless disregard and entitlement toward their peers.

> The reason is because honestly things happen in professional athletics. For football, you can just absolutely obliterate that guy on the field and that is legal. In baseball, if somebody is talking trash or disrespects you, you can get them back on the field. But when you are in regular everyday life, there are policies and laws that protect people from doing these types of things. In sports, there is not and on top of that you are surrounded by enablers who are afraid to say no to you. That is a whole other topic. You are never around somebody that says, "You know what? Sleeping around with a hundred women is probably not a safe practice." You are around people that say, "Oh my God, dude, that is incredible!

> Show me pictures." You don't even have to obey the law. The whole environment is a godly manifestation of what life is. Just running ramped with no roles to be idolized. And then put a million bucks in a twenty-two-year-old's pocket that has had no supervision anyways when they were growing up. Now you get the stories we hear on ESPN. That is what happens.

According to Hayden, there are rules of social behavior that are adhered to in a civil society but they simply did not apply in the world of elite or professional sports. He went on to describe the etiology of these altered rules as a form of entitlement, particularly linked to the special treatment that professional athletes received during their careers.

> The coolest part of being a pro athlete is knowing that God gave you talent that less than 1 percent of the world has. The way the system is set up, it really makes you feel elite. You are walking in as a young man where everything is done for you. It would be like going to a country club, where the minute your car pulls in, they are grabbing your bags and asking you if you need anything. All the conditions are absolutely perfect. You have this fake sense of, it is almost like a setup. I absolutely loved it. It is a great setup to feel like the man all the time.

It is always important to recognize the complexity of one's self-narrative when conducting qualitative research. We must remember that Hayden previously expressed how he personally tried to distance himself from any notion that he was unique or treated exclusively based on his athletic ability. However, in this context, he seems to have relished aspects of it, expressing nostalgia for the influence and attention he experienced in his previous life. In Hayden's case, it would be reasonable to assume that he is grappling with a certain level of cognitive dissonance regarding his past indulgence in entitlement and his aversion to the negative social and emotional habits it can foster in life after retiring from sports.

Finally, and in one last effort to delve deeper into the dissonance, Hayden provided a detailed account of how an entitled mindset personally affected him while he was working in medical sales after he left professional baseball. He described an irony that many sales companies face when trying to hire retired athletes.

> I told my boss, you are better off hiring the people that didn't make it in professional sports. Unlike me, you are better off hiring kids that wanted to play but didn't make it. . . . Ones who wanted to play but they just weren't good enough because that is the kid who is going to sell like his hair is on fire. The problem with guys like me in this environment is that I was so successful in sports that the doctors or customers don't want to meet with me or cancel on me, I am not going to call that guy back begging for an appointment. I don't care. I can play

> sports blindfolded. You can buy my baseball card on eBay and I will autograph it for your kids when it is convenient for me. I am not on your time; you are on my time. I would always say . . . an actual super successful athlete won't do great in this environment.

In this passage, Hayden described how he loathed criticism from his bosses and resented any occasions when customers wouldn't show him the level of respect he felt he had earned from his professional baseball career. Despite sales departments assuming that the same competitive instincts developed in sports would seamlessly transfer to the high-stakes, extrinsic-reward-oriented world of sales, they overlooked a crucial motivational aspect during the hiring process. In Hayden's case, he never held the same level of passion for sales as he did for baseball. He never shifted his identity into that of a salesperson after his baseball career. Sales was merely a job that a former professional baseball player stumbled into because the money was good and he could keep paying his bills. Despite his best efforts to distance himself from his baseball career, he mostly identified as a baseball player while in medical sales. When he faced criticism for his shortcomings as a salesman, his default response was defensiveness. He would instinctively retreat to a social-cognitive place that was more or less dominated by his baseball identity. "Well, I am just a visitor in this world, anyway. And you have no idea how powerful I was in my previous competitive career." As a visitor in the world of sales, he could always deflect his shortcomings and keep a short temper with those who might criticize him for his lack of acumen in this field.

MISSING PIECES OF SELF: THE IMPACT OF IDENTITY FORECLOSURE

Many of the participants in this study recognized and took great pride in the numerous ways in which elite athletic performance provided them transferable skills that contributed to their success in post-sport careers and lives (Jess, Issa) such as work ethic (Joe, Kurt, Jess, Deonte), communication skills (Kurt, Jess, Esteban) leadership (Kurt, Jess), time management (Juan, Jess; Chris), self-discipline (Juan, Esteban, Chris), and teamwork (Dannie).

Joe depicted this perspective when he expressed his belief that being an athlete correlates with becoming an outstanding employee, a sentiment shared by many other participants. Despite his goals being primarily centered around sports and his athletic identity, he genuinely appreciated the values and attributes he acquired through his career in sports.

> When you asked me how I identify with it [being an athlete], it was a way to separate people who can work extremely hard. I just saw it as a result of hard work and the reward for everything I did everyday. I think it separates athletes into a different category in society and that's why people want to hire athletes and that's why, you know I was staring at my phone at 12:29 waiting for it to hit 12:30 for your call, waiting to answer it. If I was five minutes early for a bus I would've missed it. I was 15 minutes early for everything. It teaches you so much about life and discipline and just the way you operate as a person. There are things you can't get away with in the athletic world.

While there were numerous accounts of positive attributes, such as the ones described above, participants also acknowledged that many aspects of the self were not cultivated as a result of sports culture, messaging, and identity foreclosure. The skills that are emphasized in sports culture stand out as excellent values and qualities but come at the cost of being developed as a whole, well-rounded person, as a human first. Some participants recognized that they were not encouraged to have a sense of self that could stand alone, a place where an internalized understanding of who they truly were could be built from. This left many with their sense of self being tied solely into what they were doing—playing elite sport—rather than what qualities they had that made them a more complex and unique individual. It also left them without important skills to manage retirement and life after sport.

For some of the participants, while attributes such as confidence were apparent during their athletic performance, these otherwise positive attributes vanished quickly in the face of retirement. Unfortunately, these traits were not adequately tethered to self identity, but rather success in sport. This gap highlights the difference in being confident in one's athletic skill versus having confidence in oneself as a person, or an underdevelopment of self.

Tim acknowledged a strong sense of identity foreclosure in his career and retirement. Being an athlete became who he was, and his struggles in transitioning and creating a fulfilling life after football were directly tied to how he developed—or underdeveloped—this sense of identity. He shared that his advice to athletes transitioning out of elite sport would be to recognize the distinction between who you are and what you do. "Get a strong sense of who you are, because you're not an athlete. It's what you do. You need to identify with who you are." This sentiment was echoed by several of the participants who recognized the distinction that needed to be drawn between being an athlete and being a person who is also an athlete (Jermaine, Henry, Erica). Henry also shared that it is important to "understand that what you do isn't who you are." He described how much of his self-worth became centered on his performance, what others thought of him, and needing to redefine his sense of self as a key role in retirement. "I was like that 1000 percent, Where it's like who's [participant]? Oh yea, he's involved with hockey. He's this or that. And before I used to be so wrapped up in my performance. Even outside perceptions and what this person may think of me, but even now it's still a struggle I think, but now you know you need to define yourself by your passion and what you think you are to people and how you can help people." He shared that while he now understands the need to develop as a whole person and utilize a broader lens to define himself that these are not habits that are easy to break and rebuilding one's sense of self takes time. "That is a huge benefit but it's not like I'm there all of the time because you still care about those things to some extent and that's just the truth. Redefining who you are as a person and not what defines you, if that makes sense."

Similarly, Issa struggled with how to feel like she was enough without her athletic identity. In this passage, she highlighted the underdeveloped nature of her sense of self and how this led to her devaluing her other identities, attributes, and eventually career choices. "I've always been a hockey player. So, now I'm just a teacher and that doesn't sound like enough. I'm trying to figure out that being [participant's name] is just enough and not feeling like I had to have something else. Just do things I'm interested in and enjoy and that's okay. It doesn't have to be competitive and perfectionist and pressure like it was when I was playing." For this participant, like many of the others, her self-concept had been built around immense athletic successes at the expense of developing self-worth and a connection to who she was as an entire person. This process increased the internal conflict and feelings of discontent that she felt while trying to navigate retirement. Jermaine identified this as one of the most important lessons that he had to learn in retirement. "You don't need to tie your self-worth to your sport. And I struggled with that and I think some other athletes do too." He recognized how much of an influence being an elite athlete had on self-evaluation and positive self-regard.

Finally, Issa shared that her struggles with understanding who she was as a person resulted in a great deal of insecurity in retirement. "I feel like I didn't know myself as well, so I second-guessed a lot of these decisions that were made, and that just made me insecure." She shared that not only did she not have a good grasp on who she was as a person, but she also began to question what her true personality might be. "That was one of my main roadblocks in my head and would in turn make me sad. . . . I was happier around my friends but around people I didn't know I was quiet. . . . That's not my personality and so I felt like I was retreating into a shell so it was definitely more sad and depressed during that time." Issa realized that this was not how she had come to recognize herself. Her sense of identity and purpose was in question, and it led her to question if all her confidence had been about hockey and not actually something she established as a core part of herself.

One of the areas that the athletes identified feeling that they had not truly developed was in their ability to manage and process failure. Tim shared "I never learned through sport how to handle failure and how to rebound from it." Similar to Tim, Arianna and Beth identified failure as a normal aspect of life that they felt ill equipped to manage in retirement. "The ability to face failure . . . to deal with failure." For some of the athletes such as Hayden, taking criticism about job performance in retirement was especially challenging given the success that he had experienced as a professional athlete. "Like dude, I was signing autographs for your kids now you are telling me my organization skills are bad?" While he eventually was able to realize that his managers were trying to help him, adjustment to this type of feedback was uncomfortable.

Beth also echoed that being comfortable with and knowing how to cope with failure was not something that she had developed. When describing the hardest thing about being an athlete she shared: "I'm sure this is a cliché . . . failure. I don't know many sports where you fail and you feel kind of like you work so hard every single day and people come to your games and your family comes and you just want to do well. I think the hardest part is dealing with failure in a positive way." For athletes transitioning into retirement, not being able to manage failure created intense emotional responses as they explored potential careers, interests, and tried to find a passion outside of competing as an elite athlete.

Similarly, Dannie recognized that she had not learned to manage expectations of herself or others or to set them appropriately based on situations and circumstances. This can be detrimental to former athletes who are trying to navigate change and unfamiliar roles in their lives. "I think I am still actively working on unwiring a bit. I had the highest expectations of myself, all the time." These expectations not only influenced her view of herself, but also that of others, including her coworkers. She realized that this tendency of holding others to incredibly high standards, ultimately, was not useful in building collegial relationships. "I think it was a bit detrimental to me and I think it still is. I am still actively having to work at managing my expectations of myself and others. I have the highest expectations of my coworkers and if they don't meet it, I'm like, 'What are you doing? Why aren't you doing your job? That is not healthy!'" While she has the awareness to realize that this mentality was maladaptive in her work life after sport, the adoption of healthier measurements of success is a process that has taken time for her to begin to develop.

Jermaine, like Dannie, held high expectations of himself to be in a continual process of improvement which led to him feeling as if he is "never really satisfied." This desire to do more, have more, be more, interferes with the ability to ever actually feel like you are enough. While this is a major motivator for achieving goals, it leads to discomfort in one's own skin and needing validation to measure success. "I'll always have that inner struggle with me, but it's good. I think being complacent is never a good thing, especially in the workplace . . . but I'm always going to have that struggle of why can't the boss see me doing this? I want to do this and stuff like that. So, I think it's a bit of a two-way struggle." For many individuals, the ability to see the positive side of an attribute allows them to overshadow the detrimental aspects, especially when the harm is directed at their sense of self.

Similar to Jermaine, Anna also has found herself struggling with never being satisfied and always looking for the next thing to focus her energy on. For this participant, this has led to her struggling to sit in her own skin and to be constantly focused extrinsically for purpose and sense of self. "As I get older, I reflect back on why I made these choices, what drove me to not be satisfied. I think that's a big thing, because I just had to fill the void and I did whatever I needed to do." While this participant used the term "void" to describe the empty space that sport has left in her life after she no longer played elite hockey, it particularly manifested when people failed to acknowledge her for that role, and when she was not channeling all her energy into competition. Yet the void that this participant continually attempted to fill with distractions never stopped feeling empty because it is not hockey that is missing, but an understanding and appreciation of herself, as a whole person. "My work has been a huge distraction. . . . It makes me be forced only to think about someone else and avoid my feelings. Which is not necessarily good." This avoidance has led to her struggling to sit with herself or without a way to focus her energy. "I don't like sitting, I feel like I always need to be doing something. I don't feel accomplished or fulfilled if I'm like 'I don't have nothing to do this week.'" She conveyed that the only moments of contentment she experiences are when she is distracted or has something to anticipate. It is evident that this participant lacks the self-awareness to perceive herself beyond the foreclosed identity of a competitor.

Self-awareness was a key factor that Tim found to be missing in his understanding of himself, including who he was as an athlete, and he shared believing that the development of the whole person was a crucial missing piece of his sports training and engagement throughout his childhood and early adulthood. "I wish my coaches had helped me understand self-awareness, helped me understand, you know, get clarity on what my strengths were, what my weaknesses are, what my challenges were and to be able to get comfortable with them, with those elements of me. It would have served me much greater as an athlete and I know it would have helped me perform a lot better. Had I had a sense of self-awareness, it would have helped my confidence." He continued, acknowledging the advantages he believed self-awareness could offer during the transition out of sports. Many of his challenges were directly linked to not comprehending who he is and what he would excel at. "It would have helped me in that transition, when there was a lot of noise. A lot of, you know, good intentioned people wanted to point me in the right direction. But without self-awareness, I was reactive. . . . Oh, you think this is the right path, you're probably right. . . . I wasn't strong at knowing what I'm good at, I couldn't follow my gut, so I just went along with what others thought I should do." For some of the participants, not having a strong sense of who they were as people, their attributes, the things they enjoy and dislike, led to an unstable sense of self and a reliance on the feedback of others as an evaluative tool of their worth.

Joe recognized that his sense of self was tied to the validation of others and that it was very difficult for him to manage situations where his performance did not equal the feedback that he received. When he was faced with a coach that did not like him for reasons that he could not identify, he became determined to change that perspective. Having perceived himself for his whole career as being someone who could overcome adversity, he shared his perspective on how he viewed himself as a player: "I was always an underdog just because of my size and the teams I chose to play for. . . . I had to earn my way there. I always overcame every ounce of adversity. . . . So I was just like this is another guy, this is just one more out of five who didn't respect me from the beginning. So, like I figured I would turn him eventually." When this initial approach to proving his worth did not end in success, this participant found himself without the internalized sense of self to realize that the feedback was not actually about his performance but rather how the coach felt about him. This led to a great deal of confusion when he knew he had played well, and the coach would not even look at him. The unmet need for validation left him often feeling "broken." Since his retirement he has tried to turn these painful memories into fuel for a successful career as a financial advisor, reflecting on how in hindsight even the painful experiences are also useful. "The last major thing it (being an athlete) taught me was to have thick skin. I went through things with hockey that nothing in life could ever compare to in the business world. Nothing will ever seem daunting the way that some things did in the sports world. It built up a good hard shell for me too in dealing with life and people." While the ending of his career was not what he had hoped, and one that has lasting effects on his overall emotional health, he recognized the uniqueness of these attributes and how they position him to be elite in other aspects of his life post sport. Yet they did not come without the costs associated with identity foreclosure.

BETWEEN YESTERDAY AND TOMORROW: ATHLETES' PATH TO RECONNECT AND REINVENT

For some athletes in this study, especially those who still exhibited high athletic identity, a full exit from sport was difficult to accept. A few participants embarked on a seemingly endless series of efforts to make a comeback to high-level competition as athletes. However, most of these attempts ultimately fell short or failed to provide the same level of satisfaction as their earlier experiences in competition. Several participants found ways to stay in competitive arenas out of fear that their identity could not expand beyond what was known. Coaching was the most prevalent example of this effort, but it was not the sole option. Other participants found novel athletic endeavors or novel ways to engage in traditional athletic endeavors.

Anna recounted how she remained committed to making a return, even as it was becoming increasingly evident that her career as a professional hockey player was likely over. "I have been trying to get back into it but I'm kind of far out now. I'm getting older and women's hockey is just growing, younger girls are getting involved. I am going to keep going back until [the women's professional hockey teams] physically remove me from the building. Once they do, I will just go back to roller derby." Anna was one of the athletes in this study who pursued another form of high-level sport after she was deselected from women's professional hockey. In her mid-twenties, she made the decision to quit her job, having just ended her long-term relationship, and relocated across the country to compete in elite-level roller derby tournaments. However, she continued to persistently try out for professional hockey teams while competing in roller derby. No matter how many times she was deselected from professional rosters, her identity remained deeply rooted in sports, and she yearned for the highest levels of competition.

Like several participants, Steve knew that he wanted to settle into a career in sport after his NFL career. One of the difficulties he encountered was the instability and transitory nature of coaching professional or college football. He talked about how he initially did work in radio and media at his college alma mater, only to discover that it did not provide the satisfaction he sought.

> Being so close to football was so tantalizing that I knew I had to go coach. I knew whenever football was ending, I was going to coach. It was a question of am I picking up my family? Am I going to coach in professional football? Division one? Or am I going to be able to make it work at a place that I care about locally? Because [high school he is coaching at now] had been asking me for years, but could I make a career out of it? I chose that having lived that life with my oldest son for the first two years of his life where we moved him from [U.S. state] to [U.S. state], [U.S. state] back to [U.S. state], down to [U.S.

> state] and back. I thought, you know what? Financially, I'm okay. I don't have to do this and I'm going to pass on that. I wanted stability. I wanted my kids to have roots.

Despite anticipating the stability and peace of a life after the NFL and a life outside of professional or college coaching, Steve shared a unique anecdote about the details of his final season in the NFL. He had presumed his career was finished after wrapping up the previous season as a 30-year-old third-string quarterback. He spent the offseason training but never signed with a team through the summer and early fall. However, several weeks into the season, he was signed by a team and was suddenly brought back to play.

> It was towards the end of the season and at the end of the year, I remember my contract was up for my seventh year and I didn't have a great feeling. I don't think they're going to re-sign me, and I went home that off-season and said, "I'm not ready for it." But I remember having a conversation with my wife like, "this might be it." Fast-forward to the April draft, they tried to re-sign me but they had also signed two other guys, and basically wouldn't guarantee me anything, other than, "We need you to come to camp. But we love you, you know how we are about you, we'd love to have you back." I said "You know what, I appreciate it but I'm going to hold out and see what happens." I still wanted to play but I wasn't going to put myself in that situation where I had zero chance and it was basically going to be less chance than I had before. And I went that whole summer, stayed in great shape, first July of my life where I didn't have football since I was eight. Just at home with my boys and it was just in a state of uncertainty. . . . I get a call from my agent: "go to this workout, go to this workout." Finally, it got to mid-October and there were no more workouts, it's purely just to see if you're healthy enough if they ever needed you in an emergency and I just . . . I can't keep getting on a plane and doing this. Because every time you do it there's a certain amount of stress and anxiety. You gotta put your best foot forward. Then I get a call out of nowhere. I'm literally changing my son's diapers. My agent calls and says, "You got to get on a plane." I said, "I don't want to do this shit no more. I told you that, I'm not doing any more workouts." He goes, "No, [NFL team] is signing you." I go, "What? [NFL team]? I don't have any connections there." He goes, "Doesn't friggin matter. They don't have a quarterback and they need somebody." So I get on a plane that day and fly down on a Friday, take my physical. I travel with the team to [NFL city] for their game on Saturday. The following Monday, they called me and said, "you're starting this week against the [NFL team]." Who was the number one defense in the league. And I had played with [NFL team] so I knew all of the guys on their team. I didn't know anybody, I knew [NFL player]. That's the only guy I knew. I called it my "Rocky Balboa moment." Like you think they're asking you to spar with the champ. "No, we actually want you to fight the guy. You're fighting Creed." . . . Oh okay, great. So that's what I felt like that whole week. Coaches hours all night, slept at the facility a couple nights, got my chance to start. It's

> an unbelievable memory for me, but I knew it was winding down. They drafted [NFL player] that following spring so I knew it was done there. But then I would get a call out of nowhere for a true workout where they're gonna sign a guy. Go out for the workout, only to find out that they held me back to sign me.

No single passage in this book encapsulates the tumult and uncertainty of the conclusion of a professional career more perfectly. Despite part of his motivation, identity, and desire to sever his connection to the NFL, there remained a deep part of him connected to the league. He even took great pride in his final return to the league, despite it being a regular-season game for a team without playoff aspirations against a league juggernaut. His pride in his preparation and unwavering focus had not waned in the end. Despite the uncertainty surrounding the end of his career, Steve had the remarkable capacity to shift almost instantly from changing his baby's diapers to leading an NFL offense into preparation for Sunday competition. This ability to seamlessly shift between these identities serves as a model for coping with the ambiguity that is almost inevitable at the conclusion of a professional sports career.

Arianna shared similar sentiments to Steve, expressing how coaching provided a means to retain her athletic identity while simultaneously acknowledging that her sense of identity was evolving.

> I think my identity has evolved a lot. I think some of my bigger identity pieces now in adulthood are staying very close to the game because I am a university hockey coach. In reflecting, I do wonder if I took [the coaching] path because I wasn't quite ready to let go of the athlete identity. I just look at it as it's the only role available to me right now. So there's that part of me that would still consider myself an athlete in a different form. Players look to me and my past experiences as a way to lead them to current experiences.

Arianna acknowledged that coaching was a way to keep some facet of athletic identity, primarily because of the profound meaning she derived from sport and competition. The opportunity to develop and mentor athletes, as well as relish the thrill of competition, allowed her to embrace multiple identities in her retirement. Later in the interview, Arianna described how despite her identity expanding to include roles such as wife and mother, even her partner was a former professional hockey player. Much of their focus in parenting revolved around connecting with one another and their son through the sport as well. Despite there being some identity foreclosure in her journey, insofar as she is still tied to athletic identity in retirement, coaching—for both her and Steve—seems to be a healthy way to engage in multiple forms of identity, with athletic identity being just one of those.

Though not tied to his actual professional sport, Hayden discusses how he and his brothers—another elite athlete—reminisce about how difficult it is to not have competitive outlets in life after sport. He explains this as the reason why they still long to golf as much as possible in retirement.

> Dealing with retirement is almost like an identity thing. Me and my brother talk about it a lot. My brother said the only time he feels like an athlete is when he goes to play golf. It is the only time I feel like I am kicking someone's ass. Every other time in my life I am taking care of the kids, doing work, doing this and that. You just feel like an average Joe, fooling around. . . . You choose to live in that golf world where they can literally avoid responsibility for their fatherhood and their husband hood and want to be in the country club all day and socialize. Just be the man.

Hayden again offers an expression of dissonance around his struggle to complexify identity after his professional baseball career. He acknowledged holding identity as a father and husband but is a bit dismissive about the meaning and significance of those roles as compared to athletic identity. When describing his time golfing, he uses descriptors such as "kicking someone's ass" and "being the man." When describing fatherhood, he expresses feeling like an "average Joe" or the burden as a "responsibility," and one that can be avoided on the golf course.

ECHOED DREAMS: LIVING VICARIOUSLY THROUGH CHILDREN

To conclude our discussion on identity foreclosure, we delve into a fascinating yet potentially harmful psychosocial facet of this phenomenon, living vicariously through their children's athletic pursuits. Some participants revealed that postretirement, they perpetuated their athletic identity by immersing themselves in their children's competitive sports experiences. This aspect of identity foreclosure, while intriguing, has the potential to negatively impact both the retired athlete and their children. Living vicariously through one's children is a phenomenon that is by no means exclusive to retired athletes. It's important to note that this was not a prevalent theme among the participants in this study. Nonetheless, it was observed among those who maintained a strong athletic identity well into their retirement. Many Americans recognize that some parents live vicariously through their children, particularly in areas such as academics and athletics. However, this is typically not something that is proudly proclaimed; rather, it is often brought up in a mocking or shaming manner when discussing such behaviors. Interestingly, it was unique to see a few participants express the desire to live vicariously through children. They saw it as a way to foster a connection with their children and encourage them to reach their full potential or experience the unique joy that sports can bring. This perspective stands in contrast to the more common view of vicarious living as something negative or unhealthy.

Anna described how one of the ways she sees herself moving out of hockey is through moving into her children's careers in hockey. This projection illustrates her belief that connecting with her future children through the sport that defined her identity could potentially help her navigate the void left by her departure from professional hockey. However, it is important to note that she has not yet experienced motherhood or marriage, making this a speculative and perhaps idealized method of coping with her loss of self in the sport.

> I am learning how to sit home on a Tuesday night and not have something to do besides hang out with the dog or have a family one day. I am hopeful that I can shift from this perspective of it being me to shifting to a family where I have a child to take care of and being friends with my child's friend's parents, or the hockey community. I'm obviously going to try to make my kids play sports. But sometimes I'm like, "Am I trying to live vicariously through them?" But I don't think it's that, I think I'm just accepting that the next chapter will have to come, kids, natural things like that. My life would be them now and watching them play, and I'm sure the next transition would be them moving away to college and I'll have to grieve at that point in my life too.

Anna exhibited a strong sense of anticipation and pride in the prospect of finding a renewed connection and purpose through supporting her future children in their potential hockey careers. While she briefly touched on the possibility that this approach might be somewhat narrow or even potentially harmful, she did not linger on these concerns or delve into a deeper exploration of the potential pitfalls. This fleeting acknowledgment suggests that she may not have fully grappled with the complexities and potential challenges of intertwining her lost athletic identity with her future role as a parent. In the end, Anna reconciles with the idea of living vicariously through her children's potential hockey careers, recognizing it as a significant way for her to connect and communicate with them. This reflects her personal history, where sport served as the principal channel for intimacy between her and her father during her childhood and adolescence. Her father's affection was primarily reserved for her due to her success in hockey, while her siblings, who were not elite athletes, didn't receive the same level of affection. This experience has undoubtedly shaped Anna's perception of sports as a crucial means of building and maintaining intimate relationships, influencing her decision to adopt a similar approach with her future children.

Hayden described how, now as a father, he is deeply invested in promoting sport—specifically, baseball—in the lives of his children.

> My wife and I built this really nice house last winter. . . . I did a basement remodel and the theme is a major league clubhouse. I have a batting cage down there, I have a 55-inch TV, kitchen cabinets, food, everything! Because I want to bring back that camaraderie of a clubhouse to my house. When my kids have their sports games or they win their game or whatever, everybody comes over to the house. . . . I want the kids to have some fun in the house and we can just operate as a clubhouse. That's what I'm trying to bring back to my local residence. Going to the kid's soccer game and them coming and flipping through Netflix. That is just depressing.

It is difficult to express this next bit of analysis without irony—Hayden literally built a baseball clubhouse in his basement. This juxtaposition is striking and somewhat paradoxical, yet it encapsulates the deep and complex relationship Hayden has with his athletic identity. On one hand, Hayden vocalized the importance of moving forward and finding a new identity in his role in medical sales. On the other hand, the creation of a baseball clubhouse in his basement symbolizes his unwillingness or inability to fully let go of his athletic past. It's as if, by physically manifesting the baseball locker room within his living space, he's holding on to a tangible piece of his athletic identity, safeguarding it as a refuge where he can always return, even as he steps into a new phase of his life. The presence of a baseball clubhouse in Hayden's basement is perhaps the most poignant example of identity foreclosure in this study. This is a clear example of suspending identity exploration for a state of almost infinite nostalgia for a past youth.

Chapter 4

Identity Expansion

Many participants in this study experienced the opposite of identity foreclosure in retirement or life after sport: identity expansion. For some, this process of identity expansion began early in life or at least well before retirement. For others, it was a harsh but necessary process that occurred shortly after retirement or deselection from sport. Regardless, for those who did not foreclose their identity in athletics, their ability to remain connected to their athletic selves appears more fluid and predicted rather than a transitional process requiring redefinition of self. Their identity as athletes was integrated into their self-concept in such a way that the expectation was that it would always be a part of who they were, even when the immediate choice to discontinue was not within their control.

THE IMPORTANCE OF ADAPTING AND INTEGRATING MULTIPLE IDENTITIES

Marshall went from being a Division-II NCAA football player to having an unprecedented seven-year career in the NFL and arena football. He described how he was able to complexify his sense of identity during his athletic career, even at the height of his athletic accomplishments. "I always looked at it like that too, like my dad always said, 'You be the biggest tough guy on the field, but you be the politest person off the field.' Because at the end of the day, you turn it on, you turn it off. And if you can't, then it's an excuse for me. Like I said, if you're carrying stuff out after a game, or after practice, that means you didn't go there and work hard enough. You just had all that time out there to be the barbarian." Marshall's ability to differentiate between his athletic career and personal life played a crucial role in shaping his complex identity. By not letting the emotional intensity and demands of his sports career infiltrate his personal life, he practiced a form of mental compartmentalization.

This separation was vital in preventing his identity from becoming entirely consumed by his role as an athlete.

Analyzing the differences between Marshall's experience with his NFL career and Hayden's journey in professional baseball provides valuable insights. For Hayden, there were hints of a sense of power and entitlement through the interview. He described feeling like a god among men as he moved down from the Mount Olympus of sport to live among the masses. This perspective hindered his ability to make a smooth transition from sports to regular life, resulting in identity foreclosure. It also created barriers to establishing trust and forming intimate relationships with his coworkers and peers in his post-sports career. For Marshall, the description of how he viewed his career in the NFL could not be starker. While Marshall did derive a sense of pride, power, and strength from his role as an NFL linebacker, even admitting to taking pride in his physically intimidating presence on the field, he was also taught by his father to treat the field as a vacuum. This was a place where he could legally and cathartically indulge in those emotions without letting them spill over into other aspects of his life. After leaving the field, Marshall was expected to root his identity in kindness and respect for others, including his peers. This approach serves as an exemplary model for a complex identity, where an individual is capable of embodying various facets of their self within suitable and appropriate contexts.

Deonte similarly detailed his process of developing a complex identity during his transition out of sport. He explained how he managed to integrate various aspects of his identity, successfully navigating the shift from his athletic career to his new endeavors.

> I was making music when I was younger, like early high school. Then once I got to college playing football, I stopped because I was so heavy on football. That's all I cared about, just football. Full focus on that. Football ended, and I looked around like, "What am I doing? What's going to bring me my joy; my happiness? Am I just going to be working forever and then that's it? What about things that I like to do?" I noticed when I graduated, seeing my friends start their jobs and seeing friends who were older who had been working their jobs for 2–3 years, it was kind of like doing the same things over and over. They didn't really have any extracurriculars. It was kind of like: work, go out on the weekends and party, and redo every single day and every single weekend. So, I saw that and thought, "No, this can't be it." Around the same time, I started my software job, that's when I started getting into music, started recording and mixing, mastering and engineering all of my own music. I do all the work on my own and I find a lot of joy in that, to the point where it's another business for me, but it's my passion too. I find my joy in stuff like that. So, I travel back and forth for music right now. I'm working on another project with a bunch of

> producers in New York, producers up here in Boston. That's where I found my true happiness. I guess, for me, it filled that gap that was missing from football.

Deonte was acutely aware of the existential abyss that many athletes face in retirement, as discussed in chapter 3. He had witnessed former teammates retire and then struggle with the transition into a mundane, repetitive cycle in the workforce. Although his athletic identity and commitment to sport were significant while he was competing, he was determined to avoid falling into the trap of meaninglessness, boredom, and identity foreclosure that can afflict retired athletes. Fortunately, Deonte had developed a passion for music before he became fully committed to football. Like many participants in this study who were encouraged to diversify their sense of self from a young age, Deonte was able to relatively quickly transition his efforts, commitment, and creative energy from football to music.

Steve recognized his own somewhat limited sense of athletic identity throughout the interview. Yet, as a high school football coach, he acknowledged the benefit for athletes, especially the young men he coaches, in broadening their self-perception as competitors, both on and off the field.

> That mindset piece, that rip-your-heart-out-and-kill-you piece on a field. I love that. I identify so much with that. I don't see that in today's athletes. I don't get the pat on the ass, helping guys, hanging out, going out to dinner with them after. That shit never existed in my world. But I acknowledge that I don't think that that's necessary. In fact, it's probably better that [my players] aren't that way. But I don't identify with that. I had to educate myself; make myself more well-rounded. I'll never be like that, but I am more tolerant of it. I know these kids work out in different pockets throughout the year and they're seeing kids. Back when I was playing, if I saw a [rival high school] kid, you didn't talk. You probably left the area. Nowadays, they don't have that hate. They're so much better about just being chill. I think it's good in some ways but that competitive piece. . . . I was never able to turn it on and off like that. No way.

Steve noted that the athletes he coaches today are quite different from how he was as a competitor. They often lack the intense competitive spirit and group solidarity that are characteristic of a strong athletic identity. Though Steve half-heartedly lamented the loss of this edge in his players, he likewise acknowledged that their social adaptability is a valuable asset that will serve them well both on the field and in their post-sport lives.

Tess described how she had parents who supported identity expansion throughout her childhood, despite her being an exceptional athlete as a child and teenager. "Yeah my parents never . . . They were very much like 'focus on schoolwork' and then you just happen to be good at athletics. It was never this. . . . I didn't ever feel like I was so good at athletics that it was uncomfortable. Because I was supported and motivated outside of sports, I feel like as I got older, they blended together. It was always more like that's done so now I have to go do homework." Contrary to several participants whose parents deeply invested in and reinforced athletic success, Tess experienced elite success in sport, but never at the cost of foreclosing her identity or curiosity in other facets of her life. Tess explained how embracing multiple identities in adulthood provides the opportunity for different aspects of one's identity to nurture and sustain each other, leading to a harmonious and unified sense of self.

> So, identity wise, I'm also an attorney and I also have a master's degree so a lot of my identity is focused or fixated around these academic achievements and then also the career route that I'm on. I identify a lot with being in this intellectual sphere. . . . I also identify myself as a sister, or a daughter, and a dog mom, and a member of the community. I think all of them have some overlap. I found when I was in law school I was competing in cycling and I was racing at the national level, and I found that if I was to achieve in one area it was easier to achieve in another because you're just used to that high expectation almost if I'm going to succeed in this area it's almost forcing me to get my shit together in this area so I can keep focusing on this area. So I actually found that they went hand in hand really well, but then it's like you don't have a great social life. At the races I found that I was getting enough social interaction that I didn't really feel like I missed it, and I wasn't into like going to bars where college law students usually do.

Tess stood out among the study participants as having successfully cultivated an incredibly diverse array of success, along with a wide breadth of interests, in her young adult life. Despite her elite volleyball career ending with a major knee injury, she moved seamlessly into law school, where she graduated at the top of her class. She wasn't just transferring work ethic from sport into her studies. She was passionate about law because she always had intellectual curiosity alongside competitive goals. Beyond this, she also became an elite professional cyclist while she was in law school after retiring from volleyball. This shift was possible because she never solely identified as a volleyball player. Instead, she saw herself as someone who cherished sports, competition, and physical challenges. Consequently, her athletic career spanned an additional half-decade, all because she was able to cultivate a breadth of curiosity and passion from childhood.

Kurt described how having a more complex identity formed through his youth facilitated his ability to endure deselection from the NFL, despite frustrations and regrets from his career.

> I did play sports but it's still very prevalent, and faith is very important to me. My relationship with God and being a Catholic, being Christian is something that is super important to me. That's going to be an identity that I hold constant no matter what I'm doing. That's part of the reason why I was so confidently able to walk away from football. I felt like I was getting the signs or feelings, whatever you want to call it, from God that it made sense for me to not do it anymore. That's why I'm very confident in that decision. Another form, I'm trying to get really good at communicating and being a good communicator both from understanding other people and being able to communicate my thoughts concisely and in a way that's easy to digest for the listener. The reason why I'm trying to do that is because I think that'll help being in a family and in the corporate world too. That's a good skill in general to have, so I'm trying to do that and work on that. I always like to be a helpful person. I have that identity.

Kurt's faith and commitment to kindness and empathy laid a solid foundation for him to redevelop his identity after his NFL career came to an end. Having a strong sense of who he was, what he believed in, and how he wanted to cultivate connections with others allowed him to have a meaningful direction in which to channel his energy once football was over. Moreover, he elaborated on how having a complex identity and the ability to adapt and adjust one's identity can be beneficial for NFL players, potentially contributing to the extension and longevity of their careers in the league. "We had players, when I was with the [NFL team], that were basically asked 'Are you going to get cut or just take a smaller pay cut or do this role differently?' The NFL is a business so the more you can mold to the system the better, the longer you'll last." Though he expressed this quote as a form of lament around his own career—reflecting on his own challenges in making specific athletic and positional adjustments that may have prolonged his career, the message remains important. Just as a complex identity can support a smoother transition out of a sports career, having an open and curious approach to one's identity within the realm of sport can also offer advantages in terms of longevity and success in a professional or elite athletic career. Individuals capable of adapting their identities can navigate shifting roles, evolving team dynamics, and the challenges that come with aging. This flexibility is a valuable asset in enduring the annual tumult of the NFL season, and it can also lay the groundwork for finding purpose and fulfillment in retirement.

Finally, Jermaine reflected on the wisdom he wishes he had acquired earlier in his career and retirement journey. He emphasized the importance of cultivating a multifaceted identity, and shared how this can facilitate a smoother transition out of professional sports while also enhancing the enjoyment and fulfillment derived from the athletic experience itself.

> You need to compartmentalize. Don't take yourself too seriously. Don't take your athletic self-worth too seriously. It ties into those extrinsic motivations that we talked about. You have to have a social life, a school life, a family life. You have to have this other stuff, and your life doesn't have to be centered around this sport. When I was in the beginning of my career, I really struggled with that. I put so much into it, I finally started to play, but it's like man, there's way more to life and to college than just playing your sport. You don't realize that when you're in it, but don't take yourself that seriously. It helps you have fun with it. At the end of the day, it is just a sport.

Arianna echoed these sentiments, describing how the advice she would give to a young athlete with elite ability would be to focus on the important task of developing a diverse identity that extends beyond the realm of sports. She highlighted the benefits of harnessing the skills and knowledge gained from sports and applying them to new and different career paths beyond athletics. This approach, she shared, can greatly assist athletes in successfully transitioning to life beyond sport while maximizing the valuable lessons and attributes developed during their time in sports.

> You've got to have an identity outside of hockey because when it's over, it's over. When it's over, what is your identity going to be? Enjoy every moment of being an elite-level hockey player because it will end. But you also don't have to let it completely end because I think there's so many components of what you were as an elite player that you can take with you into so many different other areas of your life. . . . Drive and motivation are huge traits you develop through elite sports. Relationship building would be another big one that I think has helped me immensely in my career. Working with different people at very different times would be another big one.

Jermaine and Arianna's sentiments are in line with life-development intervention models of athletic retirement that advocate for retired athletes to leverage the diverse skill set they've developed through sports as they transition to life post-athletics. Motivation, teamwork, and goal setting are indeed qualities that almost any employer would value and prioritize in their workforce. These skills can serve as a solid foundation for athletes as they navigate their way through the challenges and opportunities of post-sport careers. However, as several participants expressed in chapter 3, these traits were only present for the individual while they were competing in sport, but don't necessarily carry over into their subsequent careers post-sports, as was evident in Hayden's case. Ultimately, the key here might be what Arianna suggests at the beginning of the passage—allowing oneself to cultivate the pleasure and motivation derived from sports, without having sport dominate one's personality and aspirations entirely. This is undeniably a challenging balance to maintain, and arguably, reaching one's full potential in sports often requires making it a focal point of their identity. Perhaps the goal should be to continue to pursue sport passionately for the joy it brings, while actively seeking to expand one's sense of self. Arguably, this intrinsic drive to engage deeply in sport without having it dominate one's identity is indeed the key to developing a more expansive and robust self-concept.

EVOLVING IDENTITY: EMBRACING NOVEL ENDEAVORS POST-SPORT

To fully transition out of elite athletic competition, many participants took up new activities or hobbies that deviated from their previous athletic pursuits. For some, this involved a complete departure from athletic competition, instead choosing to immerse themselves in hobbies or passions entirely unrelated to sports. Others opted to explore different sports that offered greater sustainability and longevity, such as cycling or running. Finally, there were those who continued to engage in sport but only on a recreational level.

Deonte shared that while he likely had the capability to continue playing elite-level football for another season or two, he was eager to embrace new opportunities and challenges that lay beyond sport at the end of his career.

> I'm just trying to accomplish something else now. Like, wow—okay—I just accomplished that. I did everything I could in football for those five years, so what's next? What can I take to another level that I'm interested in and serious in? I think music is one of those things where I wonder how far I can take this and put my mind toward the same energy in how I took it seriously in practice, in meetings. Is there another level to this music stuff that I'm doing that I think really takes this to the next level? New beginnings. I'm always like, " Alright, what's next?" I was definitely not sad at all, I was glad that I got some closure there, personally. Now I can move on to my next thing and I'll figure out what's next on the road.

Deonte embraced the opportunity to explore a life beyond football, even though he could have continued his professional career. This inclination may reflect a core aspect of his personality; he is not one to become overly enthralled with a specific pursuit, but rather is captivated by the prospect of new challenges and experiences that await him in the future. This adaptability and eagerness to embrace change is evidently advantageous, aiding in a smoother transition from sports and facilitating the development of a complex, multifaceted identity in midlife.

In the early part of the interview, Tess described how her identity as an elite volleyball player almost totally dissolved shortly after her career ended. "I'm complaining to my boyfriend all the time, I just feel like people only know me as this dog mom or my boyfriend's girlfriend. My whole identity is gone." Upon following up with her on how she felt about losing her athletic identity so quickly and definitively, she shared that while she initially felt a sense of confusion and malaise, she found a way to cope by immersing herself in an entirely different athletic activity. Ultimately, despite retiring from volleyball in her mid-twenties, Tess began to redirect her training efforts and successfully reestablished a sense of self and structure in her life.

> A lot of the benefits I feel I got from volleyball was the community and then the structure that came with it, and then also the sense of identity. You're structuring your day around this two-hour practice and then you have this automatic team which becomes your friends and family. Cycling, when I got out, replaced that in the sense that it gave me structure and it gave me identity. A way to define myself as "Oh, I do this." I lived in Colorado during that time and similar to Alaska a lot of people . . . like if you don't have this outdoor pursuit, they don't really know how to define you. It's not so much what your job is but what your hobbies are.

She went on to explain how channeling her athletic identity into both a familiar and a new sport was crucial in helping her cope with her retirement following a career-ending leg injury in volleyball.

> For rehab, they said you could swim, or you can cycle since it's like low impact. I was like "Oh, I used to swim!" So, I started swimming again, then it was almost like I was almost in too dark of a place because I didn't want to be left alone in the pool with my thoughts, so I started cycling and it was the same summer my aunt was training for an Iron Man. She would go out on seven-to-eight-hour bike rides and pick me up for three-to-four-hour rides because I didn't have anything else to do so I would just start riding that way. I actually found that it is really different from volleyball because all of a sudden you went from team sports where most of my training rides are very individual and very alone, but I actually really find I like the isolation. Then it's kind of less pressure in a sense because if you screw up, it's only you you're letting down and not 13 other people because you missed the ball. If I hadn't gotten into cycling, I feel like I would have filled the gap some other way. But I feel like I might have just been a recreational runner or gone to the gym or done yoga. With cycling, I enjoy being good at it. If I hadn't found something that I was equally good at I don't know if I would have been as driven to pursue something.

Tess's transition out of elite sport was aided by her ability to transition into a second elite sport—cycling—post-volleyball. In some ways, her story may not necessarily revolve around self-complexity or identity restructuring, as she found a unique way to extend and prolong her athletic identity into her early thirties. However, it cannot be understated just how difficult it is for an athlete to move from elite competition in one sport to elite success in another. Another unique aspect of her transition is the shift from volleyball, a power sport, to cycling, a cardiovascular and endurance competition. Her ability to make this shift was deeply influenced by her curiosity, openness to sport, and how she could recreate herself through training and competition after volleyball.

Finally, as will be discussed in other parts of this analysis, Tess emphasized how she found intrinsic motivation in cycling and how this internal drive led to a deeply fulfilling experience in her life after sport.

> The first couple of races that I did, I wasn't winning, or I got last and I was like, "Oh, this is different." Then I found I still really like racing regardless of the result. . . . I think it's hard to feel like people understand this drive that you have to do it if they aren't an athlete. They're just like, "Wait, why are you going to go do this for five hours on a Saturday?" I'm like, "I don't know. I don't have anything better to do." I never know how to answer that question because I don't know. I just really enjoy this.

Throughout this project, we found that athletes who pursued sport with a stronger sense of intrinsic motivation are able to engage in competitive sports without tethering their identity entirely to their athletic pursuits. For Tess, the joy comes from challenging her cardiovascular limits through cycling. This is what she loves, but not who she defines herself as being. She is able to immerse herself in cycling and then step back, embodying a more multifaceted and complex sense of self that extends beyond her athletic endeavors.

SHIFTING THE LENS OF HEALTH AND WELLNESS: FROM ELITE ATHLETE TO ACTIVE ADULT

The development of an intuitive connection to one's body was an important aspect of transitioning to healthy relationships with food and training for the participants in this study. For some, this process included questions related to dieting and general eating habits: What is the point of eating? How much do I need? When should I eat? They experienced challenges in reconciling the long-standing habits of dieting built from sports culture and disguised as discipline with a less active and physically demanding lifestyle after sport.

This reorientation to nutrition not only allowed for the development of new nutritional habits, but also the ability to recognize that eating for pleasure and at times indulgence was no longer forbidden. Issa shared:

> My relationship with food was pretty bad because I felt like I was training and eating and couldn't enjoy things and that it had to be the way it was. That was something I struggled with in retirement from hockey, figuring out how to have a healthier relationship with food because I had been brought up on this concept of what I thought a good athlete should eat. So when I started eating that as the nonathlete and trying to figure what I wanted to do to work out, I just didn't feel well. So it was an interesting experience trying to transition. Not only not having that sport in my life but that structure and that, you know, understanding of it and health and beyond just health surrounding that sport.

REDEFINING EXERCISE, ACTIVITY, AND TRAINING

For some participants, there were uncertainties related to how they should train or whether training was even worth continuing after sport. Some kept training as if they were competing. Some stopped altogether, struggling to find the motivation and drive to train. Others navigated this spectrum in a myriad of ways that were at times creative, fulfilling, indulgent, and harmful. The main task of retirement for these athletes involved the reconciliation of what their body could do as an elite athlete and what it could do now, with the need to answer questions such as: What is my body to be used for now? What do I actually enjoy?

Juan shared that he continued to engage in training to keep himself in "playing shape" not because he wanted to go back and play but because this is what he had known his whole life and "it feels weird honestly to not work out as an athlete anymore." Erica echoed these sentiments, sharing that her passion for working out was not tempered by retirement. "I'm still obsessed with working out and eating healthy. And what's funny, like in my mind I think I work harder now than I did then, which is definitely not true. But in my mind I think that, and I think I could have been better." This perspective highlights the reflection of the participant on the joy that she had while playing and while there is a recognition of the time, energy, and emotion that was dedicated to sport, the cost appears to be a more distant memory the more time goes by.

Beth shared that she was able to find joy in exercise again after retirement, regaining the love that had been lost during the turmoil of the end of her career. "Now I feel like what I do is more like a choice, more fun, when at a point in college, it felt more like a chore, So not being an athlete is getting to choose different things to do instead of being told what to do and not really finding too much joy in it day to day."

Esteban identified the importance of remaining physically active and training in his life after retirement and the shift that he had to make in how he views the purpose and approach to training.

> When I used to work out, I worked out for myself, only me, myself, and I. I would work out for hours, I would be on the field for hours. It was all about me. So now I still work out, but since I also do it for a profession, it's now more about making my clients happy. I guess I have shifted more to like a coach type, instead of when I was a player and it was just me, myself, and I. I love to work out. I still work out every day, you know, but it's just different now.

He went on to explain that this ability allowed him to evolve his athletic identity and find a place for training in the next chapter of his life. This shift proved to be deeply useful to his physical and emotional well-being, aided in his transition into retirement, and provided purpose and structure in his life. "I kind of shifted gears to my career now, working out and staying fit, eating right. Working out helped me out big time. It wasn't even about looking physically a certain way, it was more like, for me, it was the mental part. . . . It helped me find my purpose, to help others now."

Henry also echoed the sentiments of the usefulness of training in his transition. He described how, even though he significantly curbed the intensity of his workout habits, he felt a continued sense of mental clarity and purpose in the routine of regular exercise. "I don't train the same way, but I still make time for it every single day because I think it's important and I'm a sharper person on days that I exercise than on days that I don't, so I think that's huge. I also started training differently and that part was most exciting because I don't have to squat 400 pounds and hang clean anymore. That part has been the best part of retirement, I think." Jermaine also identified the connection between training, his emotional well-being, and the ability to cope with the transition into retirement. "At least having the outlet of working out was always a good way to cope, and then when I didn't have it for a few weeks, that was really tough." For this participant, the value that exercise was adding to his life became most apparent when the restrictions from major surgery forced him to put it on pause while he recovered. The recognition of the benefit of regular exercise was also echoed by Hayden. "I like to exercise. If I am exercising regularly, nothing really bothers me." However, for this participant, this benefit is coupled with lamenting that he will never be able to truly compete again.

Henry identified this as one of the most challenging parts of retirement, no longer using the body to physically compete. "The hardest part was coming to grips with the level of competition. You'll never get back to that in terms of iconic me versus you and us versus you. You can scratch it but by no means is it the same physical output standpoint." For this participant and many others, there was a need to reorient themselves to exercise and fitness in new ways, for some relearning what their body could do, while others felt that this had been a missing piece all along.

REORIENTATION TO EXERCISE AND FITNESS REGIMENS

Most of the participants expressed a desire to maintain training and exercise regimens postretirement. However, they faced challenges identifying what it should look like, especially when performance was no longer the driving factor. Many realized that their previous training regimes were incompatible with their post-sport lives. As a result, they adapted and created new approaches and definitions of fitness suitable for their retirement phase. While others felt unsure about how to redefine their approach to fitness, realizing that for most of their athletic careers, they hadn't been the ones making decisions about their training. Instead, their workout routines had been meticulously crafted by coaches and trainers. This lifelong programming of sport specific discipline and measurement of progress against quantifiable performance metrics was difficult to translate into fitness in retirement, requiring a significant shift in understanding of movement, the purpose of training post-sport, and uncovering what they find enjoyment in.

Jess discussed her feelings of confusion and anxiety related to what to do for training and workouts once she realized her competitive career was officially over. "It was hard because I never had to work out on my own. When I was at the gym, I was with a group conditioning or doing weights, or I would be practicing for hours with them. It was hard for me to figure out how to stay active and healthy after my career was over. I was used to someone telling me what to do. I wasn't used to just going to the gym and coming up with my own thing." She ultimately discovered that redefining what an active lifestyle meant to her opened her eyes to new possibilities and ways to engage in physical activity. "I really like being able to go outside and just . . . be active in a different way." She also realized that the camaraderie she found motivating while training with her teammates was an element she could seek to replicate as she explored the next phase of her fitness journey. "I find workout classes are way better for me because people are there. It was the first time that I realized at the gym, you're by yourself, you can just stop any time. I've never realized that." While she continued to struggle with going to the gym consistently, she has made the connection that being in a group with her teammates ensured that she would do what she had set out to do. "If I'm at the gym, if we're doing planks as a group and I stop because I'm tired, everybody else gets 20 seconds added on to their plank. You don't get a choice to stop. You keep going because that's what the group is being instructed to do." The absence of external motivation and the sense of team were significant gaps she noticed in her drive to maintain a regular exercise routine in retirement. "If you're at the gym by yourself, it's hard to push yourself because there's no person there telling you have to do it, and there's no group you're trying to keep up with. It's just you." Like many of the other participants, Jess experienced the connection between mental state and fitness, however, where others found that exercise aided in mental clarity, this participant struggled to find the motivation to engage in it. "Mentally at the gym, it's been hard for me because I've never had to individually push myself like that . . . now you have to mentally, make yourself go do it." Ultimately, she echoed the sentiments of how the shift in routine and expectation of fitness requires many transitioning athletes to explore what fitness will mean to them in retirement.

Kendrick went through a similar transition process from confusion to reintegration into a new normal following his retirement from professional sports. In the beginning, he found himself sticking to his usual training routines. "I was just going crazy, still working out, super crazy, going up to the weight room and doing all the normal workouts that we normally do." He shared that it took a while for him to be able to reconcile within himself that this was no longer a necessary part of his routine and to be able to settle into a transition that redefined fitness for him. He found success by building normalcy into his training process and incorporated working out with another teammate. "Having a teammate of mine, right next to me working out, doing all the same workouts, it kind of helped the whole mind process, like okay, you're still active and all of that."

For some participants, previous injuries and wear and tear led them to increase their understanding of body mechanics and what health and fitness looked like for their bodies. Much like Henry, Jermaine shared that his reassessment of his training regimen not only brought him satisfaction, but freed him to avoid exercises that were not healthy for him, leading him to recognize what made him feel good.

> I don't push my weights unless I want to. . . . Upper body day I might push them. I push myself in certain areas. I'm more concerned about motion and flexibility, mobility and range of motion. There's no reason to push weights anymore. I love it. I don't do stuff if it's painful, especially with my back. I'll still front squat, barbell lunge. . . . I'm never gonna back squat or an Olympic lift or a hang clean any time soon. I just don't see a reason to. I still want to challenge

> myself but I'm way more concerned about high-volume stuff, isometric stuff, eccentric stuff, like going down for 4 or 5 seconds and holding it. . . . I'm way more concerned about higher volume than higher weight. I just don't see a reason to do that anymore. Physically, I feel great. I'm 225–230 [pounds] now, so I still feel bigger, and I like that. I'm just not 250 and I'm not laboring my joints anymore. It's nice, I'm comfortable like that. I walk a ton, it's just a very comfortable way for me. It's helped alleviate a lot of pressure on my low back, especially after surgery, I just feel so much better. The sciatic pain that I had on my right side is gone. It's numb, and sometimes throbs a little bit, but there's no more pain. My range of motion is so much better. I'm stretching a lot more, so that stuff is just so much better. I'm not playing and taking that pounding that was obviously hurting it a lot. So, I'm a lot more comfortable. I'm sitting a lot more, and in class a lot more. I need that.

While his body shifted in retirement, the physical improvements and relief that he felt buffered negative responses and facilitated acceptance of these changes. This development of an intuitive connection to their bodies and functional capacity was an area of positive growth found in retirement for some of the participants.

Dannie shared how recovery from ACL surgeries allowed her to grow her understanding of body mechanics and functioning in ways that she had not realized were missing from her understanding of training and fitness.

> One of the best parts of my physical therapy team was learning the parts, mechanics, and function of your body that you don't really get taught in college. All I remember of what my trainer did in college was pinch my fat for our prescreening body mass, put weight on the bars I was doing. That made me feel weak. I felt like I couldn't do it. . . . I was not taking more time to see that my lower back was messed up because of the way I was using my hips. . . . I was learning the mechanical parts of the body, taking the time to learn was just really cool. I felt like an active learner to what it means to be an athlete.

This highlighted gaps in her preparation for a life of overall fitness and functionality that were forgone due to an emphasis on sports discipline and performance. This passage sheds light on the internal struggle that was built into her relationship with her body through sports culture, with the body becoming a tool that you utilize and maximize rather than a relationship to be nurtured. She shared the impact of not only her increased knowledge about her body, but also of her ability to work with it rather than against it in retirement.

Ultimately, she describes a shift from hyper-focused sports performance to healthy athletic goal setting. "I can see if my knee is getting more flexible and how my knee is feeling in those positions, whereas before I would just jam it in and be like 'You have to be in this position, I do not care if it hurts.' Where now I am like we can make a modification. It is okay if you can't do something, you have had four surgeries." The participants in this study needed to recalibrate and realign their approach to training and exercise in their lives after sports. This realignment had a significant impact on how they engaged with physical activity, influencing various facets of their fitness routines and overall well-being.

EXPLORING NEW HORIZONS: NOVEL CAREERS POST-SPORT

While some participants found careers that aligned with and supported their athletic identities during retirement, a number of others took a different path, pursuing careers that required them to step away from their athletic selves and embrace new aspects of their identities. This divergence highlights the variety of ways in which individuals cope with the transition from sport to retirement, navigating the complexities of identity and self-perception.

This was one area where identity foreclosure and its effects on well-being were most evident. Those participants who were able to successfully expand their identity beyond sport had steady and even flourishing careers post-sport. In some instances, they could apply the skills developed during their sports careers without identifying as athletes. Conversely, those participants who struggled with identity foreclosure while transitioning found it difficult to achieve career satisfaction. While they leaned on their sports-related skills to adapt to their new professional environments, the outcomes varied significantly depending on the social and competitive dynamics of their chosen jobs.

Deonte described how he was able to merge childhood interests, athletic identity, and thirst for new experiences to forge a fulfilling and successful career in his life after sport.

> I realized I wanted to see the world, I want to meet different people from different backgrounds and go to different states. When I was growing up, I was an entrepreneurial kind of kid. Instead of hanging out with friends, I was making YouTube videos and getting heavy into video editing. I was selling stuff. It's crazy looking back, when I was younger and before I had a job, I was making money taking surveys online as a kid. I always knew I had some entrepreneurial background and seeing new people, meeting people from all across the nation and world, because I was doing that with YouTube as well, collaborating with other YouTubers from all across the country. I remembered all that because I never really forgot my past. It brought me closer to what I should be doing and what I wanted to get involved in. . . . It's cool seeing sports play a role, to still see it having an impact in my life outside of playing the physical sport. So that

> was really the coolest part. That's the reason I got to where I am right now. It's funny, regarding the research study, I really treat my work how I treat football.

A key protective factor in Deonte's journey is his eagerness to embrace new challenges, complemented by his exposure to many different forms of meaning and joy in childhood. Throughout his football career, he was conscious of his diverse interests that had been nurtured since his youth. These outside interests didn't diminish his love or commitment to football, but provided a robust safety net for reconstructing his identity and motivations postretirement. He looked forward to this new career and found meaning and fulfillment in work that had nothing to do with football.

Despite receiving additional tryouts and opportunities to hold on to his spot in the NFL, Steve had thoroughly committed to his coaching career and felt no regret about his final decision to step away from professional football.

> I just said, "No, I'm done. I'm not going to get hurt, I'm not going to embarrass myself." Even if I knew deep down, I'm not going to friggin embarrass myself. I would go in and make an account for myself. But I had a commitment, that's what bailed me out. If I hadn't been coaching, I definitely would have done it. But the fact that I had moved on into coaching and I cared so much about what I was doing there, I'm like, "No, I'm not putting my life on hold for the NFL anymore." I think that is what I said.

In his role as a high school football coach, Steve was able to maintain a connection to his passion for sports, while also likely preserving some aspect of his athletic identity in his post-NFL career. However, it was necessary for him to fully disconnect from the NFL in order to wholeheartedly commit to and embrace this new direction in his career. As discussed in the previous chapter, he experienced a purgatory of sorts around whether he was still an NFL quarterback hanging on for another chance, or if he was going to just fully step away. Despite offers trickling in, he had to be intentional about moving in a clear and distinct direction away from his personal athletic career.

Jermaine described how he threw himself into graduate school and the path toward a journalism career after he was deselected from the NFL.

> I thrust myself into writing as much as possible to stay busy. At certain points it got hard but I tried to throw myself out there and see what I'm good at; what I like and don't like. Applying to grad school was a goal for me. I was ambitious in some of the schools that I applied to. I wrote for two different websites in that time span. I was trying to get as much sampling as I could get out, to give myself the best chance to get into some of these schools. I channeled it there, and when I had gotten surgery on my back before Thanksgiving, that was tough for me because I was sitting a lot and not moving. At least having the outlet of working

> out was always a good way to cope, and then when I didn't have that for a few weeks that was really tough. I just thought, "Man, I need to go to school to fill my time and get some inner fulfillment." I attacked that. That was always good, another goal to strive for. I was always finding some sense of inner purpose, that really helped me. Through writing, trying to get my back in proper shape, or to find a career or job. I always try to find that inner purpose. . . . I definitely had my struggles in the beginning, but now I'm happy.

Initially, Jermaine grappled with numerous physical injuries and psychological turmoil, particularly in relation to his sense of self and what motivated him. Nevertheless, he was able to cultivate a new passion by diving into a completely new field. Unlike Deonte, Jermaine had no prior knowledge or expertise in this particular area, yet he bravely took a leap of faith to chase after an ambitious goal and what he considered a dream job. He went on to express his gratitude for following his passion and choosing a career that truly resonated with him, instead of settling for a job that offered more financial stability and professional security.

> Going to school has been fun, I'm learning a ton, I'm meeting a lot of great people. I know it's overwhelming for some people, but I think I'm on a good track. I trust the track that I'm on and I'm excited to be doing it. I'm going after my passion; a lot of my friends didn't necessarily go after the job they wanted to do. They just wanted to get a job, which is fine, but I struggle with that kind of security, of knowing what your future is and having that nice entry-level salary and job after college. I didn't have the same road as them, I'm taking a different path. I struggled with that in the beginning, comparing myself to others. But that doesn't matter, I'm running my own race, I'm doing what I want to do, and I'm happy. I have other goals to strive for too, which is hard, I know that. But it is fulfilling, and I like it, so I get a lot of fulfillment out of that.

Jermaine prioritized personal fulfillment over financial gain when transitioning from the NFL to a new career. The prospect of establishing a career in journalism was fraught with uncertainty, given the field's competitive nature and the difficulty in maintaining a stable career. Meanwhile, many of his college friends had already secured well-paying jobs. Regardless, Jermaine decided to follow his passion. The joy he derived from the work itself, especially in the beginning, was enough to sustain him, irrespective of whether he ultimately succeeded in breaking into the field. Engaging in this pursuit brought him fulfillment and facilitated the process of reconstructing his identity within the context of his newfound career.

The next two participants described how there was a desire to leave professional sports as they approached the point of being deselected or cut from their respective teams. Hayden's transition into a new career post-sports was driven by his commitment to a lifestyle that prioritized the stability and security of a steady job, along with quality time with his wife and children, over the unpredictable and chaotic nature of professional sports. His shift in priorities signaled a significant lifestyle change that he was ready to embrace after retiring from professional baseball in his mid-thirties.

> My uncle was in financial planning and was a professional baseball scout for a bit. He suggested I stay in baseball. I just knew in my heart that staying in baseball means you are going to be an absent father and absent husband and I do not want to be that. I'd have the coolest job in the world, but my kids are at home lonely and my wife is home alone. I didn't want any of that. I did not see that as being as valuable as being a dad and I don't really care if I am an average Joe at this point. It doesn't matter anymore to me.

Hayden was forced to move almost every single year of his professional baseball career. Beyond this, he spent half of his year living on buses, planes, and hotels on the road. There simply wasn't stability in this life, and he had endured it for so long. Even though he didn't have a passion for his career after baseball, he did desire stability and worked to find it.

Kurt experienced a profound sense of relief when he transitioned from the high-pressure environment of the NFL to a career outside of professional sports. Unlike some of his peers who thrived on the intense pressure and competition of the league, Kurt found that the demands and lack of control inherent in an NFL career were detrimental to his well-being. Securing a job outside of the NFL represented a welcome escape from those stressors and a positive step toward a new chapter in his life.

> I probably didn't realize it at the time, but looking back it was definitely the moment when I got the job at [employer]. I was so relieved. I felt so free, and it finally felt like a win that I controlled and that I got. It was so satisfying to me. . . . I was so happy, and I felt so free being able to be in control. . . . So, for me, I didn't want to be a football player just to be a football player. That's not why I did it. I did it because I really enjoyed winning. I really enjoyed competing and that's what I was good at and it allowed me to make money while doing it. Of course, I'm going to keep doing it, but as soon as I lost that, it wasn't fun. It was just like destroying my mental state and it was consuming me. Now, I know I'm not going to get cut tomorrow, so that's good.

Kurt's perspective challenged the commonly held assumption that reaching the pinnacle of professional sports is an inherently positive and enjoyable experience for all athletes. His candid account of life in the NFL, marked by overwhelming anxiety and a lack of control, serves as a powerful reminder of the complexities and potential pitfalls of a career in professional sports.

Kurt's experience as a third-string quarterback in the NFL was characterized by intense scrutiny and immense pressure. Every aspect of his performance was closely watched by the coaching staff, and he knew that there were countless others eager to take his place at the slightest misstep. This high-stakes environment can be invigorating for some athletes, as evidenced by Chris's positive recounting of his early years in the league. However, for Kurt, the constant pressure and lack of job security were draining and disheartening. This contrast highlighted the diverse range of experiences and emotional responses that athletes can have within the same professional sports context. Shortly after being deselected from the NFL, he was picked up in a stable sales career. The stakes were lower, but the environment was still competitive, and he trusted his instincts that a retired athlete would thrive in this arena. Ultimately, he did, and he described having more joy in a career after the NFL than his career as a backup quarterback at the end of a roster ever provided.

NEW IDENTITY: SAME MINDSETS

As described in the last section, some participants found joy and fulfillment in a novel career after sport. Some did not desire the change, but when it became inevitable, they embraced novelty in their careers. Others anticipated this shift and looked forward to life after sport. Either way, of those that found success and fulfillment in their lives and career after sport, many found that the skills and mindsets they had cultivated in sport allowed them to be successful in a novel career and life after sport.

Kurt described how he was able to transition into a novel career while still utilizing certain mindsets and motivational lenses that were conducive to his success in getting to the NFL. Though he expressed a sense of loss related to certain aspects of football in his day-to-day life—specifically, the physicality of competition in contact sports—he found peace in being able to leverage the skills acquired during his football career to achieve success in the business world.

> I wanted to be a starting quarterback in the NFL and win a Super Bowl because that's the best thing you can do as a football player. So, that was very much a hyperfocus on my goal. But at the same time, my mentality is whatever I'm doing, I'm going to have the goal to be the best. So, when it wasn't time for me to play football anymore, which luckily, I was very much able to come to terms with how it wasn't ah oh maybe I should keep playing, I knew it was time for me to stop. So, because I knew that, then I was able to take that mentality and transfer it over to what I'm doing now and the things and responsibilities I

> have to do now and try to be the very best at that. Yeah, it might not be to win a Super Bowl, but now it's to be a CEO, or run my own company, or be the best dad or husband in the world. It kind of was my mentality about everything and it's just shifting. Whenever I get frustrated about not being able to compete physically on the court or on the field, then it's what can I do to learn more? I've been reading a lot more, which I never really did because I never really had time, or it wasn't really a focus for me. I am trying to learn more about what I'm trying to do next. Can I do certain investments or things with my money that's going to help set up the future? Just thinking of things that I could put my mind to or energy towards succeeding and doing well. Although it might not be physical or on the battlefield, I can channel the energy into that. So that's kind of how I coped.

The desire to be elite and find the top of his field was expressed here as an almost universal trait for Kurt. This mindset would have translated to just about any career, but it certainly translated into the sales world. Kurt's sense of self was rooted more in a philosophy of success, diligence, and achievement, rather than specifically in sports or football. He elaborated on how he has seamlessly blended his identity as a football player, particularly his role as a quarterback, with his emerging identity in the sales industry.

> I feel like I have shifted identity, but at the same time I feel like I haven't, because I'm always going to be a football player to a certain extent. I played it so much throughout my life and I learned so much from the game. A lot of what is formed in my mental processes is from football. So, I'm going to be that to a certain extent, but I've also embraced this. My identity is what I am now. Maybe I have bits and pieces from my past identity still ingrained in me. I guess what I'm trying to say is that I'm not 100 percent this or 100 percent that. I'm kind of a mix of everything. That's how I look at it. Not everything is so black and white in my mind. That's a good question though because maybe I think I've shifted identity more than I have, but I feel as if I have. I would still say people look at me and say, "Oh, that's [name], the quarterback." That's probably never going to change. At least for people who knew me in college, maybe it will change eventually but not right now.

For Kurt, complexity was at the epicenter in understanding his own identity. He valued being diverse, flexible, and not tethered to any singular form of self. Finally, he went further, even describing how his new coworkers who did not play with him or may not have even competed athletically were cognizant of his complex identity in the workplace.

> I don't go around telling people I played football. It eventually comes out because they either look me up or they'll just find out and say, "I didn't know you played in the NFL!" I just say, "Yeah, whatever, not anymore." So, then

> they probably look at me a little bit like that just because to them it's, "Oh my God, a professional athlete!" It's foreign to them so they probably look at me like that. But I also think they look at me like, "He's a hard worker and good at his job." Maybe if I stunk at my job they would say, "Oh, he's just a football player." But because I try to succeed and do well and try to prove myself outside of being a football player, I think they look at me in that light. . . . *I think that's why I've embraced the transition like I have. Well there's a multitude of different reasons, but I think one of them is being able to take that competitive mindset and translate it into the industry that I'm in.*

FRIENDSHIPS AND SOLIDARITY OUTSIDE OF SPORT

In this study, participants who had some of the best adjustments to life after elite sport were those who were active and intentional about developing friendships and connections with individuals outside of sport. Jermaine described how he is certainly cognizant of how difficult it was to lose the connections he felt with former teammates. "You had your eight, ten guys that you literally do everything together with. It sucked at points, and it was really fun at other points, but you did it together. I loved that brotherhood. I loved that bond that I made. I still keep in touch with those guys today, and I still have coaches I talk to today. So that was definitely my favorite part of playing college football. Nothing is like playing on a college football team. I do think there are certain coping mechanisms that I might subconsciously make." Jermaine was one of many participants in this study who described in lucid detail just how valuable and meaningful the relationships he cultivated in sport were. He loved his teammates, loved being a teammate, and forged deep connections to those individuals over years. However, he tried to stay intentional about forming connections with family members and colleagues in his career and life after sport.

> I was at home last year for the first time since high school for that extended period of time, so it was really nice to be at home that long with my parents. I got to see my brothers a lot. I had never been home for longer than six weeks. Nothing is like being on a team. Being in class now is nice; it's nice being with people that are like-minded and have similar ambitions. But playing a sport together, lifting every day together, going to practice every single day together, nothing is really parallel to that in the real world. So, I think I find certain ways to fill that void and I still am best friends with some of those guys so that's great. But now, I talk to my parents every single day. I know that's not normal, but for me, they're still a drive away but it's enough space where it can get lonely. I do try to keep that contact with them so that's always nice. I think it's always nice, even if it's a two-minute conversation or a thirty-minute conversation, it's

always nice to have them in my back pocket and to have that relationship, to fill that void.

Though he was able to form some connections with his classmates in graduate school, he admitted these never really replicated the depth of solidarity he experienced with teammates. However, he was able to rekindle a relationship with his parents. He admitted in the passage that he does not find it normal to be a former professional football player in his mid-twenties calling his parents every day, but it doesn't matter to him. He felt a void in his social world, and the connection and intimacy he has to his parents is enough to fill that void. Finally, it is worth noting that Jermaine referred to life after sport as "the real world." He wasn't the only participant to make a similar innuendo and it spoke to just how unique the vacuum of the elite and professional sports world can be for athletes.

Henry described how he was able to expand identity after an abrupt retirement from professional hockey through expanding his relationships and being a more diligent and thoughtful friend.

> I take a lot more pride in building relationships and keeping in touch with people. Being away from home now for a long time. . . . A lot of my buddies have made their way back and like I said, a lot of guys I'm close with play college hockey. Just making sure that even though the miles have increased with all of us, the relationships are the most important. Because that year I was off, I lost that side of it and really went into a shell because I was upset and a little bit embarrassed because things were coming to an end in a way that . . . no one ever wants it to not be on their terms, right? That's the thing I take most pride in now, I call my friends all the time. Probably too much. And they all get annoyed now and stuff like that. Really, I just want to make sure I'm involved in that sense because I want to be known as the guy who cares and knows what's going on in my friend's life. I'd say relationships mean the most to me out of anything now.

Just as several participants shifted identity by finding a novel career after sport, being a socially attuned friend who valued dependability, intimacy, and connection was Henry's next phase of identity. It became a form of motivation for him. His passion for solidarity in hockey was a skill that he relied on in life after sport. Even if it was strange to those he loved, he wanted to continue to forge a strong sense of connection, even if they weren't on his team.

Finally, Henry's career after playing professional hockey has been coaching college hockey. In expressing the deep value he placed on relationships and solidarity, he went further, and described how cultivating strong relationships is the epicenter of his philosophy as a coach and mentor.

> All I really care about is the connection I am forming with my players. I think it's the best way to get the results that you want and the results you're getting paid for because I think it's the exact same as when you teach. If you're just coming down on your students like, "This isn't good," and they don't know you and they can't be vulnerable with you and they don't feel like there's something more than just teacher-student, then the performance is always going to be average. Yet, if you're connected on a level that goes beyond sports then there's autonomy in it and you do things that people value in a relationship. Then I think it just skyrockets on the performance side. The results just take care of themselves. It's like an inverse relationship . . . doing the opposite to get the results that you want.

As a college hockey coach, Henry was acutely aware of the need to produce results to keep his job. Nonetheless, he placed a premium on cultivating strong relationships with his players as a way of shaping their own motivational lens. This also offered him a space to open a new form of relationship with others outside of his former teammates. No doubt, this was still a sport-centered relationship. But this was one that existed within a context of mentorship, care, and cultivation. This new place in leadership allowed Henry to expand his identity and reestablish a center of purpose in life after his hockey career.

THE ROLE OF INTRINSIC MOTIVATION

Participants who were able to expand their identity also tended to experience a shift in motivational lens after retirement. Some of these participants were already more intrinsically motivated in their athletic careers. However, others became more intrinsically motivated and less concerned about results/rewards only after they retired from their athletic careers. This allowed them to find greater fulfillment in careers that involved more mundane work, less tangible reward, and less adulation (e.g., almost all jobs not in entertainment and media).

In the case of Marshall, the intrinsic motivation he cultivated in youth and demonstrated during his career was translatable to his professional life and career in retirement from the NFL. He saw little difference between the type of effort and commitment he would put into sport and the type of effort he would put into his position as a trainer after leaving the NFL.

> I always really pour my heart into it. I don't BS it. I don't sugarcoat stuff. I try to be as real as I can with them. At the end of the day, hard work is what prevails. Yes, you've got to have gifts, especially at that level. But it's about who works harder. I remember Coach [name] was my linebacker coach with the [NFL team]. So, I had [NFL player], he was our bigwig, he was awesome, he

> was such a good guy. Humble as they come, and he was a hard worker. Those are the guys that last.

Marshall described how his ability to work diligently, stay focused on the present, and love the task he is performing gave him an edge in the NFL. He also mentioned how some of the best players he played with embraced a similar mindset. This intrinsic motivation and devotion to the task and process transitioned into his career after the NFL. He was able to stay engaged and productive by focusing on the task at hand, being candid with his peers, and giving maximum effort.

Deonte described how accolades never meant much to him while he was competing. This mindset continues while working in the field of sales; he cares more about personal effort and integrity.

> As far as my jobs go, and accolades, I guess now, for me, it doesn't really matter because I try to . . . Obviously I want to be the best at everything that I can do, and I get that from football and sports in general. It'd be great to get accolades, but I know at the end of the day, I'm very worried about my abilities. Now that I'm older, I could care less if someone gave me something. I'm just like, "Damn, how can I perform like myself and do better?" If they gave me an accolade like, "Oh, he's employee of the month." That's cool, but I'm always like, "Did I do my best? Can I do more?" I'm always internally fighting with myself to try to be better and I don't really look at accolades like I did with football.

Similar to Marshall, Deonte finds himself more enamored with the process of self-development and growth. He appeared to have little interest in the awards or accolades he received in football or that he received in sales. He is more interested in getting better at his job, doing the work well, and finding ways to increase effort and focus on his day-to-day tasks. This mindset allows participants like Deonte to worry less about their identity and more about their self-development.

Jermaine described how his lens of motivation shifted early in his football career from one of seeking praise and affirmation from coaches to one of intrinsic motivation to master his craft on the field. He believed this shift allowed him to have few regrets after leaving football because he had expended all his energy and effort into the development of his abilities.

> And I remember something that was said when I was a freshman, and I didn't understand it, but now I understand it: "The amount of satisfaction you should get from being on the front line at kickoff and being that J-dropper and stopping that 4.6 linebacker who is going to run his head through you and headbutt you, and drive you back into the returner . . . Being able to execute that block should give you the same satisfaction as scoring a gamewinning touchdown." I

> remember thinking, "What is this guy talking about? I know what you're saying, but that is the corniest most Hallmark bullshit I've ever heard." Sacrifice for the team, etc. No guy in their right mind would agree with that. But, when I got older and transitioned to tight end, I began to love executing a good block probably more than making a catch because that almost came easier to me. . . . I loved being an integral part of the run game. I loved helping out on special teams. I loved finding any way to help younger guys at practice. . . . The process is so much more important than results. If you are always driven by results, your demise will come at some point. Some guys don't face that until they are 35, and for some NFL players and professional athletes, everything comes easy to them until it doesn't. At some point it catches up to you. I think being process driven, it's cliché, but it's the way to approach your workspace and your life by building these good habits.

In the case of Jermaine, and different from the previous participants' passages, he did not come to college with a developed sense of intrinsic motivation toward football. In fact, he was skeptical of any promotion of intrinsic motivation when it was posed to him early in his career. However, something began to shift in his motivational lens as he began to engage in the nuances and details of his job on the field. Over time, he developed a sense of engagement and pride over his ability to be attentive to all the details of his position on the team. Again, the ability to cultivate intrinsic motivation allowed Jermaine to care more about the work, his responsibilities to teammates, and much less on his identity and status as an elite athlete.

LEAVING A LEGACY: THE ROLE OF GENERATIVITY

Some participants discovered fulfillment in the experience of giving back and sharing their wisdom with a younger generation of players, teammates, and peers. This usually involved finding roles in mentoring, coaching, or teaching. Most of the time this was in sport, however, in other cases, the giving back was a form of wisdom sharing that occurred outside of sport.

Marshall retired from the NFL in his late twenties and started his own business as a performance trainer for young athletes. He provided an example of his desire to be generative upon leaving the NFL:

> I feel like you can make an easy transition (out of the NFL) if you have passions your heart goes to. Now I'm opening a business in personal training and recovery, so it's right in the same field. It makes it easier because I can help kids and people who are making the journey to where I was, so that makes me feel a little more attached because I'm still involved. I'd love to get to coaching, stay still involved in the game, it makes it a little bit easier. I know a bunch of guys

> who went cold-turkey, and they go onto something so different, whether it be sales or something. It's such a different angle. . . . Last year I was doing some coaching. That helped a lot, staying involved with the game and giving back to the kids, giving them that knowledge. It makes it special because you get to share your experience with them. There are kids out there who have that dream, anyone who has the dream and wants to do something with that in life, I try to help fold them over because I remember what it was like to have that dream and to work for it. That's what makes it really easy to give back.

He went on to examine how some former teammates he played with tried to move into careers that were lucrative but not generative. He explored how this process has played out for his peers:

> I can still feel like I'm giving back and being an asset to the community outside of just football and smacking my head around. That was kind of like my guide for what I was going to do once I was done. . . . You also have other guys who were former players who have a comeback, they talk about some of the things that worked out for them and haven't worked out for them. I remember my buddy who played with the [NFL team], when he was getting out, he was getting into life insurance, and he was telling me, "Hey, let's get you signed up so that way when it's done . . ." He was making good money, so it was tempting. It was more than I was making. But a couple of years after that he was already out of life insurance just because it was something totally different. Now he's actually doing the same thing, personal training.

After making a few years of an NFL salary, it was certainly tempting for Marshall to take the more lucrative position, if nothing more than to try and keep his lifestyle intact in retirement. Nonetheless, he had solid instincts around what he truly wanted after football and that was a career with a sustained sense of meaning. Football was fulfilling to Marshall throughout his life, and he wanted to continue in that world in some way. For him, the best way to sustain a sense of meaning in his career in sport was to become a mentor, teacher, and coach in the field. He felt that his success was due not solely to his athletic ability, but to a certain sense of knowledge imparted to him throughout his career. Good coaching mattered deeply to him, and he wanted to ensure that young people moving down the same road were given a similar knowledge base that could give them an edge.

Steve described how leaving the NFL caused several years of confusion and even depression upon retirement. He tried several careers before finding fulfillment and meaning in coaching high school football at the high school he had graduated from decades earlier.

> I enjoy the mentoring piece of the coaching that I get to do, which I think is a unique attraction to this level versus college or the pros. I truly do believe that I'm making a difference in young people's lives at this level. That look in their eyes when they look at you and when they're searching for your approval and guidance. I love that they hang on every word and it's important to them. . . . But that look and their whole life in front of them and that kind of stuff excites me and invigorates me every day. . . . I think the attraction to this for me is to be able to build a program and to build it the way you want to build it, and to mold kids the way you want to mold them. That's a special opportunity in my eyes and I've enjoyed so much of it. . . . I think nowadays, given what we're living through, between the racial tensions in this country, coronavirus, and everything else, my hat is off to these kids. I can't believe how well they have handled everything we're going through. I think back on myself 20 years ago in high school, there's no way I would have handled this as well as they have. This gives me hope that stuff we're doing now matters and it's going to help these kids, and they're going to be able to help kids down the line. There's a lot of meaning in the work.

While Marshall's approach to generativity was primarily focused on performance enhancement and guiding young players to greater success in their athletic careers, for Steve, the experience of generativity is one that sought to engage a more holistic picture of the young men he coached. He was invested in shaping them through the sociopolitical, cultural, and health challenges that they face in this day and age. His goal was to develop young men who are resilient, grounded, and socially conscious. He understood that the work he is doing with them was going to shape and serve their lives in the future. As he said, this work of cultivating teenaged boys into well-rounded and thoughtful young men was deeply meaningful.

Juan described how he felt a sense of meaning in his career after football by being able to work and share knowledge with a younger generation of athletes. "My retirement really hasn't been bad at all, just being able to use all my experience and my knowledge from being an athlete, and I think that's something to that, you know? I take some pride in just having that experience and being able to pass it along to the next generation. Just having that knowledge and being able to pass it on is important to me." Juan was one of the participants in this study whose career transition was exceptionally smooth. Despite having multiple NFL tryouts, he chose to retire. He was tired of flying from site to site and waiting for the next call. A job in football operations for an NFL team was offered to him that summer and he took the leap. Like other participants in this section, he wasn't sure whether this was the right choice when he severed from his NFL dreams. Ultimately, the ability to experience generativity in his mid-twenties was fulfilling and led to a meaningful career after football.

Esteban described how it was incredibly difficult to be released from his professional soccer team in his mid-twenties.

> I remember going home when they were telling me, "Listen, there's really nothing you didn't do. You were a great player. But right now, our team needs this." And that was so tough for me. That ride back to my apartment was so tough. . . . I was empty. Very empty. Very sad. Because deep down I knew my time had come. My plan was to do this as a career and it didn't work out that way. That was just tough. . . . So, I came back to the United States. I really, honestly had no direction at all. I was like, you know, out all the time. Partying all the time. Women all the time. I was never really an alcohol or drug person until this. I just had no direction for a while. I'd wake up every day like it was just monotonous.

Esteban had one of the most difficult initial career transitions out of all participants in this study. He went forward, describing how he was able to work himself into a more fulfilling space as it relates to a sense of purpose and identity in sport through his present career as a personal trainer.

> My approach to sport changed in a lot of ways. A perfect example is when I work out. When I used to work out, I didn't train anybody. I worked out for myself and only me, myself, and I. I would work out for hours. I would be on the field for hours. It was all about me. But now what I do as a profession is not about me anymore. It's more about making my clients happy. . . . I guess my purpose is to help others now. That's kind of what I do now. I help others. That's everyone, really. It includes a 55-year-old woman who just wants to get in shape. She isn't training for a sport or anything. But I also train high school kids who are too.

Esteban found a similar sense of fulfillment that Marshall described in working as a personal trainer in life after professional sport. His clientele is a broader group of persons than Marshall, however, the sense of purpose and joy in giving back is still present. Continuing to find meaning in his career, post-sports provided him with the opportunity to navigate through the initial grief and confusion he felt following his deselection from professional soccer. This process was essential for him to come to terms with his retirement and the significant transition it entailed.

BEYOND THE GAME: TRULY VALUING EDUCATION

The overwhelming majority of participants in this study played collegiate sports, even those who ended up moving onto professional careers after NCAA participation. Among all participants, there certainly were varying levels of commitment to academic coursework while also competing at an elite level. Nevertheless, those who truly valued their education and coursework outside of sport were more likely to utilize those skills in aiding a healthy transition out of elite sport.

Jermaine took great pride in being the only football player at his college to major in philosophy. Though he never pursued a professional or academic career in philosophy, his engagement in the field broadened his identity and provided him a source of pride and fulfillment outside of sport. "I took a lot of pride in [my academic success] too. In my five years, I was the only philosophy major on the football program. I think football and sports came easier to me naturally, whereas philosophy was like learning a new language. That was hard. Reading philosophy was hard, but once I understood it and when it clicked, that was so fulfilling. There are different outlets that you can reach and there are different ways to get that self-worth or fulfillment that you got on the football field too." Jermaine was one of the participants who initially experienced anxiety and malaise after being deselected from the NFL in his mid-twenties. In time, he found a sense of purpose and meaning when he enrolled in graduate school for his master's degree in journalism. He laid a foundation of curiosity in academic work as an undergraduate. As he said, the hard work of reading philosophy was challenging and stimulating. It was just as fulfilling as sport but cultivated a totally different skill set than what he had developed in football. Ultimately, he found he had more to rely on than just a sense of being an elite football player when he found himself without football in his mid-twenties.

Henry described how he wasn't initially engaged or prepared for the rigors of an elite college institution; however, he came to embrace education and expand his identity through this process.

> Making that jump was really tough. That first semester, I struggled academically but because you're just like, "I'm here to play hockey." That was a really cool transition for me because I went into college not really caring about school. I realized quickly that if I was going to stay there, I had to take this seriously. So, I started to and I found I loved it. Now, I really care about the continued learning and I got my master's degree through coaching. It's something that I'm extremely passionate about now. In high school I would have never read and now I have books behind me. That part is different, for sure, but it's all about the process of going to a school like [alma mater].

Though Henry was more of a late bloomer in regard to academic engagement than Jermaine, he more or less stumbled into academic seriousness in a desperate effort to keep hockey eligibility while he attended an Ivy League university. He did not expect to find fulfillment in this work but, over time, it became a reliable source of meaning and part of his identity. He expressed not only caring about being informed but showing that he is informed to his peers. His passion for academic work became a facet of a more complex self in his career as a college hockey coach.

Finally, Joe used his dedication to education and learning as a coping skill during a tumultuous ending to his collegiate career. When it became evident his athletic career was ending, he coped by throwing himself into his studies and graduating a year early. He recognized that this outcome might have been significantly different if he hadn't chosen a major that would serve him in retirement. "I took about 8–10 classes at a time junior year and I graduated in 3 years. That's how miserable I was. Finance was a hard major there, one of the hardest ones, and I tell people that it was so easy compared to everything else that was going on in my life, it was like nothing." For Joe, there wasn't as much of a pursuit of academics for the love of learning that Jermaine or Joe described. Yet, the stress of his athletic career ending led him to throw himself into the hard work of completing a Finance degree within a narrow window of time. Whether he loved the work, or the process of learning wasn't really the point. Academic work was a landing place for his motivation and purpose once it was clear he was no longer going to be an elite athlete. Though this did not become as much a part of his identity as it did for Jermaine or Henry, it allowed him to engage in a form of work that had nothing to do with hockey.

DEVELOPING AN ALTER EGO IN ATHLETIC RETIREMENT

Tess is a participant whose lived experiences are strewn throughout this chapter. Her ability to pour her athletic energies into a wholly different sport—cycling—after a career-ending injury from volleyball provided tremendous psychological relief and identity reconstruction. She described how, even though she became more successful in cycling than she ever was in volleyball, she never had a platform to express a sense of cycling identity to her peers. She described the curious manifestation of her identity as a cyclist while in law school:

> I feel like law school was very interesting. I feel like I only made four or five friends because I was so focused, and I think this was very telling. In law school there is like a banquet where they give out awards and it's like "Most Athletic," etc. First of all, I had to miss it because I was at a race, but then I was like, "I should probably win that because I've raced six national championships while in law school." But I didn't win because nobody knew who I was because I was training for these professional races. It's funny because with work, sometimes

> someone will make a comment about, say, a Tour de France racer. Sometimes I actually know that person, but you don't know how to say you know that person without going into it.

She acknowledged that she was not a self-promoting person and during her law school years, she didn't prominently display her athletic accomplishments as a part of her identity. Interestingly, she realized the extent to which she was downplaying her professional athletic success to her peers. As she reflected on this experience, she described how her cycling career took on the role of an alter ego, contrasting with her everyday identity as a law student and later as a practicing attorney.

> It is difficult to explain to my boyfriend too. I'll be out doing my own thing having all this time and I don't think he understands what it's like to go through race season with me. So trying to explain to him what it's normally like has been challenging because I don't think he realizes the time chunks it takes out. Here a lot of people talk about racing or riding or Lower 48 stuff. I don't really talk about it because I haven't quite figured out how to say, "I've actually done that." Or if people find out about stuff, I'm usually fine with it but I don't go around saying, "Oh, I've won that race," or "Oh, I won that national championship." It's just this underground secret that, if it emerges, I'm happy to talk about it, but it's very different than at [college] where you have all the teams in gear so you're walking around in "[College] Volleyball" and everyone knows. It's kind of this weird alter ego where you have work which is one area and all of a sudden you go home and change into your bike kit and you're on your bike and it's this other alter ego.

Developing an alter ego presents a potentially novel strategy for retired athletes to foster self-complexity. The majority of existing research assumes that these individuals overtly incorporate new aspects of their self-identity after the end of their athletic career. Almost all participants in this study who experienced a fulfilling retirement did actively and intentionally express their novel identity in life after sport. However, in the case of Tess, her novel identity was kept latent as she navigated life after volleyball. It is not clear why she wasn't more demonstrative about this identity. She alluded to the fact that in college sports, she was more inclined to wear her team's apparel, share meals with her teammates, and engage in other similar group activities. Perhaps in a solo sport like professional cycling, there just weren't as many clear opportunities to express her identity in such a manner. Regardless, there seemed to be a part of her motivation attributed to a desire to keep her new identity clandestine. Cycling, in and of itself, was incredibly fulfilling and a way to bridge her athletic desires after volleyball was over. It didn't matter whether she was actively expressing this identity or keeping it as a tacit alter ego. She loved what she was doing and found deep joy in the work.

Chapter 5

Exploring the Influence of Social Support in Athletic Retirement on Transition Outcomes

Social support has been found to positively influence the outcomes of psychosocial transitions. For many participants in this study, the efficacy of social support was dependent upon their readiness to acknowledge the transition from sport and the extent to which they could envision a future that included retirement. Some participants recognized the importance of social support in their transition, and they understood that its effectiveness was dependent upon their own capacity to accept, seek out, and engage in supportive relationships during the transition into retirement.

Many participants in the current study experienced a bevy of well-intentioned attempts at support during their transitions that provided comfort. For others, there was a lack of social support that exacerbated negative emotional experiences including increased feelings of guilt, confusion, embarrassment, and shame. This often led to attempts at avoiding conversations and not wanting to talk about what was happening in their lives. This was true for Tim, who shared that he had not himself begun to face the transition in his career, making conversations with others unbearable. "Once I stopped playing, I was frustrated with it. I was upset. I was embarrassed. So, I just wanted to put it in a drawer because I didn't want anyone to ask me about it anymore. They wanted to ask me, 'Hey are you still training? What's the next opportunity?' I was embarrassed to say I'm no longer playing, and I didn't have a plan, I didn't have the next thing to say." Tim highlighted the role that his own embarrassment and sense of failure played in his avoidance of sharing his experiences and emotions with anyone in his life. He became tired of being asked repeatedly by well-intentioned people for updates, feeling as if his answers fell short and were a reminder of the failure he had become. For this participant, he struggled with self-doubt and a lack of confidence which contributed to his experiencing feedback from family members as exacerbating his confusion and sense of failure.

Tim went further, explaining how these conversations put a spotlight on the void in his life where football once existed, a void that had not yet been filled with meaningful career choices. "Then it was family saying, 'What's up? How come you don't have a job? Are you in between jobs? Can't find a job?' I was like, 'I don't know, I'm trying.' I'm interviewing, I'm going out there. . . . So my self-doubt and lack of confidence was exposed when people continued to ask me, like, 'Hey, what's going on?' and I just didn't have an answer." He shared not having an idea of what the next step should be for him, not having the self-awareness to identify what his transferable skills were, or what type of career would give him a sense of passion and purpose. He became perplexed and began to follow the advice of others, even if he was uncertain about the goodness of fit, just to be doing something that would ease his sense of being lost, which resulted in many fits and starts and an extended sense of failure.

Joe also found himself trying to avoid social interactions, limiting the opportunity for uncomfortable conversations that only served to add to his inner turmoil. "I honestly didn't want any relationships at that point in my life because I was embarrassed. That's really true. I didn't want to talk to anybody. I didn't want to talk to my cousins, old friends, or anyone. I had [girlfriend] and a couple of my teammates and that was it." For this participant, it was not just about generally avoiding conversations. He found himself at a loss for what he could share with others when he did not understand so much of what ended his career. There were also feelings of embarrassment over a career that was taken away for athletes that had their careers disrupted by injuries and did not end on their own terms.

Henry shared similar sentiments. "That year, I was off . . . I really went into a shell because I was upset and a little embarrassed that things were coming to an end in that way . . . no one ever wants it to not be on their terms, right?" Beth, having her career disrupted by injury, had a similar desire to avoid talking about it, and at times to eliminate reminders of what she was not a part of. "I didn't really talk about it much with anyone. . . . I would get the games and scores and everything so sometimes I would just have to delete it and not see how they were doing and what I was missing." She shared that while she now wishes she had not taken such a huge step away from everything that reminds her of her sport, she recognized that it was a necessary part of her transition at the time.

Issa also identified the need to pull back from these conversations and focus on relationships that she knew would allow her to have space from the ongoing conversations about what she was missing. "My boyfriend supported me through it because he didn't go to college with me. He didn't play hockey, so it was easy to kind of be a way with him and not have to talk or deal with any of that. My parents would want to talk about it, talk about what the girls are doing, or how the practices are going. I just didn't want to be around them because I was so sad and heartbroken and jealous that they could continue to live out our season and play together. . . . It was really hard." While she understood that her family was trying to create normalcy while she recovered from an injury, similar to other participants, these otherwise well-intended efforts only intensified the feelings of sadness she was experiencing. She shared that she was not in a healthy enough place to have these types of conversations or to be around people who reminded her of what she could not presently do. There was a need to pull away from her sport that allowed her to ease the pain she felt at a career cut short, something that continued for several years into retirement.

Jermaine also echoed these sentiments. Yet, he was able to identify a common cognitive distortion and its impact on self-confidence—staying fixated on the opinions of others.

> People aren't inspecting your life the way you think they are. People build it up so much in their head. I was doing that, thinking "Oh people are going to think I'm such a loser. I'm training for the NFL, an empty dream. Now I'm unemployed and applying to grad school, going to even more school . . . what are people going to think of me?" They don't, and the people that are my friends, don't care. They'll be happy for me or they won't. I put too much stock into that at certain points. . . . Sometimes it's hard to realize that reality, but at the end of the day, people aren't examining your life in the same scope that you are.

He recognized that this, coupled with his continued comparison of himself to others in his life, led to a great deal of uncertainty in what the future would hold for him in retirement and decreased his sense of connection to his support system. He shared the need to realize that feedback—real or perceived—from outside people in your life only clouds decision-making and confidence in ways that are unnecessary.

FAMILIAL REACTIONS: THE BIDIRECTIONAL INFLUENCE OF RETIREMENT

For some participants, familial reactions had a significant impact on the participant's own perceptions of the retirement process. Some participants shared that their parents grieved as much if not more than they did when the participant's career ended. Family members even experienced significant disappointment when a participant's career came to an end. For these athletes, family bonds had been built at an early age and around this common interest of sport. Some found that there was a dearth of dialogue around retirement, or a complete lack of acknowledgment, as if all the emotions related to this event were repressed. In each of these examples, the connection to family influenced the retirement experience and, for some, created psychosocial stressors that needed to be mitigated.

In some cases, families tried to shield the athlete from their emotional response to retirement. For example, Esteban shared that, while his parents were extremely supportive of him, the sadness that they felt about his retirement was palpable, despite efforts to shelter him from it. "I think my father had a tough time with it. He loved watching me play. He wouldn't miss a game. My father's probably the hardest working guy I've ever met. He is just nonstop, but he always made time to go to every single one of my games. He was always there. So, I think it was hard for him especially at that particular moment [retirement] because I was upset about it and he just loved that aspect of our lives." Like many of the participants, he recognized that his familial dynamics had been built around his athletic identity. They recognized that watching their loved ones grieve the retirement and trying to navigate the transition simultaneously added to the struggles they were themselves experiencing. "I think there are moments of sadness for me for sure that I, you know, look at him and I wish he had more. . . . I still to this day, many years retired, think it's a void for him." This dual experience of grief, both for themselves and for their loved ones who were also losing the connection to their career and the role they played in it, resulted in feelings of sadness and guilt.

Jess found herself questioning what her familial relationship would be built on as she and her parents moved forward into the next chapter of life. What would she have to offer them? How would she make them proud? She explained these questions and frustrations: "Even though they couldn't be at the games . . . they tuned in to the live stats or the video every single game. They'd done that for as long as I had, and I've always heard them say how proud they are of me . . . and for that to be ending too, it was like, you know, that's one of my biggest achievements in their eyes and now that's ending." Jess recognized that, while she rationally knew that her family was proud of her, it did not erase the feeling of loss that she had in no longer having this point of connection in the relationship. "It's nice having something to show your parents, and feel proud of." She highlighted how the realignment of relationships is a major task of retirement for many athletes, adding to the many changes that they are faced with during this transition.

Through the description of participants, some families not only identified their loved ones as an athlete, but also began to self-identify with the role of supporter, fan, and cheerleader. They formed an identity around attending every game and supporting the participants. This contributed to the observation of personal grief when the participant transitioned to retirement. Issa shared her observations of her family's reaction to the injury that prematurely ended her collegiate career. "They were heartbroken because they thought they had five more games of watching me play and my team was sad too . . . but I think it hit my immediate family the most." She echoed the sentiments that sport was a connection and identity that was shared between them, and its loss was felt immensely.

For Anna, this led to a great deal of angst as she wondered whether or not she would continue to be the "golden child" in retirement. "I remember crying about it one night and was like, 'What is my dad going to talk to me about? Is he not going to like me? I provide nothing to him.'" While these thoughts were eventually soothed by her father's continued involvement in her life and reassurance that he was interested in all her endeavors, it highlighted the impact of athletic identity on all aspects of development for elite athletes. This impact includes the internalization of what the relationship with their parents is truly built on. Participants began to question whether their self-worth was based solely on what they could provide their parents with the identity of being an athlete's parent.

For some of the participants, their parents' reactions led them to question if in some cases the grief that their families experienced may have been greater than their own. Arianna described how her father likely struggled with her retirement from hockey more than she did. She described how her father, a decade later, is still grieving the loss of her career.

> I would say my dad actually struggled significantly with my retirement, probably more than I have. I'd say to this day he still struggles with my retirement. He was the person that put me in hockey from an early age and watched me develop, and I don't think he missed a single game in at least four or five of my final seasons. He traveled everywhere. I think it became a significant part of his identity, and when it was gone, I think he struggled to find out what he would do with his retirement. His retirement as a superfan . . . To this day, many years retired, and I still think it's a void for him.

Her father made the commitment to her athletic career in a similar fashion to her own, with the sports arena becoming central to a personal identity that now must be reconstructed in retirement. This required a paradigm shift, leaving both parties unsure of the role of sport in their lives and what their personal relationship will look like moving forward.

For other participants, such as Juan, he recognized that his mother's reaction to his football retirement was more about being connected to a vision about what his future would hold and difficulty reconciling with a different path. Despite the fact that he found an opportunity that allowed him to remain engaged with football in a meaningful way, his mother still struggled with the stark reality of his deselection from the NFL. "I'm not gonna lie, it was kind of hard for my mom. She always thought I was gonna be a professional football player. After I kind of made the transition to be done with it, it was kind of hard for her. She's way better with it now because she knows what I'm doing now is something that I love. But it's been fine for me. It hasn't been that hard, but at first it was really hard on my mom." The goal of playing in the NFL had been the driving force of family decisions for so long that letting go of this dream evolved from many difficult conversations. He shared that the hardest part of retirement for him was "just trying to explain it to her, how it works." He was able to navigate these difficult conversations by reminding himself of the connection and relationship that they had. "I knew that was her dream, but I knew she would, you know, come around and understand, you know, where I was coming from and once that happened, we were all good."

For parents who had invested fully in their children's athletic identities, many were left also confronting what they would do next. Where would they find the same level of passion and excitement? What would occupy their time now that their children were moving on to other careers? For some, particularly those whose children stayed in coaching, this led to them following the participant into the next step of their professional career. Arianna shared that her father "attempts to fill (the void) by coming to the games that I coach, but it doesn't give him the same high." Arianna experienced her parents missing the high from sports performance in the same manner that she did and attempting to fill the void that leaving the arena had in their lives by staying on for her coaching career.

For other parents, their child's retirement had so much turmoil and angst that they themselves were no longer able to be a part of that sport, including watching it on television, or discussing it with others. Erica, when describing her family's response to her brother's retirement, shared: "My mom can't even watch hockey now. She hates it that much, which is obviously a little bit uncomfortable because that's my husband's career." She identified that this severing of the connection to hockey after her brother retired impacted her entire familial dynamic. "We used to be like, you know, we'd always have hockey on TV. My family announced, like, nope. My brother doesn't watch it either, he told me this morning." She shared that it is hard to witness her brother, who had such a love for sport and faced a tumultuous retirement in 2018, still having nightmares about it to this day. "I think there hasn't been any closure for him, where it makes me think, yeah, I loved it, I worked hard and everything, but I knew that it wasn't my end goal, he didn't necessarily know that wasn't like what the cards were saying for him. Like, you're not going to do this for your life." For Erica, having other retirements to compare hers to allowed her to see the very significant differences in how each person and their respective families handled it. Ultimately, this provided her insight into the different way that being an elite athlete was internalized.

While intense emotional experiences were present in a number of the athlete's families, Erica experienced a complete lack of recognition from her family that she was retiring. She shared that she internalized this as being related to the different way that women in hockey are viewed versus men. "No one even thought about it. Thought about me retiring. I think more so it's just because I was a girl. That's the biggest thing, because people don't take girls' sports as seriously, at least the people that I know. Nobody even mentioned it, I never heard one word of it from anyone." This feeling of disconnect led to her having to find other avenues for support. For this participant, having been so close to her spouse and brother and witnessing their retirements, she recognized how differently she was regarded.

Hayden also shared the experience of having his retirement not recognized by many members of his family, and this left him questioning the value of his career to others. "I had fourteen years of pro sport and in my immediate family there is not a single person who asks me 'what was it like in [state] when you got traded and had to drive 90 hours from [state] to [state] and then play the next day? Nobody is interested in asking me about my career and I have fourteen years of really cool experiences that I am really the only one that knows about." This idea of how one's story may continue to live on and where it will fit into one's life after retirement is one that Hayden had to navigate in the transition out of sport. It was the question of his familial legacy that weighed on him after he retired from baseball. For him and others, this added an additional layer of pressure to identifying the next chapter, one that held purpose and meaning.

While some participants were able to count on their families to ease their stress through retirement, others came to recognize how the mutual pain contributed to the intensity of their emotional experience. Joe shared that his athletic journey, particularly in hockey, had been one that his entire family embraced. In many ways, it was the epicenter of their familial connection and purpose. The impact that his deselection from sport had on his family exacerbated his own emotional responses and transition to retirement. "My mom felt whatever I felt, times two. I think that was a huge, huge piece of this. My parents rode the whole journey with me, and they had all the exciting parts, going to USHL, getting college offers, they rode the whole journey. But I think as a mother, you can't be happy unless your kids are happy. You feel any pain your kids feel, maybe even more. She knew what I was going through and she's extremely sensitive, so it really shut her down as a person." He shared a recognition that he and his mother fueled one another's grief. However, despite realizing this, he was unable to compartmentalize his emotions due to the overwhelming sense of loss and confusion he was experiencing at the time his career was ending. "She couldn't sleep the way I couldn't sleep for years, and I hated that it did that to her, but there was no faking it. I couldn't be happy for her. I couldn't tell her things were going well, it was pretty black and white. I was either playing or I wasn't. It really hurt her." For this participant, with some time away, he saw alternative ways that he and his mother could have handled the intense turmoil at the end of his athletic career. However, these coping strategies were not readily available amid such angst and disappointment. When this level of connection occurs between an athlete, their parents, and the sport, an overidentification can materialize and shake the foundation of the relationship and family dynamic.

Despite many of the challenges that the participants faced in navigating family dynamics, some participants found that their family's support eased the transition process. Beth shared that the outward acceptance and support she felt from her father allowed her to put aside any feelings of failure or not reaching her potential that she might have been carrying. "I think they really helped, especially my dad. I mean he coached me my entire life. It was the best thing that ever happened, him accepting it and supporting it. Because I think his opinion would have mattered the most." Even for this participant who found comfort from her father, she highlighted well, in her own recognition of the importance of her father's approval, the powerful influence that family reactions and feedback play in the retirement process for these athletes.

Kurt shared that he knew that his family would support him no matter what decision he made, and he found their concern for his well-being to be a source of comfort.

> They wanted to make sure that I wasn't just doing it to do it. They didn't want me to have any regrets, you know? Obviously, she wanted me around more, but at the same time she wanted to make sure that I didn't feel like I was selling myself short on my goals. Same with my parents. Once they realized, "no it's okay, I'm very confident in this, this is a good thing." They were very supportive, and it wasn't because they were not supportive of me wanting to play football but it was more they wanted to be supportive of me and they knew that was a goal of mine.

For Kurt, the foundation of his relationship with his parents was not built around the connection over the sport itself but the connection to one another. When he reflected on their relationship, it is the place he repeatedly refers back to. "I've always known that they were in support of me with everything throughout my life and they've shown me that since I was a little kid. . . . I never questioned it." Furthermore, Kurt shared that he too was able to quell his parents' concerns about his retirement and letting go of his dreams.

> I remember my parents were concerned and they said, "I know you had these aspirations for football and these dreams for football." And I said, "Mom, you don't understand. Yeah, I had all those aspirations for that because that is what I was doing. That was my job, that was my life's path at the time, so of course I wanted to be the best I could in that. Now it's this. All those aspirations and goals that I had, they are going to translate over to this job and I'm going to be incredibly good. I'm going to kill it."

For this participant, like others, he recognized that his parents needed to understand that he was okay with the transition and that it was not going to leave him with regrets or unfulfilled dreams. Once they did, the tremendous source of familial support was a solid foundation for him to move into a life and career after the NFL.

EMPATHY WITHOUT UNDERSTANDING: FAILURES OF EMPATHY

While most participants identified individuals that they believed wanted to support them, the overwhelming theme in these experiences centered around the lack of having experienced the same pain. From nonathlete friends who had empathy but did not understand the experience of commitment and dedication that had gone into achieving this level of performance, to family members who failed to recognize the meaning and experience of retirement.

Like many participants, Tess experienced well-intentioned messages from her family members about what she would be able to do after a career-ending knee injury left her feeling misunderstood and isolated. "Even for my family, my parents would say, 'Oh, you can do this instead.'" These sentiments, while intended to help her see the many options that lay ahead, lacked the validation that she needed about the struggles that she was experiencing in the face of life without volleyball.

This sentiment was all too common for athletes who experienced injuries during sport. While attempting to send messages of positive recovery and a return to sport, families failed to convey the needed validation about the experience of being injured. For Dannie, her mother's enthrallment and participation in her athletic career created an expectation that her mother would understand her pain. However, Dannie's experience was quite the opposite in relating to her mother in retirement.

> It has been me and my mom since I was 16, so she has definitely been one of the most important people in my life. She would drive up five hours for an 11 o'clock game and drive five hours back to Boston. That was her commitment. . . . When I tore my ACL, I was beside myself. I felt like my mom did

> not view it as devastating as it was for me. When it happened to me, I knew I could never be as good as I could be. I was like, "You are not being the most empathetic or nicest to me, Mom." I was like, "This is devastating, my life is over." She was like, "You are being dramatic." I was like, "Am I, though?" That was pretty weird.

For this participant, she experienced her mother's disconnect from the depth of her emotional turmoil as an empathic failure, creating a sense of being all alone. The experience of being alone in her pain only intensified for Dannie when her teammates, in an attempt to create connection, compared their experiences to hers, rather than simply allowing space for her to talk about her unique and subjective experience. "You felt like it was this competition of who had it worse or who had it better. It was really weird, I expected my teammates who had torn their ACL to be there for me and understand the devastation and the smaller parts of not being able to do things for yourself. . . . My teammate would say 'well it was hard for me' and I would be like 'well it is so hard for me right now.'" Unfortunately, these exchanges, while commonplace attempts at relating, were ineffective. In many ways, they only served to further intensify Dannie's experience of social isolation and increase her symptoms of depression. "I felt very kind of on my own. Experiencing that aloneness for four surgeries, I think the final one, I was kind of like, 'I am depressed. I am by myself.'"

Beth echoed feelings of being alone in her struggles with the coach and school, which led to her withdrawing inward and not sharing her experiences with her family.

> I called my parents, my dad, right after and just told them about it. . . . It was an interesting standpoint, for them to be put in the middle, where they didn't want to be. So, I kind of stayed quiet and didn't talk to my family about it and they didn't ask me about it again. I tore my shoulder my freshman year. The school kind of missed the injury. . . . When I went home my parents took me to a different doctor. So, I went back to school and decided not to have surgery, just play through. And my junior year, I just couldn't play anymore. . . . I had a bit of a harsh coach. . . . It was a huge ordeal, where she thought there was no possible way it was true and went to the athletic director of the school trying to get my scholarship taken away. . . . I basically had to medically retire.

While her family was able to support her in retirement and accept that this was the best choice for her, she found the least amount of empathy from her coach, who struggled to accept the depth of her injury. Where most athletes who had to medically retire were afforded a transition and remained valued members of the community, for this participant, this was not an option.

> Where normally people who get to medically retire get to stay like a part of the team and still go to everything and ride on the bus and everything. But my coach wouldn't accept what we were saying was true, so I didn't get to be a part of anything. To be just like totally stripped and not it was hard like I just don't know, I kind of struggled. . . . Totally got rid of all my softball stuff and was just trying to pretend it didn't happen so that was hard not feeling like I can go back ever again. It went from 100 to zero really fast.

This unwelcoming approach to her retirement left the participant feeling completely cut off and isolated from a sport that had been a part of her life for as long as she could remember. While she continued to live with her teammates, who were more accepting and understanding of her retirement, it did not buffer the pain of this experience. This lack of closure and ending on terms that were not chosen by the participant influenced how she experienced the transition into retirement.

Erica, while experiencing her "world imploding" after being cut for her senior year, found her personal experiences overshadowed by questions about how her situation may impact her brother's decision to play for the same school. "It kind of turned into a bigger deal for me, specifically because my brother being a good prospect. He was in the newspapers and stuff. So for me, people were like is your brother going to decommit because the athletic director screwed you over? Oh my gosh . . . so that was like the big issue. You know, it wasn't like 'Are you okay?' it was kinda like, 'Is your brother going to not come?' For this participant, these conversations further solidified her beliefs about the gender differences in how elite sport is perceived and the significance of her performance to others in her life. Many of the participants experienced feedback from their families that placed a shadow over a career and retirement that they may have otherwise regarded with pride.

For Hayden, while he knew he had an impressive career, he was not immune to the impact of his family's assessment of his career on his own feelings about himself and what he had accomplished. "One of my struggles is that my mother looks at my career as I choked, that is a struggle for me. My uncle looks at my career as I did pretty well, but there were times I was called up that I didn't play well. Those are hard things for me to deal with." He shared that hearing repeated messages about his performance, particularly that he "didn't live up to the talent that I had" were hard to hear given how much of himself he believed he gave to his athletic career. He acknowledged that the weight of his family's expressed disappointment about his career and decision to retire made the retirement process more difficult for him. Ultimately, he was able to contextualize this feedback with the love that he knew his family had for him. In referring to his mother's disappointment, he shared: "She doesn't necessarily say the right things, but her heart is in the right place. She cares. My uncle cares. He tried every little thing he could do to try and get my call-up. I respect that." For Hayden, finding a way to meaningfully integrate his family's reactions allowed for his narrative to end with a well-played and well-earned career.

Tim also shared experiences of his family members attempting to help him that, while well intentioned, only created a larger divide between them and increased his inner turmoil.

> My mom, she's probably an enabler actually, so she enabled me at times. "Hey, let me send you a little bit of money just to kind of help you out" and you know I knew I could if I got into trouble, always rely on my mom to help me out. My mom would express her worries. . . . It's like they were walking on eggshells I think around me, not wanting to upset me, because I lied. A lot. . . . I was using lies to cover up tough conversations that people wanted to have with me. And so those people couldn't get in and they know how, I would just block them off.

Unfortunately, this created a cycle of communication and interaction that left everyone walking on eggshells and the participant eventually feeling compelled to lie to keep others from truly knowing how bad things were. Like many of the participants, he believed that the important people in this life wanted to provide support, but his defense mechanism of pretending that things were okay and lying about opportunities was a barrier to asking for and receiving help. "The next deal, this next opportunity was always something that was not solidified at all, but that I could use to get away from letting them in."

In some cases, even when participants were willing to accept help, they often were unable to verbalize the need for support or what would have been helpful to them. Issa, referring to her family and her boyfriend at the time of retirement, discussed this lack of insight. "They were feeling sad for sure but they also didn't know how to support me because I wasn't openly saying what I needed, because I didn't know what I needed. I just wanted to cry and be left alone because that was like how I felt like coping with it. So that was also something they supported me in not kind of prying and saying no let's talk about it and not forcing me to open the wound, if you will." Some participants did not discover what would have been helpful in their retirement until much later into their journeys. For Tim, he was not able to allow himself to be vulnerable enough to reveal how much he was struggling in retirement until several years in when he had divorced and begun a new relationship.

> I was working at the time, things were pretty solid and so she really encouraged me, "I see something in you, I can hear it in you and I'm in." She was kind of the first one to really support that in me. . . . So then I felt in a safe place and encouraged to be able to share that part of me and the more I'm sharing it, the

> more I'm putting it together. Oh yeah, there's something about me that I've suppressed. . . . I see how that can align with where I am today. I've been dying to talk and talk about it but haven't had the opportunity.

For Tim, while he credited "a right alignment with meeting this person," it allowed him to begin to explore a piece of himself that he had long since kept hidden. There were many individuals in his life who had wanted to talk about it with him. However, there was always a preexisting relationship that kept him from feeling comfortable unveiling how bad things were, until someone saw through his resistances.

A SHARED LIVED EXPERIENCE

Many participants recognized that they felt most comfortable talking with people who understood their experiences firsthand, particularly other elite athletes. They recognized that it was easier to connect and feel supported by someone who had walked in their shoes and understood not only the changes they were experiencing transitioning into retirement but also athletic culture and performance levels they had competed at.

While going through her injury, Tess expressed a sense that only a few people in her life truly understood the pain that she experienced as she retired. When she identified this small group of individuals, she found solace in identifying the few people who she believed could relate to the emotional loss. "I would say my teammates understood the best, quite a few of them had injuries at some point just not the sustained injury I was facing. I feel like my close friends who weren't on the team were also supportive but again didn't really understand why this transition was so hard and then some of the cross-country runners who would have prolonged stress fractures also understood because you're getting taken out of sport without wanting to. So, I found some solace in finding other people with boots to walk around with on campus." Support from people he could trust and who he believed understood the pain of an injury that impedes an elite career also played an important role for Henry, who described how he had tremendous support from friends and coaches who had competed, retired, and managed serious injuries in their careers. Their advice, support, and mentorship were essential in his transition into retirement and decision-making during a time of turmoil in his life. "I was really lucky in terms of having a lot of people you can trust who have gone through similar things and they were more on the outspoken side of saying this doesn't make sense." He shared that these key individuals helped him to move on from the "competitive side of you that wants to get back and prove you can get back and play at a level that was higher than when you left." In hindsight, he saw that there was a combination of ego and sports culture that drove his desire to return even when he was not feeling well enough to play. In the end, while battling through his inner conflict, he recognized that the long-term ramifications of returning to elite hockey were not outweighed by more time on the ice. "It came down to the point of buckling down and listening to the people you can trust and saying that there are other ways to get that competitiveness out, and that led to the coaching side of things when I wasn't sure what I wanted to do." While retirement was not what he wanted or envisioned for himself at that juncture, he recognized that it was the appropriate time. His ability to seek support from others opened doors into his next chapter as a coach and which allowed him to remain in an arena that he loves, albeit in a different role.

Steve shared a similar sentiment on the benefit of connecting with other retired athletes who are going through the career transition and identity dissolution. "I'm fortunate that a guy I played with in (state) had a 10-year career with the (team). He and I are pretty much best friends. He lives in the area. Our transitions were within 4–5 years of each other. So, I kind of had him as a buffer because I really struggled." Jermaine also had a close person in his life, his brother, who had very similar athletic retirement experience. This close connection helped him to feel understood when he was struggling to explain it to his parents. He shared that his brother expressed the need to detach oneself from the individual aspect of it and the recognition of how hard the lifestyle of elite performance is.

> The way he explained it to me was, "Man, I struggled with it when I gave it up. You know I got so much satisfaction doing that and I loved it even more than I played. I loved my career more after than when I was playing towards the end. You can love your career after sports more than you did playing." I thought, "You know, no one really explains it like that."

He identified that this conversation allowed him to see a path forward where he could have a career that he loved and have satisfaction and passion in that too. This was the first time that he had heard feedback about life after sport. "I never realized that, I was just told you have to play as long as you can, kids would kill for your spot. Your dad would kill for it." He recognized that these messages created limitations in his thought patterns about what his life could hold that were not based on what he was really capable of or what his future would entail. These messages kept his identity tied closely to athletics despite his own consistent attempts to be recognized for his many attributes and identities. "I think that your life can be just as fulfilling or more fulfilling and that never really clicked for me until he said that, and once he said that, I think it became a lot easier for me." Ultimately, Jermaine found new positive ways of viewing retirement and life post sport from those who had walked the path before them.

Joe identified his relationship with his girlfriend as being a connection point that he could not get anywhere else in his life at the time where he could see that he would not be able to take his career any further. "[My girlfriend] got me through it. She was on the division one softball team at the time, and she had a shoulder injury, and they were trying to take advantage of her scholarship wise and jerked her around a bit. So we were kind of going through it together. I had a really strong relationship at this time, she was kind going through athletic and [university] coaching and management type issues too. So we were both going through it, and it didn't make me feel like I was the only one." For many of the participants, the need to not be "the only one" permeated their stories and experiences. It helped to be able to connect about the shared experience of pain, while also having someone who had dedicated as much of themselves to their athletic identity buffered against isolation as they transitioned. Joe highlighted how this connection was a resource for him as he faced what he experienced as an unfair ending to a career he had worked hard for.

> It was nice to hear her story of her childhood [girlfriend's] and how hard she worked to get where she was and how it wasn't playing out the way she wanted it to. It was just someone else, rather than thinking I'm the only person in the world that works hard then doesn't get what they deserve from it. My ego would have been destroyed. It's a real thing. I could not have swallowed the fact that I was there, thought I was better than other guys, and wasn't playing.

This participant believed that without this shared lived experience he would not have been able to continue his education and face the emotional turmoil that he was experiencing. Knowing that he was not alone may also have helped him to depersonalize the actions of his head coach. This, coupled with the feedback from his team and other coaches, allowed him to find more balance in how he saw the events that were unfolding and to decrease the damage to his self-worth.

Erica also found comfort in those who were going through the same situation that she was, a career that was ending prematurely based on the decisions of others. "I had my classmates, because we all had the same thing. I handled it with them . . . and some people on the men's teams were like, you know, there for me too." However, for Dannie, this was a connection that she longed for but could not find in others in her life. "I do not feel like there is anybody who I felt innately got it." Even in those who she believed understood the loss of sport, the true experience of being understood remained elusive. "My best friend, who is also my teammate, got it. She also quit our senior year.

She would be like. 'I get it. You are done with soccer.' She was always there to help me. But that emotional connection to the devastation, she did not get that." Beth expressed a different experience when her boyfriend's career was ended by a coach that did not like him. She recognized that while they both were experiencing an emotional transition, that his grief experience was so much greater than hers that she found herself not wanting to share her feelings. "I would never want to talk about it. I would talk about it with other people." She expressed that the differences in their coping styles, despite having retirements that were out of their control, led to a disconnect in the ability to relate. "I was a little more positive about it. I think I saw a light at the end of the tunnel and maybe he didn't. I just didn't find purpose in being told about and saying I worked so hard for this to happen." She recognized that this type of personal reflection was a barrier to being able to move forward to her next chapter. "I saw it as an opportunity to create something new and go elsewhere, so I think I was kind of more helpful to him and he took it harder than I did." These sentiments underscored the impact of coping styles and internalization strategies on the effectiveness of the shared lived experience as a mechanism for transitional support.

Issa did not have an opportunity to connect with others with similar experiences, however, she recognized the value of these types of connections. "I honestly think an outlet to talk to somebody, that was the other thing, even though everybody else was going through the end of the year career or whatever. I felt like I was so alone because I was injured. I felt like there was nobody to talk to about my personal experience that could relate. . . . I felt like I had to put on a facade." She shared that having her career ended abruptly before the end of the season, left her feeling disconnected from the sadness that her teammates were feeling as their college careers came to a close. For this participant, without feeling understood, and without the coping skills to provide outlets for her emotions, the stress she experienced was intensified. "Having to talk to somebody really like almost break down like this [referring to her crying], but with somebody who could feel that pain because they went through it too, I think that would've been helpful." There was significant recognition among the participants of their role in seeking support in retirement. They often oscillated between wanting support and not wanting to talk with anyone about what they were going through. When they were presented with individuals who had a shared narrative, the willingness to be vulnerable increased.

OUTSIDE LOOKING IN: WATCHING IT MOVE ON WITHOUT ME

While some participants found their teammates to be a significant source of support during retirement, others quickly found themselves feeling like outsiders in an environment where they had previously felt immense connection, camaraderie, and friendship. In some cases, this served as a reminder of how fast the sports industry changes. For others, they found themselves serving as a reminder to their former teammates of what could go wrong, a feared ending to a hard-earned career.

Esteban shared that, as he found his career options dwindling and his age advancing, he quickly felt disconnected from the individuals who he had considered to be his family for several years. "Even the guys that I had relationships with from team, my teams, they didn't care. You know what I mean? They were . . . and it's fine, it's the type of life. It's cutthroat." He recognized that not only was the sports culture about surviving as long as possible, it also meant moving on and disconnecting from anyone who was no longer a part of the team.

Tess echoed these sentiments and shared feeling that her teammates, while having sympathy for her, were happy that they were not in her shoes. "I feel like my teammates . . . It was almost like, 'We're really sorry this happened to you but we're really glad this didn't happen to me,' you know?" While many of her teammates had experienced injuries, their recoveries had been quick, and they could not relate to the sustained nature of her injury. While every participant acknowledged that they knew their career would come to an end, some found themselves feeling disconnected from their team and athletic community as their identity changed.

Chris experienced a similar disconnect. This was not necessarily due to the overall sports culture, but due instead to the marked difference between his lifestyle and schedule as an elite athlete versus the one that he had in retirement. "It sucked, because I still had a lot of friends on the team, and I wasn't on their schedule. We'd hang out and I felt totally out of place. Because I just wasn't a part of what they were doing. It wasn't the same, and it was quick. Maybe it was all me, but I remember guys when I was in and those guys were out. Even that relationship wasn't the same." He shared that it changes so quickly, from being a part of the team to being on the outside. "It doesn't take long. You can walk around a locker room but within a year nobody really knows who you are. It was tough. I mean, I was the guy in the locker room with all those guys." He realized that he too had perpetuated this cycle of moving on when he was playing. Ultimately, he acknowledged how fast relationships can change in the elite performance arenas. Athletes continue to have to focus on keeping their own contracts and perfecting their own performances: "It's their world now. It's not my world anymore."

Deonte shared that, while he was somewhat aware that his football career was over, this was solidified when he returned to visit his old campus and recognized how much of what he remembered had changed.

> I snuck onto campus like two weeks ago . . . just to say what's up to the coaches because I was in the area showing a home . . . being back there, it was cool seeing everybody, but I knew when I walked into the coach's office, like yeah this is a bit different. . . . I knew at that point, that chapter is closed, forever. But it was cool being back and seeing guys I knew were still there. Because, damn, the years are flying by. There's only one more class that I still know. It's nuts how fast time flies. It felt like yesterday.

All these athletes pinpointed the connection to their teammates as one of the best things about being an athlete. Yet, most participants in this section experienced a severing of these connections when their careers ended. This was especially true for those participants who had performed beyond the collegiate level.

LASTING PUBLIC PERSONAS AND THEIR IMPACT ON ADAPTATION

While many athletes struggled when others began to view them differently in retirement, for some participants, the public athletic persona was one that persisted. Undoubtedly, this increased the challenges experienced during athletic transitions. At a time when they needed to see themselves through other identities, the one that was held on to by others was their athletic identity.

For Tess, the experience of injury and rehabilitation occurred center stage, with regular encounters that served as reminders of the injury and the limitations it was creating. "All of a sudden, everyone knows you're injured. I was in a boot so much that people started calling me boot girl. It's like a very public rehabilitation. . . . You have to tell everybody what's going on all the time because they're still wondering why you're in a boot. So it wasn't even like I could focus on rehabbing, it's almost like you have to relive everything all the time." Joe echoed these sentiments when he explored remaining on campus for his junior year after accepting that there was no way to salvage his time on the hockey team. He was cognizant of how hard it was to have people still want to connect with him. "There were a lot of donors from [school] who were trying to meet my family and people who were always trying to take me to breakfast and to lunch and stuff like that. I wanted nothing to do with that, and if I took those dates, I would have to explain what was going on." He highlighted how being at a large school where everyone knows that you are an athlete creates almost a compelling need to explain the dynamics of one's retirement on a continual basis, a task that was too daunting for someone who was struggling with his own intense emotional turmoil.

For some of the athletes, while they were able to transition from some aspects of their athletic identity in retirement, it was harder to move away from the long-standing persona in the communities that they grew up in. Jess shared that returning home brings back front and center her athletic identity because that is how others in her community view her. This created a duality between the life she was building post-sport and the continued identification as an elite athlete in some parts of her life. "When I go back home . . . I still identify as an athlete, because everyone there also still kind of knows me as an athlete. . . . When I started my first job after college, when nobody knew that I even played in college, those are the times I didn't really identify as an athlete anymore, but back home, everyone I went to high school with and a lot of my friends in high school, were volleyball players, so I kind of identified as an athlete and I feel like I still do in certain situations." For Jess, she was able to draw a connection between the identity that others had for her and the one that she began to carve out for herself. However, a shift had occurred when she was around those who still remembered her as an elite performer.

Kendrick also experienced the influence of his home community on his athletic identity and transition into retirement. He shared that while they had encouraged his athletic career with messages such as, "you're going to make it to the NFL," they were so far removed from sports culture and athletic performance arenas that they lacked the awareness of what it takes to go to "the next level." Kendrick shared that the ongoing messages during his transition from family members were, "What are you doing? Aren't you supposed to be getting ready for this [the NFL draft]?" These messages highlighted the disconnect between his experiences and what they were observing. For this participant, it added pressure to his own experiences of trying to get into the NFL. "It's tough to get in the NFL, I'm not a hundred percent healthy, not being able to really showcase my talent for the games and stuff that I missed my senior year [due to injury]. . . . I did try to go to the next level." While he felt the support of his immediate family, once they accepted his decision to retire, he shared that it took longer for others to recognize this shift in his life trajectory. "Others that were not in my immediate family didn't completely understand. That's just the notion of, you know, they attributed me as just being a football player. I think that's how they viewed me." This lasting persona in many cases left athletes navigating the complexity of retiring while being regarded by others as an athlete. This identity was hard to let go of and felt like a natural fit.

ATHLETIC TEAMS AND SOCIAL COMPANIONSHIP

Almost all of the athletes in the current study highlighted the role of the team in their lives. Working toward a common goal, struggling together through grueling practices and camps, celebrating wins, and lamenting over losses were at the epicenter of their competitive experiences. Teammates became built-in friends, in many cases regarded as family, with the connection to one another evolving out of shared schedules, the grind of training and practice, and lengthy travel schedules. This natural evolution of friendship was one that many participants found themselves having a hard time replicating in retirement, as we have discussed in previous chapters, the ease of relationships being replaced with having to make an actual effort to remain connected.

This transition created feelings of loneliness until they were able to navigate these changing dynamics. Jess expressed this sentiment: "It was hard, I was used to just seeing my friends at practice. I didn't have to be like, 'oh, let's go, like, get coffee' to hang out. Like I never had to do that. You just automatically saw them. . . . You never had to just think of something to do and then invite someone. . . . So it was pretty lonely initially because even though they were on the same campus as me, you don't have a reason to have all six of you get together anymore unless somebody organizes it." For many of the participants, retirement from sport meant a loss of the built-in peer group that had become their sole source of friendship and comradery. For Esteban, being an only child, his teammates became the closest things to siblings that he had. "It's like a family. You're with these people every day. You're training with them. You're going to eat with them. You're showering with everyone. . . . You know everything about every single teammate. Bus trips and plane trips and, you know, you just become family. You know? And I guess the closest thing I could say, when it comes to being an athlete. You develop such a family aspect because you're with them all the time. I didn't have brothers and sisters, so in a lot of ways they were like my brothers."

Juan echoed these sentiments, depicting the emptiness that is left in a place that this companionship once filled. "Being in the locker room, surrounded by the guys every day, going through workouts with the guys every day, practice, just the daily grind, with your teammates . . . I guess that's been the hardest part. You go from that to not seeing your closest friend." While he recognized that this may be a typical experience for college students after graduation, he shared that it felt particularly jarring given all of the time he had spent with them.

Similar to Juan, Jess also highlighted the rare nature of this connection, one that is hard to duplicate even within elite sports culture. "They see each other as equals but always try to push each other to be better. I probably only experienced that type of mentality once or twice in my eighteen years, but when you experience it, it changes how you take the field, how you show up as a teammate. It is addicting." Henry expressed how the relationships with his teammates throughout his sports career set the stage for his approach to relationships in retirement and allowed him to recognize what type of connections he needed to thrive. "I need real relationships, and hockey provides that even among a coaching staff. Your staff hangs out together just like teammates do, and you have that vulnerability and transparency with one another, and I think that it makes for the best work relationships." He continued, sharing that the bond created in these environments is special. Like many other participants, it was hard to replicate in other arenas. It became important to him to maintain these relationships into retirement and to recognize the unique value they had given him.

> I was incredibly fortunate. My assistant coach at [college], he is someone that I keep in touch with now and he's number one in terms of mentorship. I call him when I'm struggling like do I take this job or do I stay and he said you got to go and as soon as he said that I'm calling it in because of the trust level. We talk about things that aren't hockey, like big shit in life. We talk about stuff that's incredibly important and he was just that guy for me right off the bat. I think a big part of relationships is you trying to put as much positive energy into your interactions with people, because everybody wants to know that who they're talking to cares about them, and he did that for me.

For this participant, his connections and relationships went beyond just his teammates to include lifelong relationships with coaches who served as mentors and eventually friends.

When it came time to transition into retirement, many of the participants found themselves having to transition what these relationships would look like after sport, as they entered into the next chapters of their lives. For some, this was another change that brought about questions such as, "What do I want to do now? Not just with [sport] but in terms of relationships." Jess shared that she had to learn how to maintain friendships for the first time in her life, and while it made her a better communicator, it was challenging to adjust to this new role. "That's been challenging, especially with having to coordinate when you're going to see people and everything. I've become known as the good communicator. I am the person in the group that's like always initiating, like, 'Let's go do this, Let's go take a trip somewhere.' I try to be the good communicator, because a lot of people aren't and if somebody is not putting in the effort to like, maintain those connections, they'll go over a year without talking to someone. It just happens so easily and so quickly." For this participant, it was the first time that she realized that relationships take effort to maintain and to develop and that they are not as convenient as what she had experienced as an athlete. For some of the athletes, they have been able to maintain the strong connections to their teammates into retirement, for others, they have had to identify new ways to create the comradery that they lost in retirement. Yet, for those athletes who formed strong bonds to their teammates they were able to forge the path into retirement together, being in one another's weddings, remaining close friends, long after sport. Jess highlighted the strength of these relationships. "A lot of those people are still my best friends. . . . And it's just so much stronger than a lot of other relationships I had with people outside of volleyball, because you do fun things with other people, but it's not like accomplishing things together, going through challenges together. I think athletics strengthens relationships on a whole new level." For Jess, while maintaining these connections required intentionality in retirement, all other relationships felt superficial after experiencing such an intense bond. She expressed a void and feeling of loneliness that she does not believe she could fill with other relationships.

Issa echoed this sentiment when she explored the relationships that she would not have had without hockey. "To put it in perspective, I got engaged this weekend, the people that were there were my teammates from college." Erica also shared that her former teammates are still a part of the major events in her life. "It's impacted every area of my life, all of my friends, like my bridal party, every single girl, I played 12U hockey with." Jess also shared that after having experienced such a deep bond with her teammates, relationships in retirement seemed to lack the depth that she was seeking. "The newer friends just seem more surface level. You haven't been through things with them. . . . Not only did you go to school together and see each other longer, you went through a lot of experiences together that automatically bring you closer." While these connections were not unique to those participants whose careers ended at the collegiate level, athletes who performed at the professional level reported less direct connection to teammates at that level. Some professional athletes even recalled their college years as the greatest sense of comradery and success that they had experienced. These sentiments point to a potential difference in the experience of camaraderie and friendship across elite levels of performance and potentially type of sport.

For some of the participants, such as Tess, the relationships that she had with her teammates dissipated in retirement, which led her to identify that their connection was built around sport. Ultimately, she realized that they did not have a lot of common ground outside of volleyball. "We're definitely not as close just because time has gone on. It's interesting because in a lot of ways you don't have that much in common with the individual other than the sport, so once that ends, you don't really have a lot." For Tess, the value that she found in having a social life that is embedded in sport carried into her future athletic endeavor of competitive cycling.

> I feel like a lot of my social life is able to exist with training because a lot of other people are also going on training rides so I can have this social life and also have this outlet that exists too. I feel like when you go to the bar there's no real benefit for me. There's no dual purpose, you're just there to do one thing. . . . I think it's hard to feel like people understand this drive that you have to do it if they aren't an athlete. They're just like, "Wait, why are you going to do this for five hours on a Saturday?" I'm like, "I don't know? I don't have anything better to do." I never know how to answer that question. . . . I feel like there are barriers where I feel like it's not quite understood.

She recognized that there are a lot of ways in which her need for connectedness was met via sport and how this differs from some of the more mainstream ways in which people socialize. While she saw the value of connecting with others, she continued to be the most comfortable in creating these relationships with individuals who shared her athletic identity and drive.

Chris shared similar struggles in connecting outside of football and voiced the challenges in developing friendships as an adult.

> I have acquaintances and stuff, neighbors. I think a lot of it has to do with youth too. As you get older, everybody's busy, and then it becomes "Oh, let's do this tonight!" and then, "Eh, no." I mean certainly in that environment. . . . I can imagine if was 42 playing, like Brady, I'd probably be doing the same thing I was doing when I was 28. But that kind of camaraderie . . . my circumstances don't let me have that. . . . I know a couple of coaches I have now, I latch on to them like crazy. We bullshit and we text and we talk about football.

He shared that while his wife does not understand his need to find a genuine connection with others around sport, that it is the place that he feels most comfortable in his social life, a common ground that he can build friendships around and that fills the void for all of them. When reflecting on other coaches that he knows, Chris expressed:

> It's funny, because my wife thinks I'm crazy, and his wife thinks he's crazy, but I think it gives us this outlet. And I'm more friendly with those two guys than friends I have around here or friends from home. I'm friends with friends from home, but more friendly with them. Maybe we just fill this need. It's crazy, I can't even describe it. Even in the offseason, we talk and try to get kids to play. . . . I get along really well with the other coaches. We bond around football, so maybe that's what I do know. But that's all I've ever known. So for me to be away from football. I'm not the guy that's going to go to dinner parties

> and events and just shake hands. But put me in this environment [with other coaches], and I'm Mr. Congeniality.

For Chris, he saw a marked distinction in his comfortability and ability to connect when he is talking with people who understand the athletic identity and sports culture. While he could not pinpoint what it is about talking with those who understand him that created instant camaraderie—a bond between himself and other coaches—he verbalized this very real phenomenon for himself, much like what was previously noted by Joe.

THE POWER OF CONNECTION THROUGH ELITE PERFORMANCE AND BEYOND

Marshall approached his relationships a bit differently than some of the other athletes in the current study. He chose to hold on to a tight but consistent friend group from his childhood throughout his NFL career.

> My group of best friends has never changed up, those guys are my teammates. I think that's important too. Some people who I always see who struggle after, some of those guys maybe don't have people who are real friends with them. Some people, once they're out, they're not the same person. I was loved the same before I made it, once I made it, after I made it. So many guys I know, I hear about like, "Yeah, I lost track of this person because this person used to only care about me when I was this. Now that I'm not a big name anymore, oh well, I'm out to the woodshed. A lot of guys go through that too, that's why I say it's very important to be surrounded by the right people. God bless, I have no complaints and no hang-ups in those areas, so it's been awesome.

For this participant, he was able to see the importance of not allowing his elite athletic career to become a distancing force in his friendships. He observed how other teammates he played with were drawn toward more transactional friendships in their career. He articulated how he believed that affected their transition from elite sport, losing comradery while having to face so many other changes in their lives.

> Some teammates had the same patterns as me and then some of the high-profile teammates, that was it. You wouldn't see them out unless it was with some other big league from another team or an actor or something like that. I tell you what, usually those guys are the ones that are soul searching and looking for stuff that they don't have at that point. They don't have that fulfillment. Because like I said, it is going to run out. So, to me, having people who have been with you the whole time and have the journey, and can share it and have that before. Like

> I said I was from a very unique situation, don't get me wrong I've added other best friends as I go. But since I was 14, I've had the same core group of best friends. So, people go to college and form brand new friends. Our parents have always talked about that, like, "Wow it's crazy how you guys have been with each other from the beginning and never switched up." I had so many people that were along for it. So, at the end of it, when it all came to fruition, it made it that much sweeter that I was able to wake up in the morning being like, "Damn, I know they are so proud." These guys would be going nuts, so there are so many people living through that through me that that was so important to me.

For Marshall, knowing that he had the support from a core group of people who had been with him at every stage of his career helped to motivate him during his peak performance and to keep him grounded during his retirement transition. Much like many of the other participants in the study, Marshall recognized that a strong support network was an important factor in retirement, especially when they had been a constant in the athlete's life prior to elite performance.

Henry wholeheartedly agreed with Marshall's emphasis on the importance of relationships, not only during his athletic career but deeper into retirement. "I believe you have to go all in on whatever you want to be in life, but at the same time how you treat people, you have to go even harder at that because at the end of they day, it ends, and you want to have people there at the end when it does and you want to have people during the journey because life . . . everybody needs connection." The importance of support was the connection, intimacy, and stability it formed. Henry believed these relationships helped him to not only manage the stress of a career ending concussion, but also to have something positive to focus on as he navigated the transition into retirement. He shared that the trust that he had in his support system allowed him to make some very difficult decisions at the end of his career including entering retirement. "[My wife] said it's time. You have got to find something else. It's just like, 'Okay,' and you do and that lightbulb came on. I really respect this person or that person who means a lot to me. If they're saying it and I know they have my best interest at heart, then you just take it and you go with it." Believing in the relationships that he had with his support system allowed him to trust they would not do anything to hurt him. This allowed him to walk away and transition into retirement at a time when he was torn and considering trying to push through the pain to return for another season. While the social support these participants experienced varied, it was clear that those who had access to and could meaningfully engage with support networks were better positioned to face the stressors and nuances of the retirement journey.

Chapter 6

Psychosocial Experiences, Stressors, and the Layers of Grief

Retirement from elite athletic performance marks the transition from a highly competitive and physically demanding lifestyle to a new and unfamiliar chapter in life. As evidenced in the preceding chapters, this transition into retirement can create various challenges and substantial personal distress for athletes. Athletes are forced to grapple with multiple simultaneous losses, including the cessation of a lifestyle they have known for years and the interruption of an identity that has been central to their worldview. These losses include loss of athletic identity, structure and routine of training, relationships with teammates and coaches, loss of role and status, and loss of the adrenaline rush of competition. Ultimately, the transition into retirement is accompanied by an array of emotional responses including sadness, confusion, loss, feelings of emptiness, lack of purpose, and, for some, peace.

Some of the participants in the study described the initial periods of their transition into retirement as "dark" (Tess) and a time of great confusion (Tim, Joe). They detailed the intensity of the sadness and a sense of being completely lost. Issa expressed these sentiments: "I was so heartbroken; it was like an existential crisis. . . . It was definitely a weird time." Ultimately, these participants faced a period of trying to figure out some serious existential questions—Who am I without sport? Am I still an athlete? What should I do now?

While some of the athletes in the current study experienced abrupt, unexpected endings to their careers, several made the decision to retire, going out on their own terms. Participants who faced unexpected or abrupt endings to their careers due to injury, deselection, or limited opportunities experienced notable distress during the transition process. However, even those who anticipated their retirements or voluntarily chose to leave the sport were not immune to psychosocial stressors and emotional challenges during their transition into retirement. Even when athletes can foresee their retirement, the adjustment period remains characterized by a considerable amount of uncertainty as they navigate new career trajectories, adapt to shifting roles and life demands, and endeavor to establish new prominent identities.

All of the athletes in the study recognized that the end of their athletic careers was inevitable, often referring to this realization as their "shelf life," one that they knew to be short at such an elite level. However, this awareness did not mitigate the emotional impact they experienced when retirement arrived. This could be attributed, in part, to the persistent psychosocial stressors that they encountered throughout their elite careers, which had a direct impact on their emotional well-being. Living with high levels of stress and pressure on a daily basis can leave little room for anticipating the emotional challenges of retirement, making the transition even more daunting.

PSYCHOSOCIAL CHALLENGES OF ELITE PERFORMANCE

This study explored the experiences of athletes as they navigate the transition into retirement from elite sport. However, it is crucial to note that for many elite athletes, the feelings of sadness, grief, and psychosocial stress began long before their career came to an end. These emotional challenges were present in the later parts of their athletic careers and played a significant role in shaping their experiences leading up to retirement. According to the athletes in this study, they consistently carried the burden of a persistent fear of failure, performance expectations, and ongoing scrutiny, which significantly impacted their emotional well-being throughout their careers, often leading them to feel "mentally drained" from "the grind" (Arianna).

For some of the athletes, the impact of sports on mental health was present long before they participated in elite-level competition. Dannie expressed these sentiments: "I never really viewed myself as good on the basketball court. . . . I made JV as a freshman as opposed to the freshman team. I still didn't identify as good, because basketball was so bad for my mental health. Shedding myself of the expectations of being that basketball player and then saying soccer is what I want. It took me a while to find my voice and to articulate that to my parents and coaches." Dannie's mental health challenges, combined with a lack of confidence, led her to grapple with her self-imposed expectations and struggles in identifying what she was actually passionate about. She shared that it took her until her junior year of high school to get up the confidence to communicate what she wanted her athletic future to look like, while a very difficult process, it became one she has pride in. This participant's experience highlights the challenge of trying to navigate difficult conversations with adults at such a young age. While developmentally appropriate, it is concerning as this is often the age where decisions are made about athletic engagement, and young adults may not yet have the full capacity to effectively navigate these dialogues.

Esteban shared that, like many of the athletes in the study, his athletic pursuit led to him leaving his home and moving to another country at 17. This experience had a significant emotional impact on his development and identity as a young man. "It made me grow up. I had to grow up really fast." He identified how "mentally tough" it was to be away from family while trying to compete at an elite level without the support network to lean on. "I had no one. . . . Mentally, it was not the easiest thing to deal with. . . . To be honest, in the first two weeks, I pretty much cried every day." While he identified several ways that he feels he has grown from this experience, he recalls this period of elite competition as one that was emotionally challenging, never fully feeling as if he could share these experiences with his family. "I didn't want to worry my family."

Some of the participants in the current study identified a point in their athletic careers where, instead of competing for love of the game, the commitment became less enjoyable. Some referred to their pursuit of sport as a "chore" or a "job" (Jermaine, Esteban, Chris, Marshall). Esteban described the moment that he felt differently about competing: "I kind of lost the love for it because it was a job." In the current study, many players expressed nostalgic feelings about their initial experiences with sports engagement, describing the love and passion they once felt. However, many acknowledged reaching a point in their careers where they lost the original sense of affection and joy.

One factor that may have influenced this change is the perception that they were constantly trying to prove themselves. They were trapped in a cycle of fear and pressure to perform well that had become detrimental to their mental health. Jess depicted this well when she talks about the pressure that she felt each time she stepped on the court. "You just kind of get in this cycle of fear any time you go out to hit. If I hit it out, I'm going to be yanked. I'm going to lose my spot." Arianna described "constantly fighting" for the "ultimate spot," and the pain that was experienced by "any loss." In reflection, she recognized how far removed this took her from what was happening in the world around her. "Now that I say it out loud it does seem absurd, in the world that we're living in, that that's a huge moment. . . . But these moments in games where you weren't good enough, you lost, things happened. . . . I felt like there were tons . . . It was a constant roller coaster every day."

Similarly, Chris highlighted that the pressure that creates stress and anxiety is also the same pressure that fosters motivation.

> That under pressure all of the time, I hated it. I guess, because it's nerve-racking from season to season, game to game. That's the reason I was done. I was just frazzled because I took things very seriously. I didn't enjoy it as much the later it got. It was the next game, the next payday, the next contract. Would I want that kind of stress again? No. But I also like that stress and the pressure, like Thursday at 4, I gotta have this stuff done. There was always that pressure to perform, and at times it was great to embrace it and get that pulse going. . . . It's really hard to replicate, in the highs and the lows . . . very intense highs and lows.

He shared that this was one of the reasons that he was able to make the transition into retirement. While he regarded this as stress that he found to be emotionally draining, there was also a part of him that realized he thrives under the pressure of deadlines and obligations. For Chris, there is a clear delineation between pressure that is useful and that which contributed to emotional dysregulation. In reflecting on the success of his lengthy professional career, he was clear and candid regarding the sacrifices made to his emotional health and well-being and the price he paid for success. "That was the reason why, after 11 years, I took everything I had to take personally and expressed it out. I feel like, I guess that maybe got me there so long, but it probably shredded me emotionally."

Hayden also highlighted the toll that the pressure to perform can take on elite athletes, acknowledging the challenging reality they face. "The day you were striking out, the ground balls, the losing, that stuff beats you down, of course." Likewise, Tim explored the stress associated with one season ending and having to find the motivation to begin to prepare for the next one, a process repeated over and over throughout an elite career. "It's just, it's like man, especially when it doesn't end the way you want it to end. You don't go as far as, when we didn't go as far as we wanted to go. Those heartbreaks are real." For Tim, while the end to his career was very challenging, he also recognized that he had experienced similar disappointments and emotional dysregulation throughout the majority of his athletic career.

Kurt also shared the toll that elite competition had on his mental health. "I really enjoyed winning. I really enjoyed competing, and that's what I was good at, and it allowed me to make money while doing it. Of course I'm going to keep doing it, but as soon as I lost that, it wasn't fun. It was just like destroying my mental state, and it was consuming me." He shared that even the people in his life were aware of how much of an impact it was having on him. "[My girlfriend] talks about it all the time. She says I was like a rock when I was doing football because I was so consumed by it. Especially times when I wasn't doing well."

The notion of elite athletic competition as an emotional roller coaster was a common theme among many of the athletes in the present study (Joe,

Arianna, Beth, Esteban, Chris, Beth). Joe shared his experience with the highs and lows and the emotional stressors that are a common part of being an elite athlete. "The hardest part (of being an athlete) was the roller coaster of emotions. The ups and downs of being an athlete are extremely hard when they are down. You feel like you lose your self-worth as a human being when you don't perform well or you're not given the chance to perform well."

According to Arianna, one of the most challenging aspects of being an elite athlete is the vulnerability that comes with giving your all to something and knowing that there is a possibility it may not be enough. "I think the hardest one is being the most vulnerable when you've put in every ounce of yourself and you're still not in the position that you wanna be in because you're just not quite good enough." Likewise, Kendrick also acknowledged these sentiments by recognizing that the constant drive to be the best player on the team led to frequent comparisons with others. Although this exercise was intended to boost motivation, it ultimately resulted in negative self-reflection and diminished self-confidence. Kendrick stated: "That, in your psyche, makes you feel like you're not as good or as worthy."

Beth shared that she experienced a connection between performance, her sense of self, and her emotional disposition. "I remember my freshman year, I was doing really poorly. And there were six games in a row that I went without a hit, and I remember just getting on the bus and I just started crying. And calling my parents and just being so sad." Upon retiring and having the time and perspective for reflection, she came to the realization that the burden she placed on herself to perform was unhealthy. "And looking back now, it's so silly that not performing well had such an impact like that, when in like perspective to real-world problems, it's so minimal, but at the time, it's what's important to you, and what you think is. Not having a good batting average is so detrimental to someone's mental space."

Joe shared that a significant portion of the psychosocial stress experienced in elite competition originates from circumstances that are frequently beyond one's control, making them more challenging to handle and comprehend. "If you have a coach who doesn't like you, or a general manager, and they want to trade you or they want to sit you, that's out of your control. You can work as hard as you want and they just make the decision on you, for any reason in the world, you feel like a lesser person." Similarly, Erica also emphasized the limited control elite athletes have over their outcomes, regardless of their talent, work ethic, and dedication. "I think my hardest part was the things that were out of my control. I felt like no matter how hard I worked . . . hockey is a sport where your coach likes you and believes in you and you play or you can be the best player on your team, in my opinion, the best player on our team didn't even dress for games because our coach didn't like her. So, I think that part of it was really stressful."

The participants in the current study experienced the most pronounced shift in their relationship with coaches when they transitioned to playing at the college level. They expressed the feeling that, at this stage, some of the feedback became less focused on player development and more subjective in nature. Jermaine initially struggled to understand the shifting relationships with coaches and to manage feelings of constantly being evaluated and having to perform. "You think about your relationships with your coaches and you're under the microscope within yourself. You think about it introspectively, it's like, 'Why doesn't he like me? Why can't he see that I can do this?' Well, they think about you, but not really. . . . I really struggled with that and I think that when I understood what my role could be, how I could play and contribute, and it's not necessarily the big role I wanted. . . . it got a lot easier for me." He shared that it took him a considerable amount of time to recognize that the coaches were not focused on him as a person but within the context of the team. He found it difficult to accept that the coach's primary focus wasn't on his individual player development and that the level of energy and support he received from coaches at younger levels wouldn't be the same in college. It took him quite some time to depersonalize the feedback and come to the realization that, for the coach, he was just one of many players, and the coach's primary focus was on winning rather than individual player development. According to Hayden, one of the most challenging aspects is coming to the realization that the sports industry is primarily a business, and the focus is no longer solely on player development and success. This shift in perspective can be difficult for athletes who have been accustomed to a more player-centered and developmental approach during their careers. "It can get very, very depressing, knowing how cutthroat it is and how much they really do not care about you." Understanding that sports organizations and teams prioritize business objectives and profitability can lead to feelings of disillusionment, especially for athletes who had previously experienced a supportive relationship with coaching staff.

Joe echoed the changes in coaching support experienced at the collegiate level and highlighted how it can be a challenging adjustment for many players.

> That was the difference between this level and other levels where he doesn't care about the development of you as a player, or the development of you as a person, where other coaches did. Their job was to get you to college so they can put that on their résumé. . . . They want you to get better and to keep developing as a person, as a player. Where in college, he's like we need to win games, this is how we are gonna do it. I don't care about any of you. I sound super blunt and horrible but it's true. It's a dark world sometimes.

Joe saw himself as an underdog for numerous years and had faith in overcoming any challenge through hard work and dedication. However, he experienced a significant negative emotional impact when confronted with some of the harsh realities of elite hockey.

> I had almost a 4.0 in finance in school. I did tons of community service. I had a lot of great friends, a wonderful girlfriend, and there were days where I just broke as a human being. I thought I should be in prison for the way I got treated. I couldn't compartmentalize that I was still a good person even though one person, regarding a sport [referring to his head coach], was mad at me for something. I lost my identity as a person. I was one person. If the hockey player wasn't in good standing with himself, or with other people, my whole day was ruined.

He continued, expressing that these experiences of being so profoundly impacted by interactions with his coach had the capacity to change the trajectory of an entire day or even week for him and the emotional impact on his engagement and functioning was significant. "I wouldn't stop thinking about it the entire length of classes and social events. We were at parties where we would be celebrating a win where my coach would bench me or didn't play me. Everyone was having a blast, and I was in the corner thinking, 'What am I doing here? I am miserable.' I couldn't compartmentalize those two things." Similar to some other athletes in the current study, Joe depicted the far-reaching influence of sport and performance on all aspects of life, making it difficult to compartmentalize. He expressed that the emotional toll of poor performance outweighed any other negative events he had ever experienced in his life.

> I think the world comes crashing down on you as an athlete when things are not going well, and you can't push it to the side and be happy as the other person in you. It's just who you are and it weighs on you heavier than anything in the real world has ever been able to weigh on me. . . . I think it exhausted me and I think for a while that's probably why I was motivated to throw myself out there and risk anything. Any opportunity I had, I didn't have it anymore. It's just that period of time was very intense for me.

Joe adeptly articulated the emotional toll of identity foreclosure for an athlete. Likewise, he emphasized the detrimental impact of external feedback on one's sense of self when their entire identity is closely tied to their athletic performance. As a result, some participants experienced intense emotions that caused a shift in how they engaged with sport.

In addition to fatigue and burnout, numerous participants described internalized cognitive reflections that grew increasingly self-critical both while competing and in retirement. They attributed this to the competitive culture of elite performance and the atmosphere of constant comparison to other players. Steve explained how the development of this self-critical lens exacerbated distress when he did not perform well. "I remember every interception I ever threw. Every single one of them and I remember why I did it, the circumstances around it. I couldn't tell you a third of the touchdowns I threw. I couldn't tell you a third of them. But I could tell you every interception, the play, why it happened, how much of it was my bad, how much of it was that and the impact that it had on the game." Like Steve, Kurt described the heaviness of every play and game on his mental health, highlighting how his internal dialogue became increasingly critical and self-defeating. "When I didn't do well, it was like 'oh shoot, I suck.'" This internal dialogue was not solely centered on his performance, but instead generalized to criticisms about him as a person. As a consequence of such negative self-talk, these participants experienced decreases in self-esteem and confidence, both in their career and in retirement.

For participants such as Marshall, the mental toll that sports took made it easier for him to embrace the transition into retirement. "I had already mentally been through such a wash. The hard stuff to me was already over. . . . It wasn't obviously the same joy that you get out of it as a kid at certain points, it's just not. It's really demanding, it's a physical toll, a mental toll, an emotional toll, that you can never really be prepared for." The unexpected shift in expectations and the emotional pressure of elite performance was something participants had not anticipated. Unfortunately, it left many of them devoid of the joy and love for sport that had been a significant part of their lives until then.

Jess recognized that the physical and mental challenges that are part of elite performance, while tolerable for a period of time, "weren't going to be sustainable forever." At some point all of the athletes had to let go of careers that had been built upon intrinsic motivation, talent, and early passion. Issa also acknowledged that, at some point in her career, she had lost the passion and excitement for sport that she had growing up. "The passion is just not there. I was thinking of how I'm missing that in a way, the way I was obsessed when I was young just isn't there." For these participants, the grief process was intertwined with the need to adjust to a life that was unfamiliar. This presented many competing demands and changes as they navigate a path forward.

Even for participants who recognized the importance of multiple identities throughout their elite careers, they shared ongoing tensions that had to be negotiated to keep all of these identities salient. "Sometimes it can be kind of hard to balance and really make sure other identities don't get, you know, overshadowed. . . . It's kind of like an internal battle within yourself" (Kendrick). However, he also acknowledged that he wouldn't have felt complete if he had allowed his athletic identity to overshadow all other aspects of his life. "I didn't want to be just a typical, you know, jock person. I think if I had done that, I would not have been able to balance the tensions." He worked hard to ensure that others in his life did not, "strictly label me as an athlete" and recognized the benefits of having other outlets to help manage the demands of competition.

THE TRANSITION

For many of the participants in this study, their careers required spending over a decade in an environment that they understood and thrived in, in many ways sheltered from having to function in the world outside of sport. Their routines, habits, and commitments were geared toward supporting excellence and performance. When it all came to an end, many found themselves ill-prepared to navigate an unfamiliar and, for some, frightening world. The transition into retirement for elite athletes is a unique and personal journey that, for some, occurs in a planned and thoughtful manner. However, others find themselves abruptly unable to continue while simultaneously managing injury, disappointment, and uncertainty in the path forward. In this study, there was a noticeable contrast between those who had foreseen their careers coming to an end and had time to prepare, versus those who were caught off guard or didn't get to leave on their own terms.

Tess highlighted this distinction when she said it is the difference between "having priorities realign instead of being forced to realign them." This participant underscored the difference between a path that one travels voluntarily versus a path that one arrives at out of necessity. However, regardless of the events surrounding retirement, all participants in the study identified the transition as challenging, recognizing numerous changes and adaptations that were difficult to navigate.

As her senior year wound down, Jess recognized the multitude of changes that lay ahead, describing this experience as overwhelming at times. "I don't know it seemed like so much up in the air, so many unknowns, which was pretty scary because there's already a lot of unknowns being a senior. . . . I didn't know what I wanted to do." Ultimately, Jess recognized that the amount of time that had to be "tied to volleyball" had left her without "a whole lot of time where it's just been me thinking about what I want to do."

For some participants, including Kendrick and Beth, the culmination of their careers was symbolized by a final game, match, or play. However, the realization that their days in sports were numbered and that things were coming to an end was more of a gradual process rather than a sudden revelation like flipping a light switch. Kendrick recognized that as a senior graduating from college, what made retirement real was a series of events that led him to the realization that there would be no more games and no more locker room talks. "No doubt it was tough. I know right when the clock ended on my last game, tears just started coming down real fast. I was like this could be it. And you know, you walk to the sideline, and I see all of my guys in my grade, and we go to the locker room and everybody's just in tears. I'm like, 'Whoa, this is a lot.'"

Although the experience was emotional, he doesn't identify it as the moment it "hit him." He revealed that it wasn't until the final meeting of the season when the seniors were asked to give a send-off to the younger players that he truly began to grasp the reality of this transition. "I think it didn't hit me until we had that meeting. And, you know, our coach asked all the seniors to come up and speak just because it was our last time with the team together." Despite acknowledging the ending, he struggled to fully internalize this reality, as evidenced by the internal tensions he experienced. "My mind and body was still like, 'Hey, we gotta get ready for another season.'" The cyclical nature of performance and training in elite athletic competition left many athletes feeling like they were always waiting for the next season, which may have delayed their full appreciation for what retirement meant.

For Beth, the realization that sport was moving on without her did not truly occur until another season began and her teammates returned to the field. "I don't think it actually really hit me until they started playing games. And I obviously followed still on my social media, so I saw the outcomes of the games and so it kind of hit me that I wasn't part of it." This predictability and the routine nature of off seasons contributed to participants such as Beth and Erica feeling a delayed reaction to the concrete nature of retirement. "I don't think it really hit me until like the following September when I would have been starting up again." This may have acted as a buffer between the disheartening experiences of ending a career due to injury (Beth) and being cut from the roster (Erica) and the numerous changes that graduation and retirement would bring for participants at the end of their collegiate careers.

The conclusion of an elite athletic career necessitates changes in nearly every aspect of an athlete's life. Jermaine expressed how jarring this experience was for him, as he had spent a considerable amount of time insulated from larger societal pressures and expectations. "It's scary, you do feel really small. You do feel like the world is just this big overwhelming space and you don't know where to go. So there were definitely some tough times to tackle and that transition was not easy for me." For this participant and many others who had their routine and structure provided for them for so long, with all decisions being directed at their role as an athlete, adjusting to new roles brought about feelings of unfamiliarity, confusion, and apprehension.

Steve described the transition out of elite sport and into another chapter of life as feeling like a "complete fish out of water." In a similar vein, Tess also recognized how foreign a life without sport felt to her as she navigated the transition into retirement. "It was pretty dark. I remember being like, 'So I'm just a student now?' Then the sense of, 'Well, what am I going to do after this? Am I going to be able to run again at some point?' It got really bad, so it was a very dark time, but there's so much uncertainty about what this is going to look like. Am I going from this very active person to just sitting at a desk now and reading and like using my brain?"

The process of transitioning out of elite performance necessitated a reenvisioning of a future that does not include performance in the same way, and for many, this brought about a recognition of how significant of a role it had played in their lives. Chris described the period of transition into retirement as challenging and having to face a life that did not feel like it fit. "It's definitely not an easy transition for anybody. For me, if I was a guy who seamlessly made the transition, I'd be a guy who would say, 'Oh, it'd be fine.' But it sucked. There's some stuff I don't miss, but, you know, when you're so invested in something and then you don't have that, it's different." Similar transition difficulties were described by Henry as a starting over, letting go of an entire life and career built around being an elite athlete, and now having the daunting task of redirecting that same effort and energy into whatever the next phase of life would be. "I'm learning from the ground up, where you have to build it all the way back up and . . . I have to start at zero again and figure it out."

For many, this was the first time they had to figure things out completely on their own. They no longer had a coach to call the plays for them, to tell them how to train, what to do, and when to do it. Erica provided insight into the novelty of this unstructured experience of reality. "All of a sudden you're just on your own. You gotta figure it out, you gotta join a gym, you gotta start this whole life and . . . you have to make money to live. The whole transitional process is definitely tough." While some were eventually able to embrace this need for self-direction, for most, it took a considerable period of time to adjust to the transition. For participants like Jermaine, Arianna, and Erica, who had excelled within the structured culture of sport, this transition proved especially arduous. "I'm good within structure. I'm good when people are telling me what to do" (Jermaine); "I liked the structure, I thrived off of that" (Arianna). Erica shared that being "so used to the structure and having you do this, this, and this, whether it be time management or staying in good shape" greatly contributed to the difficulties she faced during the transition into retirement.

The substantial amount of time and energy that athletes had devoted to sports and performance left a significant void that many had not anticipated.

Tess explained that it's challenging to fully grasp the time and energy commitment put into athletic performance until the demand is no longer there. "All of a sudden, you're going to end up with 15–20 hours extra a week, so figuring out how to start allocating that time, whether it's a volunteer pursuit or some other pursuit. Just because I don't think people realize the time commitment then it goes away all of a sudden. It's like you don't have this automatic structure and you kind of flounder for a bit until you figure out other things to take in."

Jermaine echoed similar feelings when reflecting on his transition from sport into retirement, realizing the substantial amount of time and energy that needed to be redirected into a new purpose to fill the feelings of loss. As a result, these feelings of uncertainty about oneself and the future intensified the transition process. "Being an athlete in college is basically a full-time job. So when you lose that, you try to harness all of that time and energy into something else . . . certain people struggle with that. If you played sports your whole life, when it's gone, it's like, where does the rest of my time, identity, and energy go?"

Henry shared these sentiments and goes even further by acknowledging the profound emotions experienced when confronted with the disappearance of all structure, routine, and purpose. "There's a ton of emptiness in that feeling just because so much of each day was devoted to that, and what do you fill your time with? I was lucky in the sense that I was able to fill it with positives instead of negatives and I know guys that went in the opposite direction right? Use things or take things that are negative and take them into a harmful direction." For Henry, while he recognized that he attempted to channel his energy into positive outlets, he observed that many of his colleagues had not found similar coping strategies. Unfortunately, their choices only intensified the challenges of retirement. He shared that he could empathize with how difficult the period immediately following the disconnection from elite sport can be. "It was just tough the first initial summer where you are not skating and training every day. That part was . . . You're trying to fill it with something else. . . . That first summer was just tough knowing it was going to be different."

Despite quite a successful career transition from the NFL, Marshall understood that the adaptation process was appropriate considering the significant dedication they have given to their sport throughout their career. "Obviously once you come to the end of your professional career, it's tough and it takes a while to adapt because it's something I've been doing since I was seven."

Several of the participants discovered that they had large amounts of unexpected free time. "I kind of had all of this free time that I wasn't used to having anymore" (Jess). For participants like Issa, the surplus of free time during retirement resulted in rumination on the circumstances that brought their careers to an end. This unhealthy pattern of constantly dwelling on past events proved difficult to break, as she lacked the coping strategies needed to navigate through this challenging period. "I was ruminating on it the whole year, from that moment until graduation that was on my mind every time I walked around campus. . . . I didn't know how to cope with it so I think that was part of the challenge . . . and feeling kind of helpless in that way."

Even in retirement, the comparison to others did not cease for Anna. She continued to compare her adaptation and emotional responses to those of her peers. This introspection led her to recognize that she might have been experiencing a greater amount of internal tension in the face of retirement compared to others. "It's been extremely tough for me . . . when it all came to an end, having that realization. . . . I remember a lot of my teammates at the time at (college) were like 'Oh, I'm so excited. I'm ready to move onto the next chapter in my life.' I was in an absolute tailspin because I was like, 'What am I going to do?' I was wondering how I was going to fill my time."

As Arianna started to discern what her connection to sport would be in retirement, she experienced a shifting range of emotions while contemplating the life that lay ahead and attempting to comprehend its implications for her continued connection to sport. "A sad moment where you know, they welcome you to the alumni and you're like okay, I'm one of these old washed-up ladies now, here we go [laughs]. I get to go for beer league and move on with my life . . . a constant combination of emotion." Much like many participants in this study, Arianna perceived the traditional retirement path to be lackluster in comparison to her previous experiences with elite competition.

Deonte echoed this sentiment and described the transition period as a time when passion and purpose seemed to have dissipated, leaving behind a persistent question of how to rediscover those elements in whatever the next endeavor may be. "I was trying to figure out what was next. There was definitely something missing from my life because once you go from doing something every day for five years straight, you know what I mean, and then it's over it's kind of like uhhh [laughs]. So, I was really trying to find that . . . passion. I didn't want to be stuck in a job where I was working but I didn't enjoy it or love it like how I did football. Because football was my job for five years." For participants who have been deeply connected to a career that elicited intense emotions, including the highs and lows of performance, the absence of that career makes it incredibly challenging for them to sit with themselves and confront the void it leaves behind. However, for some participants, the newfound freedom was liberating, granting them "more time to do what you want to do" (Juan). Yet this freedom was only advantageous when the athlete had a clear vision of how they wanted to fill that time. Even in those circumstances, the contrast between an athletic lifestyle and a retirement one could still be stark and challenging to navigate.

Steve expressed the complete contrast between the world he was leaving behind and the one he was entering during his retirement. "I had a new family, I had two young boys. I went from being in the NFL and going 100 miles an hour every day to woah. That was the only thing I ever dreamed of doing and now it's over." Although he experienced an initial sense of shock while adapting to being a "100% stay at home dad," Steve also acknowledged that his success and family dynamic provided him with opportunities that other players might not have had. "I had my life in order and you hit these points where you get depressed. I can't imagine not having that financial backing and that family to go through that." Despite recognizing his privilege, he understood that it did not shield him from the challenges of transitioning into retirement. He reflected on how much more challenging it might have been for those without the same level of support and stability that he had.

Amid the changes in their lifestyles, as explored in earlier chapters, some participants confronted the tangible challenge of redefining their relationship with food and exercise regimens in retirement. These aspects of being an athlete had become so deeply ingrained in their identities that many of them felt uncertain about how to approach this aspect of their lives as they transitioned away from competitive performance. The regular schedule of training and practice, which was inherent in their athletic career, automatically prioritized their athletic pursuits and overall health. In retirement, participants were faced with the responsibility of making these decisions for themselves. With the absence of training and exercise as mandatory daily demands, participants no longer had external pressure to allocate time for these activities. This change left some struggling to integrate physical activity into their lives, consequently increasing the risks to their psychosocial functioning.

For Deonte, maintaining a healthy and consistent workout regimen was challenging during the initial years after retiring from football. This difficulty stemmed from transitioning to a new career that demanded his time and the absence of external pressure that once existed to be in the gym regularly. "In football we were working out every day, seven days a week. I remember when I first graduated, it was tough getting in the time to work out, because you have your responsibilities, your job, so it's easy to forget about the gym. I didn't quite get into a big groove until this past year, so it's been two and a half years. Now, I work out like 6–7 days a week. When I first graduated, the first year, it was probably twice a week." As a result of this disconnect, Deonte experienced psychosocial stressors, symptoms of depression, and changes in body composition. However, this situation ultimately motivated him to rekindle his love for being physically active and seek a healthier lifestyle.

> I gained a lot of weight, a lot of bad weight. I knew that I had to start working out more. There were a lot of things that happened throughout my transition from fifth year to my first job. . . . I had nowhere to live for a brief period of time. So, I was living on my aunt's couch for a month and a half, two months, when I started my first software job. My commute was insane, like an hour and a half back and forth for like two months. It was definitely a difficult first couple of months. It made it difficult to actually exercise and stuff like that. . . . I was definitely depressed for a bit. I knew it was just the struggle of life and just a part of the journey. I knew I would eventually figure out a good schedule that would work for me, and that whatever would happen with my job, I would make it work. I love being active and healthy and just knowing that I feel good.

Even with the presence of stressors that created both tangible and perceived barriers to exercise and overall well-being, he managed to rediscover the sense of relief that exercise and movement brought. Over time, he successfully created his own balance amid various competing priorities, allowing him to prioritize his physical activity and well-being in a way that worked for him.

While many of the athletes had extensive experience with juggling competing priorities of academics and sports in college, there was ongoing external pressure from coaches to ensure that prioritization occurred. In retirement, the understanding of the positive outlet that physical activity can provide must be rediscovered. The relationship with exercise must be rebuilt from a place of pleasure and well-being, disentangling it from its previous purpose of solely improving sports performance.

Retiring from elite competition can be a complex and emotionally charged experience for athletes as they attempt to redefine the purpose of activities in their lives and cope with the loss of the structured identity that their sport provided. Kendrick advised against resisting the transition from an athletic career to retirement. He emphasized that doing so can hinder the ability to move forward due to the considerable emotional and psychological challenges involved. "I think a lot of people have a tough time acknowledging what's coming next. They try to fight it. They're like it's not over. . . . When you acknowledge what's coming next, I think you'll be able to open up a little bit more room inside of you to start taking those necessary steps to move into the next area." Kendrick recalled that his ability to accept what was happening allowed him to concentrate on pragmatic, subsequent actions. "I know for me, acknowledging it was over . . . and I remember it like it was yesterday coming after that first weekend after the season was over and like 'Okay, I need to go up to that administration office and get my résumé in order because this is the first step that I need to take to make sure that I can be ready to start applying for jobs.'" While previous research suggests that transitioning away from athletic identity leads to improved adaptation

(Lavallee et al., 1997), Kendrick believed that this approach may be a key factor to avoiding a complete disengagement from one's athletic identity. "Reflecting and accepting . . . who says that your athletic identity has to be killed out, like can never be there anymore." Kendrick, adept at managing the tensions of multiple identities, had developed the ability to retain and balance more than one identity while readjusting priorities when required. "It's just being able to have other stuff kind of raised up a bit more and ready for other identities to emerge."

This was something that Dannie initially struggled with in her transition into retirement. Including repeated injuries and struggles with depression, she initially grappled with the loss of her athletic identity. However, over time and through introspective growth, she has started to undergo a change in perspective. She articulated a shifting from a sense of losing her identity to recognizing that "the identity has stayed pretty solid with me. It has just taken me looking at it differently." Her experiences underscored the fact that transitioning from a successful athletic career to retirement entails self-discovery and adaptation, which is complicated by the distinctive psychosocial stressors experienced by athletes and the profound sense of loss they encounter.

LAYERS AND EXPERIENCES OF GRIEF

The majority of the participants in the study described feelings of grief due to the significant loss of elite performance in their lives. However, the manifestation of this grief varied, with several factors influencing how athletes coped with the emotional process and adjusted to life after sports. For some, this included a profound loss of identity, loss of role and status, as well as the disruption to routine and structure and the loss of career aspirations. The process often involved anguish as they attempted to find a path forward in their post-athletic life. Some participants experienced grief that manifested as episodes of depression (Dannie, Tim, Joe, Arianna, Deonte), characterized by various symptoms that added complexity to the retirement process.

Hayden succinctly articulated the difficulties that he perceived as both he and other professional baseball players approached the end of their careers. "It is . . . something that a lot of athletes struggle with. It is almost like PTSD, to get thrown out of one arena to another and expect everything to be fine." Hayden emphasized the lack of attention given to the significant transition that retirement represents and the disregard for the grief experienced by retiring athletes, who are often expected to seamlessly move into the next phase of their lives.

Some participants no longer had the external identity of being an athlete to define themselves and shield them from the emotional challenges of everyday life. Participants like Chris found retirement to be an emotionally intense experience, accentuating the significant contribution of their athletic identity to their sense of self. "Since I've been done playing, your ego, your identity, your confidence, constantly gets kicked in the balls for a long time. That's the reality of it. Because when you play professional sports, the fence that's around you is amazing." He conveyed that while people often transition between jobs and careers, there is little that compares to the profound difference between being actively engaged in professional competition and having to transition to the other side. He described it as "a divide so intense that I can't even put it into words."

Although many athletes acknowledged the existence of life after sports, only a few had prepared for what this next phase would entail, and only a few of the participants had anticipated the emotions they would encounter when confronted with retirement. A prevailing theme was the athletes' sense of unpreparedness for the retirement transition and the multitude of unforeseen nuances they had to confront. In some cases, the participants' lack of preparedness led them to hastily seize the first opportunity that came their way (Arianna, Erica) or experiment with various possibilities, seemingly struggling to find their footing for an extended period (Tim, Esteban, Chris). While a few of the participants had a clear plan for their next steps, others felt entirely uncertain about what to do next, what transferable skills they possessed, and how to embark on the process of self-discovery.

Dannie shared that she did not feel that she had the tools necessary to manage the end of her career. "You are not given the resources or even guided. We never had conversations of what it would be like to graduate or leave soccer. We never had resources to deal with that transition. It was like your season is over and you are bummed . . . the transition, the mental health part, and just the mentality of soccer and being a collegiate athlete, I feel like we got a disservice. I got a disservice a lot of the time." For Dannie, not only did it make the transition into retirement more challenging, but it damaged her connection to her alma mater. "I would be so much more inclined to go back to my school and to participate in alumni games if I felt I had left on a good note. . . . I had no interest in wanting to stay connected. It was just like your four years of collegiate soccer is over, good luck." Feeling unsupported during this transition soured her relationship with the place where she had performed, formed relationships, and once felt connected. It resulted in a disconnection from her alma mater, which held significant memories and experiences.

Marshall highlighted the significant contrast in retirement experiences when the transition is unexpected or not on the athlete's terms. "I see guys who struggle with that a little more because when you're cut short, you're not really understanding. It's abrupt, it's quick. It's a lot easier if you're going out on your own terms. If you're not, it's a whole different perspective, a whole different angle." When athletes are unprepared to relinquish their athletic identity, particularly when their career ends in ways that do not meet their expectations, they may find it more comfortable to hold on to roles in retirement that enable them to maintain a connection to the sports culture.

Erica expressed these sentiments in reflecting on her early career navigation: "My first job out of college, I worked in hockey because, you know, that's everything I knew. . . . I worked in hockey for a year . . . so it was kind of a moment of like, let's get on with your life." Although this participant eventually returned to coaching part-time, she first had to establish a career she was passionate about before she could genuinely assess the role hockey would play in her life over the long term.

Arianna revealed that her decision to follow the expected path into coaching left her questioning whether it was genuinely what she wanted or merely a choice she made to hold on to her athletic identity. "I'm a university hockey coach . . . in a lot of reflection about that sometimes I do wonder if I took that path because I wasn't quite ready to let go of the athletic identity so I just took the only role that's readily available to me right now." While this choice enabled her to retain her identity as an athlete, she now recognizes that it also contributed to her struggle in allowing that aspect of her identity to evolve and change. "There's a way in which being a coach creates a kind of immortality as an athlete, right?"

The experiences of being unprepared were further amplified by the lack of recognition and understanding from others about what they were going through. Many participants reported feeling disenfranchised both by the people around them and by their own internalized perceptions of what is expected and appropriate during retirement. Tim shared that the pain that he experienced was immense and not something that he wanted others to bear witness to. "I internalized and didn't want to show people my pain. I didn't want to show people for fear that it would be 'just get over it, man. Move on. Just let it go.' and yea maybe there was some truth to that, but I was not ready to face it." For this participant, the pressure and expectation to immediately pursue a career, coupled with his inability to find something enjoyable and fulfilling, resulted in symptoms of depression and hopelessness. He internalized messages about what a successful retirement and transition should entail. When his own experience was filled with disappointments and perceived failures, he found it challenging to separate appropriate grief responses from his emotional turmoil.

Joe also faced disenfranchisement during his traumatic retirement, as people who admired his elite career seemed to shame him for the pain and heartbreak he went through. "Yeah, it's tough, right? Because people would look at me and say you are the 1% or the .01%. You got approved to go to the USHL, you have tons of college offers, you got to live the life. You got a full ride to college; you got this whole amazing life from sports. People would look at me and be like, 'You're so lucky, you got so much more than so many other people would get. Why aren't you grateful?'" These messages only served to devalue his grief experience. "I had earned all that and got shit on."

Like Tim and Joe, Issa struggled with the expectations to swiftly move on, disregarding the emotional turmoil surrounding her retirement. She felt that the time she needed for reflection on her career and to find balance between the traumatic ending and the overall success was not available to her, given the circumstances of her pending graduation and perceived expectations from others. "I felt that there was this expectation of what was next instead of just like yeah that was a really good career, good things happened. It was just like okay; I have to move on and think about something else." Issa, like several of the other participants (Jermaine, Hayden, Erica, Chris), did not feel connected or passionate about the next chapter of her life including a career, hobbies, and relationships. This lack of connection also extended to how sports and training would fit into her life, a topic previously explored in earlier chapters. Instead, she experienced pressure to move on from her grief, with others in her life failing to acknowledge the depth of her emotions. With her retirement already pending before her career-ending injury, and graduation also on the horizon, her anguish regarding the circumstances that ended her career was overshadowed, disconnecting her from everything that once felt familiar. "It was kind just like, not necessarily in the past and no one cared about it, but it was kind of like, okay now the thing you are dealing with is the concussion symptoms."

This participant's decision not to be open with anyone about what she was truly experiencing resulted in a lack of support that, in hindsight, she realized might have been helpful in coping with the heartbreak. "Not feeling well and having to put on a facade of being well for my teammates . . . I felt as if I couldn't be as vulnerable about what I was actually feeling with anyone. That's why I kind of retreated into my own shell because I knew I could be real with myself, and I didn't want to be real with them. The pain I was feeling in my head and my back . . . the heartbreak I was feeling . . . it would have been better to talk to them about it, but it was easier for me not to." Feeling isolated in this experience and burdened by the weight of her emotions, she withdrew from her teammates and eventually distanced herself from hockey entirely, retreating into solitude. She expressed grappling with significant internal conflict as she tried to navigate the reality of graduating from college alongside the overwhelming feelings of emptiness and grief. "Because you're graduating, so you're like all right all right gotta get your career, that's the next step of your life, but I don't feel that passion about it. So what is my next passion? I didn't know where it was. It was just so hard to figure that out, what that was for me. When I couldn't figure it out, it made it 10 times harder. I didn't know where to go. I felt helpless. I don't know what to do now." Despite recognizing the significance of social support throughout her athletic career, she came to realize that, in order to work through her grief, she needed to create some distance from the pressure and well-intentioned feedback from others. Similar to Tim, this participant also found it difficult to let others witness her pain, especially as she struggled to process it and experienced symptoms that didn't resolve as quickly as she would like.

The circumstances surrounding retirement had a lasting impact on many of the participants in the current study. Joe characterized his retirement not only as a challenging experience at the time, but one that continues to haunt him to this day. "When I tell you this is the worst thing I had to go through in life, what happened to me, it's the truth, and I have nightmares about it and I wake up and I'm so happy I'm in my regular life." For Joe, the source of distress extended beyond just the ending of his career; the unanswered questions have made it extremely difficult to process the whole experience.

> I still really don't know to this day. If you put me on a lie detector test and said how good, you really were and did you deserve it? I would tell you I'm one of the best players on the team. So, when I go to bed at night now, I'm doing really well. I love my job, life's really good. I don't think about it during the day much but I find that my subconscious won't let it go and most mornings I wake up with his coach in my head and like I haven't talked to him in years. I just can't get away from it. It hasn't left me yet because it's almost like it's unsolved. . . . It's still there, my subconscious has not left. It's been 2 years and I can't get it go away. . . . I can't live and be fully happy full time. I'm pretty happy, but my subconscious won't let it go.

Joe continued, revealing that he has yet to encounter a conflict or challenge in his life that compares to the anguish and confusion he experienced when facing deselection. The process of being forced to walk away from hockey and making the heart-wrenching decision to prioritize expediting his education during the remainder of his time in college, all to escape the painful reminders as soon as possible, was an incredibly difficult experience for him. He shared:

> Finance was a hard major there, one of the hardest ones and I tell people that it was so easy compared to everything else that was going on in my life, like it was nothing. I just had to go to college to be a regular student. . . . I'm still on the roster, he was like look, you're done, I'm not playing you. If you don't want to transfer that's on you.

This marked the start of his withdrawal from hockey and all its aspects, redirecting his energy toward graduation to create space for the healing process to begin. "I'm not wasting my time every single day, for 3 hours at the rink and working insanely hard at the gym doing all of this for you to not even look at me." He shared that his inner determination helped him to arrive at the decision: "Let's just get out of here and start your life." For Joe, this experience was the most disillusioning of his career, one that significantly impacted his relationship with hockey and his athletic identity for the foreseeable future.

In the study, many athletes found that maintaining a connection to sports eased their transition process. However, for some participants, although they still enjoyed a strong foundation in training and exercise, they needed to detach themselves from their sport to avoid reminders of the pain they experienced during retirement. Joe shared his continued love for training and fitness: "I still work out all the time." However, like others, his training fundamentally shifted in that it did not include his sport. "The one thing I haven't really done is skate. So I'll do all different types of physical activity, and people invite me to play hockey all the time and I don't do it." For this participant, even though he acknowledged the significance of training during retirement, he wasn't prepared to confront reminders or triggers related to the end of his career. The lack of closure in his retirement has had a significant psychosocial impact, not only on himself but also on his family.

Much like Joe, Tim experienced a challenging ending to his career and felt profoundly lost in retirement. He devoted a significant amount of time to seeking ways to revive his career, which hindered his ability to process the loss he had experienced. "I refused to believe it was happening." Over time, he has faced significant difficulty in looking beyond his struggles and acknowledging the successes he achieved in his football career. Although he has managed to take his jerseys out of a drawer, symbols of his career, and hang them on the wall, he still feels distant from the pride he would like to experience.

> I look at the jerseys framed in here and the medals and I look at it as a cost. . . . I wish I could look at that and go, a career well done, and effort well done. . . . It just meant that something was taken away from me and I am unable to get it back. I cannot go back and get that even though that's where I would like to be. That's right, that's who I want to be. . . . That's what gives me fulfillment and the joy in my life and it's been taken away from me. I spent a lot of years trying to figure out how to get it back.

While Tim believed that he made progress in grieving this loss and finding a path forward, the sorrow continued to be an ongoing and intense part of his retirement. "That window, that door closed and so for a lot of years for me, that was something that was taken from me and was just that it was something that I didn't get closure on."

Similar to Tim, Issa grappled with feelings of loss and a sense of having something taken from her. She described the career-ending concussion and the process of coming to terms with an ending that she did not choose, along with the trauma associated with it.

> The doctor looked at me and said you're done and so that was the moment where it's like yeah, holy shit, fuck, yeah, I'm done. That was really hard to hear and also a little lack of empathy on her part the way she said it. So that moment was pretty defeating and that was like the start of like okay then what's next? I don't have hockey, yes still have this team but it feels different and weird because I can't play with them. I have never missed a game or practice. So, to be forced to miss a game because of a stupid situation was really hard for me. So, those words, "You are done," was a really hard pill to swallow.

These words are still etched in this participant's memory today. For Issa, losing her identity so close to the end of her career was a devastating blow that left her emotionally and physically unwell. "It was hard because I knew I couldn't play because I was unhealthy, my brain was not in a good place and the subsequent whacking and whiplash on the ice made it hurt so much more and I knew it was gonna end. I knew my competitive hockey career was going to be over in a matter of weeks after my senior game, but for it to be taken away from me before I was done was so hard, and it made me have a weird connection with hockey which I never thought I'd have."

Similar to Issa, Henry also experienced a concussion that abruptly ended his professional career. He shared that he too faced difficulties in finding a path forward under such challenging circumstances. "I was just always feeling like this just sucks. There was a lot of 'woe is me' attitude when there's a million other stories that are the exact same. Just overcoming that and just knowing that it was the end, there was a lot of self-awareness that needed to happen." Yet building self-awareness for these participants was a gradual process, one that forced them to confront the impact of a traumatic ending to their careers on both their mental and physical health. Issa shared that she had to come to terms with the fact that this one traumatic experience was weighing heavily on her life, preventing her from fully reflecting on the fun and successful career she had. "This experience left a way harder feeling in my gut, that one experience outweighed 18 years of work." She recognized that the traumatic closure of her career had significantly impacted the entire narrative of her identity as an elite athlete. "That's part of the challenge, when I think of hockey, I think of that because it was the last bad experience I had . . . compared to . . . you got a great career and you loved playing hockey. . . . The first thing I think of is the injury and the way that it ended. . . . I think that trauma of the way it ended clouds some of the really awesome positive memories that I have with hockey. The way it ended wasn't positive." Connected deeply to chapter 2, which explored the recurring theme of "Who am I now that sport is gone?", several participants experienced a crushing sense of identity loss, intense emotional pain, a feeling of emptiness, and longing for their past athletic career. This manifested in all aspects of their lives, including their relationship with nutrition and exercise and how they perceived these constructs in a retirement lifestyle. For those participants who found it hard to accept that retirement, this disconnect exacerbated mental health symptoms.

BODY GRIEF: MY BODY FAILED ME

Many of the participants experienced a sense of loss during retirement as they no longer had the ability to use their bodies for engaging in elite performance and competitive activities with others. It became a comparative reflection of what my body could do in the past versus what it can do now. This often included periods of body grief as they confronted changing bodies that no longer fit into their internalized athletic ideals. The experience was not only marked by dissatisfaction with their changing body compositions, but also by the physical limitations they encountered in their performance.

Arianna expressed that one of the most challenging aspects of leaving sports was coming to terms with the reality that her body was no longer capable of elite performance. "I was seen as being elite in a certain sphere. I was better than the large majority of my peers in one very small area of life. I was very disciplined. I would say that the component of physical fitness for me where I felt like I was at my elite or optimal fitness." During retirement, Arianna had to come to terms with reconciling what her body had achieved in the past versus what it was capable of now. This emotional struggle complicated the transition process, as she clung to a performance level that very few will ever achieve. No doubt, this rigid clinging to what one's body was once capable of made it immensely challenging to let go. "That's an area I feel like I'm never able to attain again. It was hard for a long time to know that I was never going to be what I was, in terms of what my body could be performance-wise. So, I had to adjust once I realized I wasn't going to be elite anymore. It was the first time I needed to figure out what to do and pay for fitness classes and make my own schedule. That was when I realized I am on the fitness for life track. I'm not on the fitness for elite athlete track anymore." In retirement, the redefinition of what training looks like diverged from the familiar, training to perform, prompting many athletes to explore new training and fitness options. For Arianna, this process involved trial and error as she navigated unfamiliar training methods, which were at times complicated by struggles to accept the limitations of her postretirement bodies and manage her self-expectations.

Dannie described how she found difficulty assessing her own training limitations even after retirement. Unfortunately, her inability to temper her expectations of elite performance led to repeated damage to her body.

> It was just I didn't understand that I had this expectation of myself that I had to still be that soccer player who I was when I was twenty/twenty-one. And the expectation, the expectation was for four years that I was going to get back to that collegiate level of soccer. Never mind that I was 23 and had had three major knee operations. I gave myself no wiggle room, I was never kind to myself in that way. It was habitual, that was who I was. I didn't understand and it really did take me having the fourth surgery to be like okay this is the fourth one in five years, this is not okay.

For this participant, the injuries became a means to recover and return to elite performance, as she refused to let go of her identity as an elite athlete. This mindset led her to ignore the impact on her body. This cycle created a perpetual period of purgatory, where she felt lost in a cycle of injury and the push for recovery, unable to find a clear path forward. "I didn't realize that I didn't exist for 3–4 years. That is why I kept retearing my ACL." She shared the need to redefine health and wellness in retirement. The only healthy path forward became acknowledging the ongoing damage she was causing to her body due to the habits she had developed around performance and the messages she had internalized about what her body should be capable of doing. "I needed to change how I view being active, how I view being healthy—I had this kind of come-to-Jesus moment where I was like it is wellness. I need to be wellness and not high-level soccer and tearing my ACL. . . . It was hard to realize my body couldn't do the things that I wanted it to do or I was used to it doing. That was a hard realization. . . . It has taken two years of active practice and active awareness, but yeah the process sucked. I was just down on myself physically and mentally." While the movement toward accepting her post-sport body was necessary, it was not an easily attainable process and often accompanied by feelings of grief over what her body had become. She described the challenging process of trying to reformulate her understanding of physical activity and her search to redefine herself as a different type of athlete. "It was the first time I went to a hot yoga class. I'd never really done yoga and I was terrible at it. It was totally new for me and something I definitely wanted to try. I knew I was trying to evolve into a different type of athlete at that point, or at least a different type of fitness. I can even remember where the class was still. It was my moment to be like, 'OK, I'm definitely veering paths in life to change.' I think in one sense it was freeing. I could choose what time I worked out or when I worked out." Although Dannie expressed the desire to redefine physical fitness into a wellness approach post-sport and to establish a new connection with her body, her strong attachment to her identity as an athlete and the desire to stay close to the arena made perceiving and accepting change more complicated for her. The shift in understanding fitness and redefining post-sport athleticism emerged as a recurring theme for many participants. It became a task they had to confront while reconstructing their identities in retirement. Body image and athletic ideals had long been integral to their identity as elite athletes, aspects they had dedicated immense focus and time to achieve peak physical condition and composition. However, when confronted with a shift away from this peak in retirement, athletes often faced psychosocial challenges in response to the loss of their athletic identity.

For Tim, the struggle to come to terms with the end of his career, combined with a lack of awareness about healthy food consumption and activity levels post-sport, exacerbated symptoms of depression. The transformation of his once-familiar body of an elite athlete served as a constant reminder of the inner conflict he was experiencing.

> I was continuing to, for years, this is how I ate, this is how I train to keep my weight on. I just continued to do that. I would continue to eat and train, but now I had other responsibilities, so I had to reduce the amount of time I would train. So I gained a bit of weight, not a ton, I got to maybe 200 pounds and I'm carrying this big frame. This thing that I'm no longer in and it was just a lot of conflicts and confusion, I guess a lot of confusion. I still, in my mind, was eating and kind of thinking about training and working out, but I've got this career, and I need to find opportunities. So there was just a lot of confusion as to who the heck I am right now.

The struggles that Tim experienced in his transition to retirement were influenced by the internalization of the ideal body and training for sports performance. Balancing the financial demands of having a family with his strong desire to return to elite performance proved difficult, and he struggled to accept that this was no longer an attainable goal. The continued connection to athletic identity may have exacerbated struggles in adapting training and eating habits and, ultimately, accepting the altered body composition that often occurs during retirement.

LOSS OF SELF

For the retired athletes interviewed here, the sense of loss extended beyond just physical functionality. It encompassed a genuine struggle with the profound discomfort of charting an unfamiliar path forward where their core identity no longer fit. For some athletes, this experience led to significant angst, to the point where they saw little purpose in continuing life without being able to uphold their previously established sense of athletic identity.

Hayden expressed that the loss of his baseball career and the transition into the unfamiliar world of sales, where he was no longer seen as a professional athlete, resulted in a sense of psychosocial disconnection. He shared, "I feel invisible sometimes," as he had to start from scratch to build a reputation in this new field and navigate new roles and relationship dynamics within his family. Similarly, Anna also shared struggles with the profound divide between being an elite athlete and what came next in her life. She described feeling the loss of her former self deeply. Reflecting on the process of grieving, she said: "It is like losing your comfort, your best friend, everything. There are so many layers, you could even attribute it to your identity, your self-worth, everything."

In the current study, athletes underwent the process of experiencing the loss of various aspects of themselves and questioning what remained, especially for those participants who experienced career-ending injuries. Tess described how she felt this sense of loss in the aftermath of her career-ending knee injury: "I would say I struggled with it. . . . I just remember that time period and I had no idea . . . like, I couldn't run, I couldn't do all these things that used to be a part of me." As they sought to reconcile what their bodies could do and what their connection to their athletic identity would look like, some of the participants felt the need to take a step away from sport and the reminders of their past selves.

For Issa, it wasn't so much that she questioned what her body could do, but that she was afraid of being hurt again. The concussion that ended her career had left her fearful that the one thing that had brought her immense passion and joy—playing hockey—might also cause years of permanent physical and cognitive damage.

Dannie also recognized the necessity of taking time away from her sport to allow her body the chance to fully heal. She knew that if she tried to kick a ball, her internal drive would push her beyond what her body could handle at that moment. "I had to be kind of dramatic and say, 'I'm not touching a soccer ball for two years.'" Suffice to say, this may have not been her only motivation for abstaining so severely from soccer. She also seemed to be working to reconcile the discrepancy between what her body could do while competing versus what it could do in retirement. Her strategy may have subconsciously involved narrowing the gap between her past and present physical abilities. "I had to say that because when I want to touch a soccer ball next, I want to feel strong and able bodied to do whatever I can." While this decision may have originated from a place of psychosocial stress, she shared that it ultimately provided her with the necessary space and time needed for healing. "I did not touch a soccer ball for almost two years. It wasn't awful and I was still doing other things. It allowed me to explore other ways of being active."

For some participants, there was a profound sense of loss related to the physical toll that sports performance had on their bodies, a feeling that was unparalleled outside of elite competition. Henry shared that he misses the physical sensation of having worked hard in training or a game, the feeling that signifies giving everything he had and expending all of his energy on a task. "I miss feeling sore. I haven't felt that type of sore in five years where you're just physically tired, of being done, but it's the price that you pay." Hayden echoed missing the intensity of training to perform. "I loved the workouts, I loved training until absolute exhaustion, I loved hitting a million baseballs, you've got blisters that are killing you. . . . I don't know, man, I just absolutely loved it." Like Henry and Hayden, Kurt shared that he missed "the physical aspect of competing physically." Yet he recognized that it was also taking a toll "but especially toward the end there was the struggles, it was almost like a relief for me." Like Kurt, some participants basked in having a break from these exact feelings. Jess reflected positively on the hiatus from serious training, saying, "I might actually be able to have a day where I'm not sore for once."

A significant part of the grieving process for these elite athletes as they moved into retirement was the fear of being forgotten, having to come to terms with the reality that they no longer lived in a world where they were known primarily as athletes. They would encounter many people who had no idea about their previous athletic identity. Tess shared her experiences in navigating the shifting views that others had of her as she became known as an attorney. "It is kind of interesting to navigate that when you think of how people perceive you and you're just like if they saw me they would only think these things about me and they wouldn't even know that this part really matters to me because it is not something I am pursuing right now . . . because you're not devoting a lot of time to it nobody sees you as this person anymore." Oftentimes, this shift in how others viewed participants' identities happened more rapidly than the athletes' own internal shift. This could lead to feelings of being misunderstood and lost as they witnessed their athletic identity fade away. Beth described how quickly after her medical retirement and being pushed off the team that she started to wonder if others even remembered that she had been on the team. "I wonder if anyone knows I play softball, but I feel like then it really changed. . . . Now certain things happen, and I totally forgot to mention that I played softball in college." She shared that she did not have a career to positively reflect on and share with others, which has left something missing. This feeling likely contributed to her burying her athletic identity during her transition into retirement. "Like making it that far. Most sports, you can go pro and do stuff like that, make it that far and kind of having nothing to show for it. I feel like I'm missing that aspect of being a part of something or feeling good at something that was widely accepted is not good, not something that is a small thing and oh that's good like something that people could actually see and be like wow. That's kind of hard." For Beth, the loss of identity was made worse by the need to redefine success in new endeavors. Measuring performance, which had once been second nature, now felt like a challenging task in her postretirement life.

The grief experience often brought forth a myriad of behavioral and emotional reactions in participants as they tried to make sense of the pain and confusion they were feeling in the face of retirement. Henry described his observations of how grief manifested in his behavior and emotions: "That part externalizes as mood changes and being bitter for a good amount of time where your identity just isn't there anymore and what you connected yourself to just wasn't there. I think that was the biggest part I struggled with, just what's next and who am I next?" While he was eventually able to transition into a coaching position, others remained stuck in a cycle of attempting to find purpose and passion that fell short of truly filling the void left by elite performance.

Even for those who found contentment in the next chapter of their lives, there was still a lingering sense of discontent that they could not shake. Tess shared being content with her successful teaching career, having pride in her accomplishments, and still not feeling truly fulfilled. "I feel like, yeah, this is great, but this is it?" This sentiment was also shared by Jermaine, who, despite finding multiple things he is passionate about in his life after sports, he still felt a sense of being incomplete. "I'm not as passionate about what my chapter is going to be as when I was playing. I'm trying to handle it the best I can . . . just trying to keep as busy as possible." Like Tess, Jermaine had many aspects of his life that he loved and found success in, but the feelings of grief continued to linger.

For other participants, the emotions they experienced were much more intense, leading to more significant psychosocial symptoms that sometimes impeded their functioning. Dannie shared the intensity of her emotions as she faced her fourth surgery: "I just hit complete rock bottom. I have anxiety and panic attacks, but I had never been depressed. I was depressed for probably four or five months. . . . I felt so defeated." She shared that working through the depression she was experiencing required her to accept that her body could no longer perform in the manner she wanted it to, a form of body grief that many athletes experience during retirement. "Just going through a depressive state and realizing I have to let go of that to get better. That was the hardest part of the transition." For Dannie, the lack of resources available to help guide this process left her feeling significantly unprepared for retirement and with a sense of "doom that kind of happens." The lack of support and guidance during this critical transition contributed to her struggles in navigating retirement effectively.

For other participants, the journey of discovering who they are after retiring from sports is still ongoing. Despite having careers, pursuing multiple interests, and finding some passions, they continued to grieve the loss of their former selves and search for new identity and purpose in retirement. This process of self-discovery and adaptation will be a journey that continues for quite some time. Anna described the ongoing search for a life that fits well after retiring from sports. The process of finding a new sense of purpose and identity remains a significant focus in her post-sport life. "I sat down last night and tried to figure out who do I want to be, what kind of person, and what are my core values? What can I do now that would give me some sort of identity, purpose, and make me feel fulfilled? I'm trying to work on these things and coming into the next identity of myself or how I want my life to move forward, because obviously I'm not going to play hockey forever and even with work, I feel like for a little I focused heavily on work to fill that void and I feel like I need to find something else." The process of reidentification for retired athletes also involves finding a place for sport, their competitive drives, and physical well-being in their retirement. As we have seen with the athletes in the current study, this may entail exploring different forms of physical activity, recreational sports, or even coaching or mentoring opportunities to maintain a connection to the sports world while adapting to a new role as a retired athlete.

For Tess, she recognized that this feeling of what comes next was not unique to her, but a common experience in the transition to retirement. "I feel like it was weird because you're leaving and then you're like 'wait so do I just run charitable 5ks now?' What do you do . . . nobody seems to know . . . I did a marathon the first year I was out, to also see how my leg would do. . . . I guess this is what people do." This experience is similar to participants who lamented that they have now been reduced to beer leagues or recreational teams that did not have the same level of camaraderie after being at the pinnacle of their athletic careers. This can be a challenging adjustment that requires accepting a new reality and coming to terms with being seen as part of the "old guard" while still being relatively young. As seen in earlier chapters, some retired athletes coped with this transition by trying to prove that they are still in prime physical condition and seeking alternative forms of athletic competition. Engaging in different sports or fitness activities allows them to maintain their competitive drive, stay physically active, and retain a sense of identity as athletes. While the redirection to other forms of athletic competition or physical performance may serve as a bridge for some retired athletes, providing a way to stay connected to their passion and cope with the emotional challenges of leaving professional sports, others may find that this exacerbates their grief experiences.

Tim's experience highlights the complex emotions and challenges that retired athletes can face when they try to hold on to their athletic identities. Despite trying to find a sense of success and fulfillment by joining the USA track and field team to continue competing, he was still unable to escape the overwhelming sense of failure that affected both his employment and personal life. He shares that in retirement from football, even the performance highs became the lows.

> I am driving home, and I get home, I parked in front of my house, and I just start crying. Tears of joy, but the tears of it was almost two-year process of training for this and I had been struggling in my career and outside of sports and I just kind of threw myself into this. At the time I had started a family and I was in tears because I was walking in the door as a success, but yet I felt like a failure. Because I wasn't bringing home a paycheck, it wasn't like I was bringing home a brand-new career to help my relationship and my family. And so, I was successful, yet I felt, it was the first time, like I just felt like a complete failure.

For Tim, finding something he was passionate about in his post-sport life was a positive step. However, he acknowledged that true success would come only when he could reconcile his love for sports with the demands of his life outside of elite competition. He realized that he had not yet fully explored who he was outside of his athletic identity and the impact of identity foreclosure on his ability to process retirement. It's not uncommon for individuals to use distractions and avoidance as coping mechanisms when dealing with the immense loss that retirement from sports can bring. However, as he has recognized, relying solely on these strategies likely hindered his ability to find true fulfillment and purpose beyond his athletic career.

Despite finding fulfilling careers after retiring from sports, some participants still grapple with a sense of loss, underscoring the ebb and flow nature of grief. The camaraderie and sense of belonging that comes from being part of a team were identified as deeply cherished aspects of the participant's lives, experiences that they were not able to replicate in retirement. Jermaine eloquently expressed the unique benefits and rewards that being an elite athlete had brought into his life. He acknowledges that these experiences could not be easily found in other areas of his life. "There are certain things about football that I will miss a ton that cannot be replicated, like eating in the dining hall with my teammates and locker room stuff. The grind of the weight room. That can't be replicated." Although reminiscing is a natural part of life, Jermaine found it challenging to fully accept that these experiences were in the past, leading him to repeatedly dwell on his former athletic life and experiences with his team. "It took me a lot of years to, you know, stop thinking about what I did at this time, or with this group." This loss of camaraderie can be a significant source of grief and a reminder of the meaningful relationships and shared experiences that were a central part of their athletic identity.

Steve revealed that despite his impressive athletic career and finding purpose in a football-related profession in retirement, there still lingers a void regarding what his career could have been. This feeling is difficult for him to overcome and leaves a sense of unfulfilled potential. "It burns me to this day. There's an emptiness in my career that won't ever be filled. I go in waves with it, sometimes I'm better with it, and then I have weeks where it still sucks." He tried to balance this perspective by acknowledging what he accomplished in his career, how he provided for his family, and built a life centered around them. Despite these achievements, he found himself caught in the ebb and flow of grief, sharing a mix of emotions and reflections on what could have been and what he has accomplished. "I don't think I'll ever conquer it. . . . It'll always be a bit of a void there." For this participant, his life was filled with many things he loved, but there was still a missing piece, a personal purpose that had not been left unfulfilled in retirement and was not something that could be replaced by things outside of himself. He also expressed attempting to redirect the same passion and dedication he had for football into his family life, trying to find a new source of purpose and fulfillment.

> My mindset shifted from where you always did everything you could to be the best quarterback or best athlete you could be. You need to take everything you got right now left that way and turn it into being the best father and husband you can be. And I failed so many times. I had so many days where I'm like, "This sucks. I gotta do something." I love my wife, I love my kids, I'm over the moon about having a baby and everything. But it was still like "I need something in my life."

It is important to acknowledge that the emotional intensity and grieving process during retirement can be an exceptionally challenging aspect of adapting to life after sports, and not all athletes can manage it. Some participants shared stories of loss related to former teammates and the distress experienced in retirement. Hayden offered a salient anecdote about a former teammate who tragically died by suicide shortly after his career in professional baseball ended:

> One of my friends actually committed suicide. He was a major leaguer. . . . A guy like him, hair-on-fire type of player, high energy. Willing to crash through a wall for the team. He was the guy in the middle of the party and in the middle of the locker room just raising hell. All of a sudden you have that behavior outside of all that. You are getting arrested. Then all of a sudden it crashes down, and everybody is no longer happy with you being the wild man. People are like, "dude, calm down." So, whatever is going on—depression, anxiety, concussions, head trauma—I don't know. But they make the decision that they don't have any more value.

This highlights the depth of the complex and emotional journey athletes may encounter as they transition into life after sports, a process that frequently involves grappling with mental health challenges.

Steve shed light on the mental health struggles that can arise during retirement, recounting the loss of a teammate who faced difficulties in navigating this transition. "When I was coming up, I mean you heard about it, but mental health has become such a big deal. Not that it hasn't always been but it's just come to the forefront so much. You know? I had a teammate at [university] who killed himself. He drank himself to death. He was a really good player. You hear about that and it's just like, 'Holy shit.' You got to take a step back sometimes. I've had enough of those moments in my life where I think I've gained some perspective in that way." While many participants have made significant progress in processing and working through the grief associated with the end of their athletic careers, they recognize that the work is not done.

Similar to Steve, Issa recognized that the journey of processing grief is ongoing, and there is still more work to be done. "Clearly, I cry every time I talk about it but I definitely feel like it made me move in a way that I never thought I would. . . . I still feel conflicted about the whole thing. To say if it was good or bad . . . I guess it's more of a heartbreak and pain than it is something that is totally terrible and a bad thing that happened in my life. Which is why it's so weird to describe how it feels." Issa offered a compelling portrayal of the growth that can emerge in the face of trauma and loss, demonstrating that pain and progress can coexist.

Anna echoed these sentiments when she shared, "It's been a tough journey that I'm currently on the road to trying to recover from." Like Anna, Joe recognized that while he has come a long way in processing his grief, there is still work to be done. "I have to go to bed at night for the rest of my life, and I'm hoping that kind of fades in the next 5–10 years, not knowing what the hell I did wrong. It's bizarre." This feeling of powerlessness had a profound influence on how this participant and many others coped with their retirement and the grief that accompanied it.

POWERLESS: WATCHING THE DREAM COME TO AN END

Many of the participants in the current study expressed a sense of powerlessness as they faced the inevitable end of their athletic careers (Joe, Tim, Kendrick, Beth, Erica, Jermaine, Tess, Henry). Whether the ending was abrupt and unexpected, leaving them feeling lost and confused, or anticipated, as in the case of college athletes who knew they wouldn't continue professionally, the transition often felt beyond their control. Some vividly described the experience of counting down the remaining games, feeling the career slipping away, slipping through their fingers. Players who were forced to retire often described the process as being drawn out, with various challenges and emotional struggles. Some attempted to prolong the ending, which only added to their angst and uncertainty. Others experienced lengthy periods of mixed messages from coaches and organizations, leaving them feeling lost and alone in their retirement journey.

For Joe, this period was agonizing as he tried to reconcile his coach's seemingly arbitrary decision to refuse to play him with the positive messages he received from everyone else on the team. While he appreciated the good intentions behind these messages, they only increased his feelings of being alone when they did not translate into outward support or action. "I was like an emotional roller coaster. I would go and have a good practice and one of the assistant coaches or someone would say something really nice to me or drop me a really nice text . . . and that happened a lot where people would try to support me from the outside but wouldn't have the balls to go to the coach about it." While this discrepancy added to his sense of powerlessness and confusion during the retirement process, making it even more challenging to cope with the loss of his athletic career, it did serve the purpose of confirming that he had not done something to deserve the treatment that he was receiving and to realize that others saw what was happening to him. This validation, though bittersweet, provided him with some comfort and support during a difficult time. "Some of the other people on the staff would say things to me because they knew what was going on wasn't fair. These things would mean the world to me and they would change my day. My assistant coach came up to me and said something really nice about what he saw at practice or my attitude or whatever." He shared that while in retirement, he has been able to gain perspective on how much external validation was controlling his self-esteem at the time. During this tumultuous period, any negative feedback was devastating. "If it went the other way, if it was bad. I was a wreck and like I couldn't think of anything else. I was miserable. I couldn't leave it at the rink. I brought it home with me." This prolonged and ambiguous process of deselection intensified his grief experience and left him feeling suspended in uncertainty, struggling to find a clear path forward.

Henry described the ambiguity he experienced when he was wrestling with whether to return after a serious concussion as being in a state of "purgatory," where one chapter ends and the other has yet to begin. "I didn't feel great . . . because you were just saying purgatory in the sense that I wasn't doing anything. Your sense of belonging or looking to find something bigger than yourself just wasn't there." Similarly, Issa echoed the experience of retirement as feeling like a purgatory, with one foot in the past and one in the future, while being stuck in the middle with one's pain "What do I do next to move onto the next thing? Because I don't want to keep being sad about it but I also don't want to be in between and in limbo." This sense of being in limbo, unable to fully let go of the past and uncertain about the future, contributed to the emotional challenges of retirement and the process of grief.

Like Joe, Esteban expressed the overwhelming sadness he experienced when he realized that despite his exceptional performance, there was no spot for him on a team. He had exhausted all available opportunities to play professionally and had explored every avenue in search of a team that would roster him. "I remember going home and they were telling me (coaches), you know listen there's really nothing you didn't do. The 'you know, you were a great, great player, just right now our team needs this.' And that was so tough for me . . . that was just . . . the ride back to my hotel was so tough. It really was." He shared the realization that his career had come to an end and the pain of sitting with those feelings, a sense of hopelessness that added to the challenges of his retirement. "It was empty, very empty, very sad. Cause deep down I knew my time had come you know. It was tough . . . it was tough, you know?" For Esteban, his relentless focus on athletic performance had left him unprepared for what might come next in life after sports. He had not considered or planned for a future beyond his athletic career, which made the transition into retirement even more challenging and uncertain. "My plan was to do this career for the rest of, however long, it didn't work out that way." He shared having to accept that "there was nothing more I could do playing-wise" due to the small window for international athletes in professional soccer and having to force himself to let go of the pursuit. "I can't just keep going in circles here . . . it was just . . . that was a very tough time." For this participant, the foreclosure of his athletic identity made his transition very difficult. After many years of reflection, he recognized that the opportunities running out forced him to finally explore other options for his life. "In a weird way, it was just me finally having to go in a different direction, cause for so long all my eggs were in one basket." The lack of preparation added to the sense of loss and confusion he experienced during this period of his life.

For Jermaine, his experience was similar as he watched his opportunities fade away. After choosing to return for an additional year of eligibility with the hope of being selected for the NFL, he faced the disappointment of COVID-19 disruptions, which diminished his chances. He described the inner conflict of trying to convince himself to let go of his dream while still holding on tightly. "It was really hard. My lowest lows. It was overwhelming, stressful, I hated not knowing. I mean, I think that's everyone, but I just hate not knowing. Man, I'm doing all of this for nothing. I'm trying to stay ready, but it's not like the teams care. They're going to keep going, so I really struggled wrestling with that at points." For this participant, this moment served as a stark realization that decisions in professional sports were more about business than the players' experiences, their desires, the sacrifices they had made, or the impact of COVID-19 on their careers. It was a moment of awakening to the fact that the industry's priorities might not align with his personal aspirations, and the reality of this business-oriented perspective was disheartening and difficult to come to terms with."They don't care about me, they have higher priorities, they're trying to field a team . . . they're going to keep moving. So, I really struggled with that because when I think about how I put my whole life into this, I played football my whole life, this is why I came back a 5th year at (college), and I played well, and I got everything I wanted in terms of winning a (award) league championship . . . coming up short is heartbreaking." He eventually had to face the reality that even without the impact of the pandemic, there was never a guarantee of success in making it to the NFL. He had to come to terms with the possibility that his dream might not have materialized regardless. However, the missed opportunities and disruptions caused by the pandemic left him with lingering questions and a sense of dissatisfaction about the way his athletic career ended. "I also knew that it might not have been meant to be. I might have fallen short regardless of if it was a normal year. I just think that area of not knowing really killed me." The uncertainty and "what-ifs" surrounding those lost chances added to the complexities of his retirement experience, making it more challenging to find closure and acceptance.

Ultimately, Jermaine's attempts to stay positive had left him unprepared to cope with the uncertainty of his future. He had to confront the need to let go of his core belief that he could make it to the NFL and come to terms with the ending of his athletic career. "You just think it's going to work out for you, you're staying just getting ready and staying ready, trying to be as positive and optimistic as possible. . . . It's nothing but positive thoughts and optimism, and when it crashes down like that . . . you're a big fish in a small pond and then you go to all this ambiguity and you do really feel small, like oh God, this could be it, but you don't want it to be it. What am I going to do now?" This process also required him to reimagine a future that did not involve professional football, which was a significant challenge for someone who had devoted so much of his life to pursuing that dream. For this participant, realizing the finite nature of elite athletic performance and the "shelf life" of professional sports helped him come to the understanding that even if he did achieve his goal of making it to the NFL, there would still be a need for another chapter in his life after his athletic career. "I knew there was going to be a life after football, I also knew that if I was gonna make it . . . it might have been 2 or 3 years because that's what the average shelf life is for a guy like me in the NFL. It's gonna be less than 2 years, or 2 years, you know what I mean?" This recognition was a pivotal moment in his transition process, as it allowed him to shift his focus from solely pursuing athletic achievements to exploring and developing other aspects of his identity and potential. While the disappointment of missed opportunities remained, he started to embrace the idea that his identity and worth were not solely defined by his athletic performance, but rather by the person he was becoming and the opportunities that awaited him in the future.

MISSED OPPORTUNITIES AND UNANSWERED QUESTIONS: IT SHOULD HAVE BEEN ME

The feeling of missed opportunities and unfulfilled potential was a common theme among many participants as they looked back on their athletic careers in retirement. Some expressed a sense of being cheated, as if external factors or circumstances beyond their control had prevented them from achieving greater success. Others felt a personal sense of disappointment, believing that they had not fully realized their potential or accomplished all they had hoped for in their sports careers. This reflection on missed opportunities highlights the intricate emotional journey athletes undertake during the transition into retirement as they wrestle with the changing aspects of their identities and aspirations.

For participants like Beth, the missed opportunities were not solely related to continued playing but also the chance to remain part of a team. She experienced a shoulder injury that forced her into medical retirement, and recounts that her coach's reluctance to accept this decision led to her being removed from the team. She compared her experience to those who were able to medically retire and still be part of the team community, which had been her hope when announcing her retirement.

> Yeah, so honestly what I could have done, which is what I was probably picturing was like for most people, football for example, when someone retires from football they see them down on the sidelines every game. And sure, maybe they

> don't get to travel and take part in the bus rides, but they sort of practice and go to all the events and honestly like where I saw it . . . that I wouldn't be able to play, but I would be part of it. There's so many like cool parts outside of playing sports, community service events and we did so many things as a team that you think maybe if she took it better, I could have still done that, like most retired players, so that kind of sucks.

Despite the sense of missing out on important team experiences, Beth also acknowledged that the abrupt ending to her membership on the team pushed her to explore other aspects of the college experience that she would not have been exposed to if she had continued playing. "Maybe it helps me, maybe I would have been worse off there every day and not playing but wishing I was. So, I don't know, it's like I wish I could have been part of it, but then maybe it's nice that it was ripped like a Band-Aid, so I wasn't sitting there sad, wishing I got to play." Nevertheless, these are not questions that she will ever find answers to, and ones that intensified the grieving process.

Like Beth, Issa's career was cut short due to an injury, leaving her with a sense of unfinished business and a longing for closure. She shared that she has been plagued by feelings of having missed opportunities to find closure and grief over the loss of the narrative regarding her retirement that she had long become attached to. When reflecting on the concussion that ended her career with five games left in her senior year, she shared that she will always wonder what her relationship with hockey could have been if she had been able to retire at the end of the season. "I don't know if I had played all of the games if I would feel so heartbroken. I think I would have obviously been sad but like I said it would've been on my terms and it would have been the last game, the final whistle, the final buzzer you know? Versus someone being reckless and hitting me from behind. That I think is what made it so hard because it was not on the terms it should have been on but instead it happened the way it happened." For this participant, the overwhelming feeling was that the ending of her career was stolen from her. The narrative that she, her teammates, and family envisioned for her collegiate hockey career was abruptly cut short, leaving her with a deep sense of loss and a feeling of being robbed of the closure she had anticipated. "I still think about the fact that it ended in that way and it's hard for me to obviously talk about [referencing that she was crying]." Issa found it challenging not to imagine a different ending to her career, one that might have brought her the closure and peace of mind she yearned for. This constant contemplation of what could have been further complicated her adjustment to retirement and added to the emotional turmoil surrounding the loss of her athletic identity.

Joe shares a similar experience of being trapped in a state of wondering what his career and its conclusion might have been like if he had been given a chance to showcase his skills. Beginning his journey as a top prospect with dreams of reaching the NHL, and scouts affirming his potential, left Joe with a persistent sense of being cheated. He recognized how much of a negative emotional impact it had and how much of the college experience he missed out on as a result. "If everything would have been going normal for me and I was just a normal guy on the team, then it would have been out of this world, fun, enjoyable. It would have been the most amazing couple of years of my life. But I was dealing with the dark side of sport in my life." This participant not only perceived the ending of his career as being robbed out of the college experience. His deselection also impacted his friendships in ways that he struggled to reconcile for quite some time, adding to the distress and internal tensions he experienced. The emotional toll of this unfulfilled potential and the resulting impact on his relationships was profound for him. "I had a hard time trying to distinguish okay, this is my best friend, he knows how good I am. He knows what I'm going through. He's my roommate, he sees me every night and the coach loves him and the coach looks at him as a son and he won't say anything. So is it just not his business, or is he a bad friend? Is it his responsibility? I came to the answer that it's not." While this helped him to accept that his best friend had sympathy but would not take action to support him, he could not shake the nagging belief that if the situation had been reversed, he would have made a different choice. "I probably would have if it were the other way around and I've done it in the past for other people." For many participants, the pain experienced in retirement extended beyond the actual events of leaving their athletic careers and had a significant impact on various aspects of their lives, including relationships and daily functioning. The grief and emotional turmoil they faced during this transition affected how they interacted with others, how they viewed themselves, and how they navigated their daily activities.

Experiencing the premature end of their careers, while witnessing other players and teammates continue to excel and find success, left many participants grappling with mixed emotions. Despite understanding that being an elite athlete comes with a time limit, and not all careers unfold as planned, it was difficult for them to avoid wondering why their paths were cut short while others thrived. This was true even in situations where the athlete had embraced the ending of their career. Kendrick shared, "There are days when I'm like, 'Whew, man, I'm glad I'm done. I don't have to go and do camp right now. I'm glad I don't have to go do this or that.' But there are other days where I was like, man, I see them play, like (alma mater) won the league this past year, and I was like, 'Man, that should have been us. I wish I could play right now.' I miss just walking onto the field."

Similarly, Kurt, who felt that he had a positive ending to his career, expressed conflicting emotions when it came to watching football on television after retiring. "I ended on my good note and I did the best I could. . . . It was hard for me to watch the NFL after I left the NFL. It was hard for me to watch the [team] after I left the [team]. It was hard in a way because I wasn't there, but I wanted to watch because I wanted them to win because I knew the players. I would watch them to root them on but it was also hard watching players that I knew on the other teams . . . because I know I'm better than that." Despite feeling content with his performance and giving his best effort, he found it challenging to reconcile himself to his new role as a spectator rather than an active participant in the sport.

While genuinely happy and excited for their teammates' achievements, some of the participants in the study felt a twinge of jealousy within themselves. These conflicting emotions emerged as they compared their own situations to the success of others, and they questioned their own capabilities and choices. This internal struggle intensified the emotional journey of retirement, as participants reconciled the desire to be supportive while coping with their own sense of loss, unfulfilled aspirations, and the internal experience of guilt for being jealous of another's success. Henry articulated this well when he shared: "It was tough in the sense that you see guys having success and personal success and you're like 'I should be at that level right now.' But on the flip side you have really close friends who have success and you are really happy for them. I don't know if that's yin or yang or what that would be. It was tough in the emotional sense because you would be happy for some guys and the other guys and teenagers you feel like you have to be out there doing it." Henry, like several other participants, found himself grappling with feelings of jealousy when he observed his friends continuing to be part of the team environment, enjoying the camaraderie that he had now lost in retirement. "I really follow friends closely that are still playing and I probably get a little jealous at times when the guys are hanging out at a hotel or on the bus or on the plane together." This jealousy was a natural response to the stark contrast between the vibrant team experiences of his friends and his own postretirement life, which lacked the same level of social connectedness that he had enjoyed for his entire career.

Similar to Henry, Issa also grappled with feelings of jealousy and envy as she observed her former teammates continuing their athletic careers while she was forced into retirement due to a career-ending concussion. "I was definitely jealous, I was so jealous that they get to have this last practice or like I love that drill or, you know, just doing it with your friends and practicing with your friends. Those experiences and moments are everything." This emotional struggle highlighted the challenges that athletes face in transitioning away from the close-knit and communal atmosphere of sports teams and adjusting to a different lifestyle in retirement, one that for this participant involved a great deal of pain and uncertainty. Issa emphasized the contrast between a concussion and a visible physical injury, describing how the concussion felt like a betrayal by her own mind. This internal nature of the injury made the loss she experienced feel even more profound and difficult to convey to others. "I had to not go, not because I physically couldn't do it, but I was unwell. Being in the hockey rink and like the passing and banging of the puck on the board was just clinging in my head. I physically couldn't go, so that also made it harder. It's not like I twisted my ankle and could still be in it, my body wouldn't allow me to be there. So, it was even more jarring to not be able to be a part of anything because I was injured in my head. . . . It was a mind trip . . . It felt really unfair." Issa's description highlighted how the intangible nature of her injury and the associated mental health struggles contributed to a deeper sense of loss and disconnection during her retirement process.

Jermaine echoed the difficulty of witnessing others living his dream while in retirement, acknowledging the challenge of redirecting his thoughts and focusing on his future. He candidly recognized the role that jealousy can play during this transitional period. "You see the success of my peers and other people, and you get jealous and compare yourself to others." While he realized that this did not serve a purpose in retirement, it was still a challenging dynamic to process. "That doesn't get you anywhere. It's your life, you're running your own race." The process of reconciling oneself to one's own retirement while witnessing others' continued success can be emotionally demanding and require a deep introspection and acceptance of new life paths.

Joe reflected on the damage caused to his self-esteem by constantly comparing himself to his teammates, and in hindsight, he realized the negative impact it had on him. He spent several years wondering why he couldn't receive the same treatment as his teammates, and this affected his confidence and self-worth. "I would have an amazing practice and he [coach] wouldn't even look at me and there would be guys that were horrible and they messed up a whole drill . . . the coach would greet them with a smile, a high five, and would never bat an eye at the bad things they did. I would be rumbling inside, 'I don't get this, what is going on? Why is this fair?'" For Joe, the challenging experiences of comparing his treatment with preferred teammates and feeling like his career fell short were excruciating at the time. However, in hindsight, he recognized that these experiences increased his resilience and shaped who he is today.

Like Joe, Henry also reconciled feelings that his career had fallen short and the lack of closure with the overall success of a well-played career. While his career ended prematurely due to a concussion, he believed he had an easier time making the decision to retire because he did not experience regrets about the effort he put into his career or the opportunities available to him. "I think I had an easier time getting out of playing because I knew I had given it all I had all the time. I had no regrets in terms of the path I took. You make mistakes but, you know, these mistakes lead you to certain places." It is possible that this reflection captures the experiences at the time of retirement or is influenced by recall bias from reminiscing on past distressing events. However, this participant credited the ability to have pride in the hard work and dedication he put into his career as aiding in the transition process and helping him find a peace that initially eluded him.

COPING PATTERNS: MANAGING FEELINGS OF GRIEF AND LOSS

In the preceding chapters, it became evident that certain athletes encountered challenges in discovering effective coping and adaptation methods during their transition to retirement. Consequently, some resorted to unhealthy coping strategies, such as hastily accepting new jobs, avoiding anything associated with their sports past, denying the reality of retirement, and attempting to fill the void with various activities. While these coping mechanisms may have provided temporary relief, they were ultimately detrimental to the participants well-being and prolonged the transition process. On the other hand, some athletes managed to embrace more effective outlets that alleviated the difficulties they faced while navigating this phase.

Some of the athletes focused on physical outlets in retirement, pursuing endeavors that they hoped would help keep them connected to their athletic identity (Tess, Anna, Tim). After Tess suffered a leg injury that made it impossible for her to continue with impact sports, she made an effort to discover alternative physical outlets. However, she soon realized that her grief over retiring from her previous sport affected her choices. "For rehab they said you could swim or you could cycle since it's low impact. I used to swim so I started swimming again and then, it was almost like, I was almost in too dark of a place because I didn't want to be left alone in the pool with my thoughts, so I started cycling."

Tim recognized that utilizing athletic outlets to cope with the feelings of loss in retirement was a key factor in rediscovering the sense of self he had lost. After struggling for eight years with his retirement and not being able to find anything that he could truly feel good about doing including a career trajectory, he turned to track, hoping to fill the void. "As soon as I started training for that, I was back. Like I was me, despite all the failures, all the pain, all of the heartache. I was mentally broke, financially broke. Once I got back into running and training for something. . . . I was myself again. I felt like me." For Tim, while this outlet did not improve his financial situation or lead to immediate employment success, he felt that he had found "the missing pieces to my puzzle." Through engaging in another form of competition, he managed to restore the sense of fulfillment and energy that had eluded him during retirement. For the first time in a long while, he started receiving recognition for his athletic prowess, rather than being defined by his lack of direction and perceived life failures.

Similarly, Henry found himself connecting with health and wellness as an outlet during his transition into retirement. He shared that focusing his energy in this manner provided opportunities to explore what resources existed and served as a distraction to the pain of his transition. Although these coping strategies didn't eliminate the inner turmoil and sadness he was going through, they did help him reconnect with self-care practices and provided valuable knowledge that now benefits him in his coaching career. "I really dove into health and wellness, so that was a great year for podcasts, books, etc. I was able to get into reading again and it was a huge positive dive into something that helps me out a lot now in terms of lifestyle and connecting with guys and having more resources just from learning about it." For this participant, when he reflected on the role that coping skills played in his transition to retirement, he recognized the positive aspect of redirecting his energy into the potential next step. However, he recognized that in doing so, he had not processed the loss that retirement was bringing to his life. At that point, he hadn't fully comprehended the intricacies of adjusting to life after elite athletic competition, which is a complex and challenging process in itself. The coping mechanisms he utilized provided a helpful distraction but didn't allow him to fully come to terms with the profound changes retirement brought, both personally and professionally. "Honestly, I didn't do a good job with that. I would read and listen to podcasts and stuff like that and I dove into the health and wellness side. I read books about coaching and internalized a lot of that competitive angst that you're missing because that part never leaves you. Whether I'm playing sports against (wife) or golfing with friends, that part will never leave me but not being able to do that on the level it was before, that part was the hardest thing." As the ending of their sports career becomes more difficult and unpredictable, the athletes in the current study tended to create greater emotional distance from their sport while going through the grieving process. The challenges and uncertainties surrounding their retirement may have led them to disengage from the sport they once loved, as a way to protect themselves from further emotional turmoil and to find a sense of closure.

In response to her coach's refusal to accept her medical retirement and removing her from all aspects of the team, Beth took a drastic step by discarding all the reminders from her sports career. "I felt maybe because it was such a bad experience, I didn't want to be walking around with that stuff and people . . . not that it matters to anyone, and say you're not on a team." This strategy, similar to Tim describing "putting his career in a drawer," provided distance from the painful events and a greater ability to avoid uncomfortable conversations that she was not ready to have. Yet, these experiences could not be compartmentalized forever, and the decision to discard all of the items that connected her to softball was one that she later grew to regret. "It didn't matter to me, obviously, which is kind of sad but now I look back and I'm like God I wish I kept some of my shirts because now I would be happy to say that I played on a softball team there, but my senior year. . . . I had such a bad last couple months that I just didn't want anything to do with it." While these coping strategies may have served to protect her from the ongoing reminders of the loss she was experiencing, in hindsight, she came to regret this impulsive decision. These mementos held sentimental value, representing her hard work, achievements, and cherished memories from her sports career. By discarding them, she discarded a part of her identity and personal history that she later realized was essential to preserve.

Some of the athletes attempted to transition to recreational levels of performance (Erica, Tess) to ease the transition and while many eventually found a way to "reset their expectations" (Tess), moving from a highly competitive and goal-driven environment in division one sports to recreational levels can be a significant adjustment. Erica, in particular, expressed that one of the most difficult aspects of this change was the loss of the culture and shared vision that had been an integral part of her Division One experience. The sense of camaraderie, shared goals, and strong team culture that often characterizes competitive sports at higher levels was not as prominent in these recreational settings. "I had a very hard time transitioning from division one to club. The commitment level in terms of everybody, you know, working their hardest every day to achieve a common goal. . . . I feel like club is a hobby that I do on the side." Transitioning to a recreational level where performance is not emphasized can create a cognitive dissonance for athletes like Erica. While she could have rationalized that it was not a priority for players at this level, her internalized approach and high-performance expectations clashed with this more laid-back atmosphere. "For me, it was my life's work at that point." She expressed that being able to adapt to this environment required her to let go of her ego. "I probably thought in my head, I'm above this."

For both Erica and Tess, there was immense frustration in the lack of skill and commitment associated with recreational leagues. "I still played rec volleyball, which is also difficult when you go from elite level to just whoever shows up for open gym, and you're like, 'this person has no idea what to do. 'You're almost more frustrated'" (Tess). These sentiments were also echoed by Erica. "I started getting angry, like I'd say for the first month I was cocky and then I was just angry and annoyed because I was not with my division one teammates but with girls that didn't come from that." Like Tess, Erica was able to eventually realign her expectations of a club team and find a way back to the fun that she had long lost in her career. "If this is just like a joke or if this is just a hobby, or like essentially in my mind this is intramural pick up that, you know, some beer league guy could come play in, then I'm just going to take college and make up for the last three years I spent being a division one athlete, and I'm going to have fun." There was a significant emotional adjustment to playing at this level "it was kind of a learning curve for me" (Erica) and one that "was a fun social aspect" (Tess). However, it served its purpose in providing something to focus on for at least a brief period of time until they realized that "it isn't the same" (Tess). Both participants eventually realized that this new experience could not replicate the same level of fulfillment and competition they had once known in their elite careers. The intense drive, sense of purpose, and high-stakes nature of competitive sports was missing at the recreational level.

For Tess, taking part in recreational sports didn't align with her vision of the athlete she wants to be, and it also failed to serve as a suitable intermediate step in her retirement journey. Instead, it only served to intensify her feelings of confusion about her postretirement path. "It's this weird thing where you don't feel like you're a recreational cyclist, you don't fit in with that, but you're not racing either." Tess goes on to share that she was losing the love for sports in general after so much exposure to elite competition. The demanding nature of high-level competition took a toll on her ability to enjoy being active and athletic, especially in the very sports she used to compete in. "I struggle right now, we'll go backpacking and this is fun but not really. . . . I miss racing . . . but at what point am I just not okay with accepting, do I feel like I'm settling?" Yet, for this participant, she recognized the importance of transitioning toward finding satisfaction in non-elite athletic endeavors. She understood that embracing this healthier mental and physical space is crucial for her overall well-being. While it might be a process that takes time, she remained hopeful that she will be able to achieve this in the future. "I think it's a place I want to get to. Your body at some point will break down and at some point you'll stop getting a PR at that point."

Tess found herself questioning the timing of stepping away from elite performance and reflecting on the legacy she wished to leave behind. She described grappling with the desire to make the most of her elite career while also considering her long-term physical and mental health. "Would it have been better to have gone out on top or do you just keep going? I want to keep going, so even if I'm riding this fading star, it's like instead of going out when I'm peaking and wondering what was left, I would rather get to the end and get dead last in multiple races and be like okay, I rode this out." Despite this introspection, she was not prepared to let go of the competitive aspect of sports, signifying the core complexity of the retirement process.

This crossroad is one where athletes must come to terms with their changing roles and aspirations, while holding on to the essence of what has driven them throughout their careers.

Some participants (Tess, Anna, Dannie) proactively sought professional support to navigate the emotional challenges that arose during their transition into retirement from elite athletic careers. Tess shared the thoughts that led her to seek counseling. "I didn't feel like I had a good grasp on my thoughts, it was so easy to keep digging this hole of 'yeah, my leg's going to get amputated' and all these things like it's never going to recover the way I'm used to. The college counselors, because I was like maybe I should go see them and I was recommended to go and deal with it, but it's like your college counselors don't really know how to deal with stuff like that." She shared that she was later able to reconnect with a therapist from back home who was able to help her "focus on identifying other parts of myself that I identified with and working through it. If I don't have athletics, what else would I maybe be interested in pursuing?" Having seen the value in being able to work through this connection, Tess says, "I would say find a good therapist, which I tell everybody so they can all fully flourish as individuals." Similarly, Anna has also been engaging in therapy as an avenue to work on "coming into the next identity of myself and how I want my life to move forward." She has become aware of her tendency to fill the void left by hockey with busy tasks, avoiding the need for difficult internal conversations and self-reflection.

Dannie also discovered that therapy was immensely beneficial during her transition, particularly in addressing the need to change her thought patterns regarding sports and her approach to health. She encountered numerous challenges in embracing physical therapy and allowing herself to heal properly, as her persistent drive to push harder impeded the process. "Me going 100 percent is really me going 60 percent. They would tell me you have to stop that. That is just how my brain is wired. My therapist said we are going to unwire that and take your expectations down." Through therapy, she worked on shifting these thought patterns and learned to find a more balanced approach to her athletic journey and overall well-being.

During the study, some participants turned their attention to hobbies as a way to cope with the transition into retirement. Jermaine, for instance, embraced writing as a transition and coping strategy, using it as a tool to explore and identify what the next chapter of his life might entail. "I thrust myself into writing as much as possible to stay busy. At certain points it got hard. I tried to throw myself out there and see what I'm good at, what I like and don't like. . . . I wrote for two different websites in that time span. I was trying to get as much sampling as I could get out to give myself the best chance to get into some schools. I just thought man I need to go to school to fill my time and get some inner fulfillment." For Jermaine, writing served as a means to reflect on his experiences, aspirations, and potential paths moving forward. He shared that finding purpose in his life and setting goals for things that he can work for and achieve have always been important aspects of success and motivation for him. "I was always finding some sense of inner purpose, that really helped me. Through writing, trying to get my back in proper shape, or to find a career or job. I always try to find that inner purpose." Whether it's trying out new activities or rediscovering past interests, these hobbies offer a valuable avenue for self-expression and self-discovery.

Issa shared that when she faced the devastating circumstances of being injured and having to end her career prematurely, she did not possess a significant set of coping skills to handle the situation. However, during her retirement, she has been able to develop and acquire coping mechanisms to navigate the emotional challenges that arose from the sudden end of her athletic career. "If I am feeling stressed out, going out for a walk, I do yoga and meditate. Things that really help me when I'm feeling overwhelmed that I didn't have at the time that comes with experience finding those interests. I didn't have those things because my whole life was about hockey." Issa further emphasizes the importance of integrating coping skills development into athletic training and support systems. She believed that equipping athletes with effective coping mechanisms will enable them to manage the various stressors they may encounter throughout their athletic careers, including potential injuries and the eventual transition into retirement.

> Those types of support for athletes are more open. Mindfulness is something we can do and expose it because that makes a huge difference. Talking more about how journaling can help you. That was something that really helped my mental health and trying to figure out how I was feeling. . . . But if I had those when getting injured, I think it would've been a lot easier to not only deal with the injury but to deal with it. I can't even go back and play anymore and have one more game. The end of transition and end of my career at school would've felt different and would've been helpful for sure.

While she might not have had these coping mechanisms at her disposal when she was initially struggling to accept the ending of her career, her subsequent experiences in retirement showed her the immense benefits they can provide. Ultimately, Issa came to realize that these coping strategies may have helped her find healthier ways to cope with the loss and uncertainties of leaving her competitive athletic career behind. She attempted to underscore in her description of her transition, the importance of supporting athletes in developing coping skills throughout their careers, as these tools can become invaluable during times of significant change and transition.

EXPECTATIONS OF PEACE AND THE REALITIES OF RETIREMENT

For many of the athletes, there was an anticipation of the peace that they may find in retirement; the dream of how the career would end with one chapter closing and another one opening. While some experienced their retirement exactly as they had envisioned, for others, it took time to reach that state of peace. Yet, for a portion of the athletes, retirement did not bring the expected peace they had hoped for. Instead, it remained an elusive space that proved unattainable within the context of their post-athletic life.

Several of the athletes in the current study were able to achieve a sense of acceptance and closure by reflecting on their careers as a whole. To shift the lens from the pain of retiring to a larger view of a career well played, accomplishments hard earned, and having had the opportunity to be elite athletic competitors. Jermaine shared, "I think giving it my shot and it not working out, gave me peace. It gave everyone around me peace of mind that I did give it a shot, and it didn't work out. . . . It doesn't work out for that many people in the grand scheme of things. I got to a point where 99 percent of athletes don't even reach. No need to feel bad about myself for that." This perspective allowed him to reflect on how rare it was to have even gotten as far as he did. It helped him gain perspective on the uncontrollable nature and longevity in sport. By reframing his outlook, he found solace in recognizing the value of his experiences, the dedication he put into football, and the opportunities he was fortunate to have as a high-level competitor.

Jess reached a point in her retirement journey where she could genuinely appreciate the bittersweet nature of the experience. This perspective allowed her to embrace and acknowledge both the highs and lows of her athletic career, recognizing the mixture of joy and challenges that came with being a competitive athlete. "At the end, I did really find that sense of peace, of like, I've done everything I wanted to do with sport. And it's gotten me to like the most incredible places and opportunities. It was like a bittersweet parting, because it did feel like it was time and I was at peace with it ending, but it was just really hard." Yet, even for Jess, this sense of peace did not come without pain. This bittersweet appreciation reflects the depth of emotions that many retired athletes grapple with. She was cognizant of the richness of her career while also acknowledging the inevitability of its conclusion and the associated pain of losing it.

Steve underwent significant perspective shifts during his end-of-career phase, where he found himself in a holding pattern attending training camps and workouts, only to receive news that he would not be signed by the teams. Through this process, he came to the realization that his time as an NFL player had reached its conclusion. "I was just at peace with it. It wasn't like all of a sudden they're going to have an epiphany and that this 34-year-old quarterback now can have a 6 year starting career with us. That wasn't going to happen." During these moments of uncertainty, Steve had profound insights, recognizing that what he stood to lose by staying and trying to continue playing was as significant as what he might gain from prolonging his career. These reflections made him realize that the costs and potential drawbacks of persisting as an NFL player outweighed the potential benefits. This self-awareness and thoughtful consideration led him to make the decision to move on from his professional football career.

For some of the participants, the journey into retirement was marked more significantly by pain and internal conflict, delaying their sense of peace until a much later stage in their retirement when they had ample time and space to reflect without the immediate sting of the transition. Beth echoed this sentiment, "I just definitely felt more at peace now, before I wasn't feeling great, hence throwing away all the items [softball gear and memorabilia]. Now I just have a positive memory. I can honestly say that like I miss playing, I miss my friends. I think now I am more accepting of what happened and happy with the choices I made and all the memories that I have from it." The process of reaching a place of peace involved allowing the initial emotional turbulence to subside and gaining a more profound perspective through contemplation and introspection.

She continued, describing a conversation with her coach postretirement when she ran into her on campus that helped to bring some closure to the situation. However, even with this conversation, it did not entirely replace the sadness she felt about ending her athletic career. "I actually ran into her at a doctor's appointment on campus. . . . We kind of talked. She basically just said, she kind of said sorry and she told me, no matter what, if I wanted to come back on the team. I said thank you, but this is a medical decision, this isn't because I don't want to be on your team, and I never heard from her again." While Beth can recognize that this conversation was a nice change from the "really aggressive and defensive" behavior she had previously experienced with her coach and allowed her to release some of the negative energy she had been carrying around. Ultimately, this sense did not give her peace or change her perspective about the end of her career. "So, her saying that I guess made me feel a little bit better, but still not great." Coming to terms with being injured was already a difficult process for this participant, but the situation became even more challenging when she had to medically retire and subsequently lost her role on the team. This loss took away any comfort or solace she had hoped for, as she saw her team moving forward without her. What made the situation even more distressing was that she was no longer allowed to remain a part of the team culture she had been a part of for so long. The emotional toll of both the injury and the loss of her team role compounded, leaving her with a sense of profound loss and longing for what had once been a significant part of her life.

Similar to Beth, Henry shared that while he knows that he made the right decision to retire and not risk more damage after his severe concussion, there was no feeling of peace or contentment following his decision. Instead, he recognized the pressure that was on him to decide what his next chapter would entail. "Making the decision, I didn't really feel relieved at all. It was like okay now I need to pony up and figure it out." The decision to retire placed a new burden on him to figure out his path beyond sports. This highlights the complex emotions that can arise for athletes when they retire, as they navigate the process of moving on from a career that has been a significant part of their identity and lives.

LETTING GO OF THE DREAM

Henry shared that, after he was able to accept that his career was ending and acknowledged how bad he was feeling physically, he was able to direct his attention to trying to break into the coaching arena. Becoming a coach presented an opportunity for him to remain involved in the world of sports and share his expertise and knowledge with others. "I always knew coaching was the top of the list but getting into education too. It's really hard to get in, you know what I mean? You have to sacrifice and cut your teeth a little but it came down to the point where that's the avenue that made the most sense. It took a long time to get there and a lot of this suppresses the ego and the competitive side, where you see your buddies playing and off doing their thing. That is probably the hardest, knowing you're not in that place anymore." He further elaborated that arriving at acceptance was not an easy journey for him. However, he recognized the wisdom in listening to the advice and experiences of those who had retired before him, as well as the support and care from his friends and family. He acknowledged that, deep down, he knew that if he ignored their perspectives and didn't heed their warnings, it would be a mistake. "This is going to suck so much, but you're a fool if you don't make the right choice when someone gives you the answer to the test." This willingness to learn from the experiences of others demonstrated his maturity and the valuable role that external perspectives can play in shaping one's decisions during significant life transitions like retirement.

Arianna shared that she arrived at the natural conclusion of career, having taken it as far as she could. She acknowledged that if there had been an opportunity to continue, she might not have been as open to transitioning to a different role. "I had no choice. I don't know how long I would have dragged the career out for if I had a choice in the matter. But when you're five years is up . . . It was forced." For this participant, her unwillingness to let go of her athletic career might have played a role in her decision to abandon her initial idea of becoming a professor and instead accept a coaching job. This shift allowed her to find a space where she could "almost recycle that world again."

Jermaine recounted his decision to stop pursuing opportunities in the NFL and instead shift his mindset toward the next phase of his life. Making this choice necessitated a change in how he viewed his athletic career and required him to ask himself difficult questions rather than merely following the expected path.

> Do I love it? Do I want to keep training? And I got to the point where it wasn't doing very much for me anymore and I kind of got everything I could out of it. . . . The process is so much more important than the results. I didn't think I wanted to do it anymore. . . . I was driven by fear. I wasn't 100 percent in it. . . . If I looked at myself in the mirror at 40 years old and hated my life, and had to start all over, that's my nightmare. Even if I had a nice secure job or a nice family, that's the thought that kept me up at night.

Jermaine had reached the realization that he was ready to prioritize his health and move forward with his life. Yet, the fear of potential regrets added complexity to the decision-making process. While he recognized that there were "greener pastures at the end of the tunnel," it did not buffer him from the doubt and insecurities of the transition. "I struggled with that, like, why can't I get this? They don't care. That's not how it works, the sooner you realize that reality, it's way easier." This conflict between prioritizing his health and considering the potential missed opportunities in professional sports showcases the difficult choices athletes often encounter during their transition out of competitive sports. Making decisions during this transition can be emotionally challenging, and considerations about potential regrets can heavily influence the choices athletes make.

FINDING SILVER LININGS AND GRATITUDE

In the midst of the grief and sadness that often accompanies athletic retirement, some athletes are able to find silver linings and positive aspects in the process. Having suffered so significantly during the end of her career, Beth explored her observation of the differences in the transition process between herself and her boyfriend who had been deselected. "I think I was a little more positive about it. I think I saw the light at the end of the tunnel and maybe he didn't. I just didn't find purpose in being sad about it and saying I worked so hard for this to happen. I saw it as an opportunity to create something new and go elsewhere, so I think I was kind of more helpful to him and he took it harder than I did." She recognized that while they shared similar struggles, she felt better able to cope due to her desire to remain as positive as possible. This ability to find silver linings highlights the resilience and adaptability that many athletes possess as they navigate this significant life transition.

Marshall reflected on his journey in professional football and shares a valuable perspective. He acknowledged that the true blessing lies in the fact that he had the opportunity to play at the professional level, recognizing how rare and challenging it is to achieve such a feat. Despite any disappointments or feelings of dissatisfaction along the way, he viewed his career as a series of stepping stones, each contributing to his growth and experiences as an athlete. "The only thing you take with it is the blessing that it got to happen, because there's millions of good guys out there who probably had an opportunity to make it and didn't, just because it's so hard to make it. . . . I was able to play professional football, if on the way out I was disappointed or felt anything less than satisfied . . . it's different stepping stones." This sentiment also recognizes that the path to success in sports, like many aspects of life, is filled with ups and downs. A focus on the process over the immediate results is deeply beneficial in navigating careers and career transitions. The overall journey holds its own significance beyond just the intermediate outcomes.

As some participants have had time to distance themselves from the events surrounding their retirement, they have found the opportunity for positive self-reflection. During this period of introspection, they have come to appreciate the person they have become and the manner in which they transformed challenging situations into successful careers. Joe shared that he harnessed his pain and grief to fuel his work ethic, using these emotions as a driving force to transform the narrative surrounding his experiences. Instead of dwelling on what happened to him, he channeled his energy into focusing on how those challenges paved the way for his future success.

> I can control what I can control, no one can stop me if I put in the extra work, I am going to get rewarded for it. I am going to be extremely successful, every kid that got preferential treatment for no reason from this coach is going to have a hard time, and I know that because they never had to go through things like I did. . . . Now I have a hard shell and now I'm going to be successful because of it. . . . It's just my mind structure where I'm using it as motivation to never let something like that happen to me again. . . . I went through insane and hard beatings so real life's a breeze. That's the positive that I'm taking from all of it. My career has been really good so far in the past two years. I've done extremely

> well, and I plan on doing extremely well in the future and I think so much of it is because of what I went through in some twisted way.

Even though the memories of his retirement remain exceptionally challenging, Joe channeled all the energy he would have dedicated to hockey into graduating early and positioning himself for the next phase of his life. Though this process served as a distraction, it also helped position him for the future. Through reflection, Joe has recognized that few future experiences are likely to be as challenging as what he has already faced, and he uses this realization as a reminder to cope with stressors in his daily life.

The athletes interviewed for this project discovered the resilience and strength within themselves that enabled them to navigate difficult transitions and forge fulfilling paths beyond their athletic careers. This positive self-reflection serves as a testament to their ability to find purpose and fulfillment in the face of life's changes, demonstrating the importance of self-awareness and adaptability as they move forward in their post-athletic lives.

Chapter 7

Navigating Athletic Retirement

Insights and Implications

For roughly the last half-century, scholars have extensively examined athletic identity and identity foreclosure concerning elite performance to gain deeper insights into their influence on athletes and their emotional well-being. The present study looked to add to the existing body of research by focusing on athletic identity and identity foreclosure in the context of elite performance and its impact on athletes' emotional well-being. Specifically, in this study, we closely examined the intersection of grief within the context of athletic identity and identity foreclosure among elite athletes, aiming to understand how the experience of grief may be intertwined with the loss of an athletic identity during retirement.

Qualitative research looks to center the subjective lived experience through open-ended questions that require deep reflection. Our project was able to place these narratives at the center of our analysis throughout the work. Undoubtedly, one of the biggest limitations of our project was that we had to rely on retrospective self-reported narratives of participants. It is certainly possible, if not likely, that participants were blinded to certain aspects of their transition or that they exaggerated other aspects of the process. We made extensive efforts to ask and reword questions in the interview process to ensure we were getting as valid an account as possible. Yet, whenever self-report is at the epicenter of social scientific research, lack of self-awareness can and will always provide limitations.

As mentioned in chapter 1, the participants in the present study acknowledged that sports culture, which begins at a young age, not only played a role in shaping their identities but also influenced their identity foreclosure process. A rigid sense of athletic identity, if it occurred, was shaped and established at a very young age, well before participants had the autonomy to make independent decisions about their personal interests and life paths. This early formation of their athletic identity was primarily influenced by external sources, including family, peers, teammates, and coaches.

Their earliest memories of engaging in sports at around 4 or 5 years old involved receiving reinforcement and recognition for their performance from significant individuals in their lives. These reinforcement patterns contributed to a strong association between participants' earliest sense of self-worth and their achievements in sports, making their athletic identity a central and defining aspect of their identity from a very young age. For example, and as mentioned in chapter 1, Hayden conveyed that the positive accolades he received reinforced his athletic talent and solidified his identity as an elite athlete. "I was 11 or 12 years old when the locals and my family really started to talk. I started to get headlines in the local newspapers about my performance. . . . You just run with it, then my personality starts kicking in."

The participants in the study highlighted the considerable impact of external influences and expectations on how they perceived and embraced their athletic roles throughout their careers. While the overwhelming majority genuinely enjoyed sports during their upbringing, they also expressed concerns about how sports culture shapes young athletes and potentially limits their developmental opportunities. Furthermore, they expressed concerns that sports culture may prioritize early specialization and intense training, which can lead to limited curiosity and exploration of other interests and passions. The emphasis on competitiveness and success often overshadowed other aspects of participants' development, such as education, social skills, and personal growth. Anna, lacking family influence emphasizing the importance of education, followed the advice of coaches who emphasized that her scholarship was primarily for playing hockey. "To this day I don't know if my coach was joking but he looked at me like, 'You know you've got all this money to play hockey, right? Not to take Bio class.'" Despite being a student-athlete at an academically elite American college, she revealed that she had been exposed to messages for a long time emphasizing that hockey came first, and school—or anything else—came second. As a result, it became easy for her to prioritize her sport over her education, leading her to miss the opportunity to adequately prepare for her life after sports. The prevailing belief that hockey was her primary focus made it challenging for her to dedicate the necessary energy and focus on her academic pursuits, ultimately impacting her post-sport life preparation. This decision became one that she regretted as she faced significant social, professional, and emotional challenges in finding a sense of purpose and a fulfilling career during retirement.

In general, engaging in appropriate levels of physical activity and participation in sports is linked to improved physical and mental health outcomes in children and adolescents (Bean et al., 2014; Brenner et al., 2019; Chang et al., 2020). However, sports culture, especially at a young age, can be unnecessarily intense and excessively competitive, transforming what should be an enjoyable and developmentally appropriate experience into a risky environment for these young athletes (Brenner et al., 2019). It often emphasizes early specialization and rigorous training regimens to achieve success in a specific sport (Bean et al., 2014; Jayanthi et al., 2013). Although this method might result in immediate improvements in athletic performance, it can and often does have adverse effects on other critical aspects of a young athlete's development (Brenner et al., 2019; Chang et al., 2020). Despite being a key feature of sports culture, there is a significant ongoing debate regarding the true necessity of early specialization, with some recommending that the sole focus on one sport at the exclusion of all others is not necessary until late adolescence (Jayanthi et al., 2013). In fact, research indicates that participating in multiple sports at early ages may lead to increased success in adult sports endeavors (Brenner et al., 2019), whereas specialization and the pressures associated have been correlated with symptoms of burnout.

Sport specialization arises from a combination of factors. Though it is not unique to American culture, it adeptly encompasses many modern American values—the drive for athletic achievement, financial incentives like collegiate scholarships, a pathway to acceptance at elite colleges and universities, and aspirations for professional or elite recognition, often shared by both parents and athletes. Nevertheless, this early focus on specialization comes with significant emotional costs for athletes and their families (Bean et al., 2014). The intensified training demands may lead to social isolation, hindered academic performance, elevated anxiety and stress levels, disrupted sleep patterns, reduced family bonding time, and psychological burnout among young athletes (Bean et al., 2014; Jayanthi et al., 2013). Participants in the current study shared experiences of witnessing burnout in their peers. They noticed that those who engaged in year-round sports activities tended to experience burnout over time. In contrast, some participants, such as Kurt and Steve, who had the opportunity to play multiple sports until a later stage in their high school years, felt that this diverse engagement helped prevent burnout and fostered a healthier relationship with sport. "All year-round sports stuff, they burn out. I played multiple sports all the way up until senior year of high school when I had to decide for college, so I didn't burn out" (Kurt). The observation of burnout in peers underscores the potential negative consequences of early specialization and the relentless focus on a single sport. Engaging in multiple sports allows young athletes to experience different physical and mental challenges, which can foster overall growth. Dannie attributed her mother's support and willingness to let her try various sports, including Irish step dancing, cheerleading, soccer, softball, and basketball, as a key factor in helping her remain humble about her athletic abilities. This openness to exploring different activities also contributed to her receptiveness to various ways of utilizing her skills beyond the realm of sports in retirement. This early diversification provides athletes with opportunities to develop various skills, work with different teams, and experience diverse coaching styles.

The impact of early sports specialization was evident among some of the participants in the study, as they made the significant decision to leave their homes before the age of 18 to pursue their sports career (Anna, Esteban, Joe, Henry). This early departure from home highlights the immense dedication and sacrifice required to pursue a specialized athletic career from a young age, potentially affecting their personal and family dynamics. Joe shared that he had a diverse background in various sports like baseball, basketball, and lacrosse, in addition to hockey. However, he had to make the decision at the age of 13 to specialize in hockey. "It got so competitive with other sports—with baseball and travel—that I had to choose hockey in the summers over everything else." This choice to specialize in hockey at a relatively young age highlights the challenges young athletes often face when balancing multiple sports and the pressure to focus on one sport for maximum performance and opportunities. For this participant, his coach forced him to decide between an opportunity of a lifetime hockey camp or continuing to play baseball. "I remember when I was 13, I was a pretty good baseball player and my travel coach said to me 'you can't play on this team if you don't come to this tournament,' and I got invited to this really exclusive hockey camp. He basically said that if you go to this camp, you're done. You can't play baseball for this township. You can't get anything else. You have to commit to it." At the age of 13, Joe was already involved in a dedicated training regimen, working closely with a personal trainer and a nutritionist to enhance his athletic performance. However, these commitments came at a cost, as he recalls having to sacrifice the opportunity to engage in "regular kid things" that most children his age typically enjoyed. "I didn't have friends in high school. . . . I was just on my own little island where I would get out of school an hour early, go skate for a couple hours, eat dinner, then go to practice, come home and shoot pucks at night."

At the time, Joe didn't perceive any void in his life as he was entirely immersed in the world of hockey. However, it took several years before he came to the realization that he had more to his identity beyond being a hockey player, something that has only occurred in the wake of his retirement.

> This has been a really interesting year and a half, where I finally separated it. I'm like wow, I'm a regular person. I have a working brain, and I'm a functional member of society and I have a job that I'm good at. I like learning and I like reading and I can try to learn how to play golf, play the guitar. This is the first time in my life where I am able to compartmentalize that guy and kind of get

> away from him. . . . That was naturally done to me based on what my life was and where I was living, because I was a hockey player.

Joe came to recognize that his life had organically revolved around hockey, primarily due to his unwavering commitment to the sport and the environment in which he lived. This singular focus on hockey overshadowed other aspects of his identity and life, making it challenging for him to see beyond the athlete persona he had developed and limiting his experiences. After experiencing significant loss in his sports career, Joe gradually gained the perspective to realize that he had other interests, passions, and dimensions to explore beyond the hockey world. It took time, but he eventually embraced the idea of a multifaceted identity outside of sports. This awareness allowed him to expand his previously foreclosed sense of self and embrace the person he was beyond being solely defined by his athletic pursuits.

Many participants also experienced significant challenges and trade-offs during their athletic careers, leading them to reflect on whether the personal costs ultimately outweigh the benefits they gained from their sports pursuits. Juan expressed that his sports career came with significant costs, particularly in terms of his relationships with friends and family. "I feel like I really had to sacrifice a lot. . . . Whether it's time with friends and family, that's a big one . . . the whole time at college, I spent every summer at school and only went home for major holidays." Erica, now a coach, shared her observations of players facing significant challenges due to the pressure to perform at a young age instead of simply enjoying the game. She noticed that "starting at 11 years old, girls are stressed, they're stressed out, their parents are putting immense pressure on them."

Similarly, Jermaine recognized that the coaching and training he received during his early football career were reflective of a broader sports culture that encourages young athletes to prioritize sports above all else in their lives."You're programmed not to shut it off. . . . It shouldn't consume your life, but it does. You have to eat right, sleep right, stay on top of your books so you can practice and do your football things. . . . But that's real in every single sport. Your life is centered around it and it's hard to shut it off. But being able to shut it off is the best advice you could give to any college athlete." The prevailing sports culture often emphasizes the importance of relentless dedication and singular focus on the pursuit of athletic excellence. As a result, young athletes may find themselves fully immersed in this mindset, with sports taking center stage in their lives. The participants in this study eventually came to the realization that they spent much of their youth constantly looking ahead, never allowing themselves to pause, explore, and fully enjoy their experiences. The intense drive to achieve and excel in their athletic careers often kept them focused on the next goal or milestone, leaving little time to savor the present moments or explore other aspects of life beyond sports. Beth shared: "Honestly, my high school friends and I talk about this all the time. . . . I remember all my friends in high school and I were so looking forward to our scholarships and playing college. And then looking back now, we all agree that playing in high school was the best time of our life. It was the most fun we had." She shared recognizing that looking forward kept her from enjoying the moments that she had. While recognizing that forward thinking is developmentally appropriate for adolescents, she cautioned against letting the pursuit of future goals overshadow the importance of enjoying current opportunities. "I would say not to miss opportunities, because you're looking forward to other things and just enjoy every second for what you can. . . . It really just goes so fast." This perpetual forward-looking mindset led these participants to miss out on the opportunity to fully appreciate and embrace the richness of their experiences along the way.

Henry shared similar sentiments about missed experiences due to a sense of forward focus. Furthermore, he expressed how this focus can lead to missing out on valuable experiences in the present. By always looking ahead and fixating on future goals, one may inadvertently overlook the significance and richness of the experiences unfolding in the here and now. "Just remember the journey because I think, and I'm like this too, it's like what's next and how can I keep this going, so with that what's next focus you forget about all the good that's happened. . . . Don't forget about it. . . . Don't sacrifice next year to not be able to remember or take pride in the previous 19 or whatever I used to have." In Henry's perspective, a fulfilling and well-lived career is characterized by striking a balance between the motivation and drive to achieve more and a deep sense of appreciation for what has already been accomplished. The sacrifices and experiences shared by the participants in the study resonate with the growing concerns surrounding the legitimacy of the long-held assumption of a connection between early specialized training and future athletic success (Bean et al., 2014; Brenner et al., 2019). As more athletes and researchers shed light on the long-term implications of early specialization, questions arise regarding the impact on overall physical and psychological well-being, the risk of burnout, and the potential for injuries due to repetitive stress (Bean et al., 2014; Brenner et al., 2019). Moreover, the limited exposure to various activities and interests during critical developmental years raises concerns about the broader personal growth and identity formation of young athletes.

Even among athletes who were not exposed to early specialization, they expressed concerns about its impact on the development of young athletes. Steve shared that he gained an understanding of the harmful effects of early sports specialization from his coaching experiences. Steve, who had previously been a three-sport athlete, did not face the same pressure to exclusively dedicate himself to one sport, like some of the other participants. "I hate everything about specializing. . . . You don't have a proper perspective when you're in that world. When you're 13 years old and you're basically told 'Don't worry about your friends, we'll take care of school, don't worry about other things you might have that you love. Your path is football or baseball. We're going to play all summer; we're going to go to every invite. We got to get you exposure.' The kid is 13, he can't even spell exposure. And then the pressure, I see it all of the time." Steve shared that his most significant challenges as a coach stem from his difficulties in effectively communicating to parents the adverse effects of early sports specialization on the overall development of young athletes. "The piece I can't do anything about, no matter how hard I try, is the parent piece. And I wish I could get through to the parents . . . because they are doing irreparable damage to their kid. . . . They're trying to do what's best for them, but I often think how much of this is about you and not your son or your daughter. . . . I'll talk to parents about it and they'll nod their head like, 'yeah I totally agree with you' and everything I tell them not to do, they do they do the following summer."

Consistent with previous literature, the results of the current research indicates that the essential aspect in the relationship between sport specialization and mental health is not necessarily the specific type or quantity of activities young athletes participate in, but rather their continued enjoyment of the sports experience (Brenner et al., 2019). Steve shared that during his athletic career, mental health was rarely addressed or discussed, and this realization has influenced his approach as a coach. As a coach, he has made a conscious effort to change the narrative by creating a supportive environment for athletes to openly talk about their lives. "When I do things, I know there is a ramification of how I talk to a kid. I don't know everything about that kid. Maybe he is driven, but maybe he's really vulnerable, maybe he's a fragile kid in some ways that I don't ever see. Maybe his homelife isn't great. So, I always try to strip it back and say, "Talk to me first about you. I'll talk to you about the football piece after that. . . . I want to hear how your day is going, how school is going, how's your family?" Steve underscores the importance of being aware of the impact that words and interactions can have on the young athletes. By prioritizing their well-being and creating an open and supportive space for them to share their thoughts and feelings, he is better able to support them not only as athletes but also as individuals with unique needs and aspirations.

For all the athletes in the current study, as we saw in chapter 5, the initial love and passion they had for the sport eventually diminished, and an overwhelming feeling emerged that it had turned into a job or a chore. Kendrick characterized the transition into college as a significant shift in the demands of sports in his life, accompanied by psychosocial pressure arising from the emotional and physical challenges he faced. "It's a job, especially when you get to the collegiate level, you have all these classes, you have papers, you've got practice, you've got to lift. And then you know, you've got games where you always get beat up and you're never a hundred percent. . . . It's a lot." Much to his dismay, the sport that once brought him joy and fulfillment transformed into something that felt more like an obligation. Kendrick shared that enjoying playing is one of the biggest things elite athletes should focus on. "If you're not enjoying it, you're eventually going to get burned out, and it's not going to feel the same, and it's going to feel like more of a job than something you are really enjoying." His experience confirmed that finding joy and pleasure in the sport itself is fundamental to managing psychosocial challenges and avoiding burnout while competing at an elite level, a sentiment echoed by many of the athletes in our study.

Jess also offered a cautionary note against turning sports into a job too early, emphasizing the negative consequences of losing the joy and passion that sports can bring to one's life. "Keep going if it's still fun for you, once it starts feeling like a job, if you're in like 8th grade and it feels like a job, you've got a long road ahead of you. If you're having fun and it's not about the mental toughness for you yet, it's not about politics or anything outside of the sport itself, just try to focus on having fun, because that's why we all started playing in the first place." Jess's advice underscores the importance of maintaining a healthy and balanced perspective on sports. A sentiment echoed by Erica who shared her perspective on the importance of allowing young athletes to continue deriving pleasure and fulfillment from their athletic pursuits without undue pressure and demands. "I think it's important that they don't lose sight of that (that they are more than an athlete) and that they have fun, and that they remember to be kids and enjoy it."

Participants in this study acknowledged that intense focus and dedication to their athletic careers was instrumental in achieving the elite level of performance they reached. However, this singular focus also had a significant impact on their psychosocial stress during elite performance and the ease of transition into retirement. They discovered that they were ill-prepared for the emotional challenges associated with retiring from their sport. The messages they internalized throughout their athletic journey, emphasizing the importance of playing for as long as possible, left them without a solid foundation for envisioning what their post-athletic lives should entail.

Jermaine expressed that he had never considered the possibility of finding a fulfilling and purposeful life after sports because the messages he received early on did not encourage exploration beyond his athletic career. "I never realized that. I was just told, 'Kids would kill for your spot. Your dad would kill for that.' I think that is true, but your life can be just as fulfilling after sport and that never really clicked for me." It took time for him to realize that there are other avenues in life that can provide fulfillment and purpose beyond being an athlete, and this realization came after he questioned and challenged the messages he had internalized throughout his athletic career and development. Similarly, Chris, like many other athletes, did not give much thought to the transition into retirement. This lack of preparedness, combined with the burnout he experienced, hindered his ability to find the internal motivation necessary to explore and diversify his identity in retirement. "I wish I was more motivated for the transition, but I didn't ever think about what the transition would be like. I wasn't really motivated to look, and when it happened, I wasn't motivated to do anything, and I do regret that. I think I would be a better person and a better dad if I had something to light my fire and get me going."

As discussed in chapter 5, the psychological burden of elite competition and performance weighs on athletes well before they reach the stage of retirement, with recent research identifying elite athletes as a high-risk group for mental health challenges (Balcome & De Leo, 2020) such as anxiety and depression (Rice et al., 2016). This risk tends to increase during the transitional phase into retirement for athletes or other major disruptions such as injury. The unpredictable nature of an athletic career as well as the mental health struggles arising from the competitive sports culture can significantly influence the coping process during retirement.

Participants in the current study described their experiences as an "emotional roller coaster," where they encountered day-to-day fluctuations in emotions and challenges (Erica, Joe, Tim). Erica expresses the intense stress and pressure associated with the weekly process of waiting to find out if they would be included in the lineup for the upcoming games. "It was really stressful, he would post a lineup like Thursday before games and like, you know, your heart would be pounding as you walk up to see if you're playing. I think that was really hard, whether I noticed, knew it at the time or not. It's like so much stress. . . . There were a lot of negatives." This aspect of competitive sports can contribute to heightened anxiety and anticipation, as players eagerly await the decision that could impact their participation in the game and their role within the team. In line with previous research, the participants in the current study encountered numerous athletic-specific stressors, including injuries, performance pressure, fatigue, and organizational factors such as poor coach relationships and unsupportive coaching styles (Rice et al., 2016). The constant pressures athletes face throughout their careers can impact their motivation, and some of the participants in the study struggled to find effective ways to cope with these stressors. Jermaine describes the pressure to always be on. "It's tough, you're supposed to be the best, train to be the best, and train harder than the guy next to you. Pass your peers, you only have so much willpower and energy. . . . There are other parts of your life."

This participant acknowledged the importance of self-care and taking time to decompress, rather than constantly being connected to the athletic identity.

In addition to the messages they received about the importance of performance, the athletes also acknowledged how their athletic prowess elevated them to a significant social status at a young age, creating an environment that treated them like celebrities. They recognized the detrimental influence this celebrity status had on their development, creating a glorified sense of self, specifically related to their athletic identity. The recognition and admiration they received for their athletic achievements further solidified their identities as athletes and reinforced the perception of their worth being tied to their performance. Anna shared that transitioning from a lack of confidence in high school to suddenly being at the top of the world in college, where they felt like she could do no wrong, was a significant culture shock. Erica described the elated feeling that came along with being recognized as an athlete on a division 1 campus. "I liked the title; I liked everything it represented. . . . The athletes have their special clothes that they would wear, and even in my classes I would have team-issued gear and everyone looks like, 'There's an athlete in my class.' So, I always had this almost superiority thing, which is so embarrassing to say, but honestly, that is what it was." She shared that her most fulfilling moments as an athlete did not actually take place on the ice but rather during the instances when she was celebrated and admired by fans for her athletic accomplishments. This acknowledgment from the public served as a powerful validation of her hard work and dedication to her sport, one that she still enjoys to this day. "It was a huge deal, I was like signing autographs in the concourse with a line of maybe 50 kids or parents. . . . I think that's my peak athletic moment, not even in a competition."

These sentiments were echoed by Joe sharing that there is a lot of clout associated with being a collegiate athlete on campus. "Everyone knew who you were. The teachers knew, they were extra nice to you. It was a complete culture shock for me seeing how much people cared about me. It was a massive part of my identity." Hayden likewise acknowledged that the culture of sports competition is designed to glorify the athlete's sense of self, and he admitted that he thoroughly enjoyed this aspect of being an athlete. "It really makes you feel elite. You are walking in as a young man where everything is done for you. It would be like going to a country club where the minute your car pulls in, they are grabbing your bags and asking if you need anything. All the conditions are absolutely perfect. I absolutely loved it." This positive feedback loop within the sports culture can contribute to the powerful allure of sports competition and the sense of self-gratification experienced by athletes.

Henry also enjoyed the positive regard that came with his athletic accomplishments. "There was definitely a time in my life where I relished in the favoritism that you get from what you were doing athletically." Different from the previous passages, he also highlights that while being in the public eye as an athlete can come with recognition, admiration, and a sense of accomplishment, it also brings its own set of challenges and pressures. For Henry, he recalls watching his peers struggle when the admiration dissipated. "Some guys really struggle when they are not treated the same anymore because they are not in hockey." Joe similarly identified that this was a struggle he personally experienced. "I think it's easy to get wrapped up in that. I struggled with it, not being 'special' anymore. Where you feel like you're something then you're not once you're done."

Additionally, athletes in the public eye often face scrutiny, criticism, and judgment from both fans and media (Cosh et al., 2015). This constant spotlight can take a toll on their mental and emotional well-being, leading to stress, anxiety, and even negative effects on their self-esteem and self-worth. Consistent with the previous literature, the heightened presence in the public eye magnified the psychosocial challenges reported by the athletes. Kendrick aptly emphasizes this idea, stating: "External pressures put immense weight on you, and when you don't meet their expectations, which are often unreasonably high, it can be really damaging to one's athletic identity." He reflected on his high school experiences, which underscored the importance of finding a balance between the external noise and judgments to safeguard one's emotional well-being. "I had a lot of pressure when I was in high school, athletes everywhere have pressure, high school, college, everyone. It's one of those things where you go and have a great game and people praise you, but once you have a bad game, you can see this with Lebron, they try to tear you down, like, 'He's not good,' or, 'He's playing bad.'"

Kendrick's insights highlight the challenges athletes face in managing the external expectations and pressures while preserving a healthy and positive sense of self within their athletic identity. Chris echoed these sentiments and conveyed the burden of negative feedback that elite athletes often face. "Everyone knows who you are, which is great, but there's also negative to that, it's very intense when people aren't happy with you, whether it's opposing fans or your own. . . . It's just a hard profession." For many athletes who were deeply immersed in the highs and lows of the performance narrative, maintaining psychosocial well-being, and not letting the pressure impact them was a challenging task.

Equally troubling is the correlation between the idealized self-image of elite athletes and the romanticized public perception of their careers. This connection may significantly discourage athletes from discussing the stress they experience. Hayden identified this experience as "there is a piece of you that doesn't feel human. It's a really weird experience. . . . It would baffle people if you explain to them that the job sucks right now, baseball is horrific, and you were so down about it." Many of the participants received messaging that portrayed their athletic career as the dream job, perpetuating a fantasy created by the external world. This idealized image puts pressure on athletes to conform to the expectations of others and "give them what they want" (Hayden), which can have the unintended consequence of disenfranchising athletes' actual distress experiences.

As presented in the current study, by perpetuating the notion that elite athletes lead perfect and stress-free lives, society may dismiss or invalidate the genuine challenges and emotional struggles that athletes face throughout their careers and in retirement. This disenfranchisement can create a barrier for athletes to express their true feelings and seek the support they need, as their distress experiences are not fully recognized or acknowledged by others. During Jermaine's attempt to discuss the fading opportunity of making it to the NFL and his desire to explore other aspects of his identity, the messages he received from other important people in his life played a role in intensifying the distress he experienced during his transition. The lack of understanding and empathy from those around him marginalized and invalidated his psychosocial experiences, making it more challenging for him to navigate through this period of change.

Deonte highlights the role of feeling misunderstood and the experience of stigma in the challenges of transitioning to retirement. "It's hard, especially today, we have the stigma, you have your parents behind you saying you should be doing this, your friends saying you should be doing this, your coworkers looking at you like you're crazy. . . . They're like 'what is he doing?' There's so much stigma." Historically, the understanding of challenges in athletic retirement predominantly revolved around individual factors within the athletes themselves (Cosh et al., 2015; McGannon et al., 2022). This individual-centered perspective overlooks the broader systemic and societal factors that can influence athletes' retirement experiences, such as the sports culture, support systems, and opportunities available for post-athletic careers (Cosh et al., 2015). As a result, athletes' transition experiences may be overlooked and even labeled as abnormal or pathological, despite being a common occurrence in the retirement process.

The overwhelming majority of participants in the current study identified the period of transition as challenging, however, the grief experience of the participants was notably differentiated by the level of identity foreclosure they experienced. This finding aligns with previous research, which links high athletic identification to increased challenges during the transition to retirement (Fortunato & Marchant, 1999; Lavallee et al., 2007; Manthey & Smith, 2023; Menke & Germany, 2019; Miller & Buttell, 2018). The fundamental difference explored in the study was the distinction between "who I am" (personal identity) and "what I do" (occupation or activities). Participants were divided based on whether they primarily defined themselves based on their role as athletes (personal identity) or if they considered their athletic career as one aspect of their life.

For participants who experienced severe foreclosure of their athletic identity, their transition into athletic retirement was marked by considerable challenges and difficulties including feeling lost, experiencing symptoms of depression and anxiety, and engaging in denial. Other factors, such as the quality of their social support networks, the circumstances surrounding their retirement (Alfermann et al., 2004), and the attainment of their sports-related career goals, also contributed to their overall experience during the transition into retirement (Park et al., 2013). Athletes who believed they had done everything possible to succeed in their sport, or who achieved the goals they had set for themselves, experienced an easier time accepting their retirement. As explored in chapter 4, this study aligns with previous research, highlighting the connection between positive social support and successful adjustment to retirement. However, what sets this study apart is that for many participants, the mere presence of supportive individuals was not enough to facilitate the transition process. The athletes themselves needed to be in a mindset where they could accept help and be prepared to embrace the transition, making this aspect unique to our findings.

The distinction between planned and voluntary retirement versus unplanned and involuntary retirement can result in varying emotional reactions and coping strategies (Alfermann et al., 2004; Küttel et al., 2017; McGlinchey et al., 2022). Notably, the level of control an athlete has over the decision to retire has been found to correlate with the degree of distress experienced during retirement (Silver, 2021). Athletes who have a greater sense of agency and control in making the retirement decision are often better prepared for the transition and may experience lower levels of distress compared to those whose retirement is imposed on them involuntarily (Alfermann et al. 2004). Similar to the previous research, the current study found that, while none of the athletes were immune from the challenges of the transition to retirement, those who perceived the decision to retire as being out of their control had a significantly more difficult time adjusting to the change and experienced the most intense grief reactions. The lack of agency and autonomy in the retirement process seemed to amplify the emotional distress and hurdles faced by these athletes as they navigated the post-sports phase of their lives. This observation holds particularly true for athletes who have faced a career-ending injury. Research has shown that these athletes tend to encounter more significant challenges in social and emotional adjustment to retirement compared to those who retire voluntarily or due to other reasons (Lavallee et al., 1997; Martin et al., 2014). The sudden and unexpected nature of a career-ending injury can shatter an athlete's sense of identity, purpose, and future plans, leading to heightened psychosocial stressors during the retirement transition.

Many athletes in the current study expressed that even in retirement, they found themselves stuck in the pattern of constantly trying to prove themselves. This perpetuated the cycle of striving to stay relevant, a mindset they had become accustomed to in their athletic careers. Now, faced with life beyond sports, they were confronted with the challenge of proving that they were more than just athletes. Kurt expressed his desire to be recognized for his personal attributes rather than solely for his past athletic accomplishments and working hard to prove himself in his current career. "I don't go around telling people I played football. It eventually comes out because they either look me up or they'll find out and say, 'I didn't know you played in the NFL.' So, they probably look at me like, 'Oh my God, a professional athlete.' I try to succeed, to do well and to prove myself outside of being a football player, I think they look at me in that light." This pattern of needing to validate their worth beyond their athletic achievements underscored the long-lasting impact of the sports culture that places immense pressure on athletes to define themselves solely through their athletic success. Even in retirement, the athletes felt the weight of expectations and the need to demonstrate their value in other aspects of life. Despite having a more balanced perspective on identity development and receiving ongoing messages from his parents about developing all aspects of himself, this participant still experienced the influence of external validation. This suggests that the culture of seeking approval and recognition from others, especially in the context of sports, can be pervasive and challenging to overcome.

For athletes such as Joe who had not fully foreclosed his athletic identity, there were still serious difficulties faced in the transition process. Though he had dedicated the foreseeable future to his hockey career, the impact of his traumatic deselection process has brought about significant distress and an intense grief reaction. Even though he has built a successful career after sports, he continues to grapple with grief, and the events that led to his retirement still haunt him. It seems he is caught in a state of uncertainty, torn between the narrative that marked the end of his athletic career and the confusion surrounding these events that hinder closure. Joe has aspired to embrace a post-sport narrative of success, happiness, and resilience, qualities he possesses, but he struggles to fully internalize this new version of himself due to a disrupted worldview. In a similar vein, Issa shared that it took her 3 or 4 years to begin to move forward from the traumatic ending of her career and to find a way to heal the fear that connected her mind and body.

CONSIDERATIONS FOR SUPPORTING IDENTITY DIVERSIFICATION

While extensive research on athletic retirement underscores the significance of preparing athletes for this life-changing transition (Chang et al., 2020; Miller & Buttell, 2018), the retirement process brings forth various psychosocial stressors, and effective preparation is crucial in mitigating their impact (Menke & Germany, 2019). However, despite this recognition, there exists a lack of consistency in the application and approach of such preparation interventions. Prior studies have proposed that interventions tailored to educate retiring athletes on identity expansion, coping skills development, and social support building have the potential to influence the severity of mental health symptoms and foster resilience during the retirement period (Menke & Germany, 2019; Miller & Buttell, 2018). Research has shown that athletes in career planning prior to retirement experienced higher levels of perceived self-efficacy when transitioning to retirement (Martin et al., 2014). Additionally, these athletes have been found to engage more effectively with available resources (Alfermann et al., 2004). Despite these research insights, the athletes in the present study revealed that they did not have access to formal resources or interventions. Surprisingly, when Tim sought information online about athletes' struggles, he discovered that while mental health challenges were well-documented, strategies to support these athletes were lacking. "I found the articles that are out there on depression and athletes, anxiety, suicide, and all these nasty things. But I didn't find any information around here's how you can help. Here's how athletes can be supported. Here's how I did it. Here's the playbook." This finding underscores a significant gap in the support systems available to athletes, particularly during their transition to retirement. Although mental health challenges among athletes are acknowledged, there is a pressing need for more comprehensive resources and targeted interventions that address the unique psychosocial and emotional needs of athletes as they navigate life after sports.

From an external viewpoint, introducing opportunities for elite athletes to diversify their identities before retirement may appear to be a reasonable intervention to enhance the transition process and reduce postretirement challenges. However, it could be ill-timed and impractical to expect elite athletes, who are intensely focused on staying competitive and extending their careers, to engage in activities that might divert energy from their primary athletic pursuits. The drive to continue competing at a high level may make it challenging for them to explore other interests or potential post-athletic pathways during their peak performance years. As such, finding the right timing and approach for offering such opportunities to elite athletes requires careful consideration of their current career demands and goals.

Although there exists an extensive body of research concerning the challenges athletes encounter during retirement, particularly regarding identity foreclosure and the necessity for diversification, there is relatively limited discourse on the precise role that sports culture plays in influencing these challenges (Cosh et al., 2015). Experiences of the participants in the current study underscore that while identity foreclosure indeed influences the adjustment to retirement, it is possible that this focus on identity foreclosure may be directing attention toward the outcome rather than addressing the actual root cause of the problem—the very culture of sports. This culture perpetuates the belief among athletes that foreclosure is the sole path to attaining elite status, which as we have seen in the current study, is not the case. Previous research has demonstrated that athletes who dedicate themselves to both their academic and athletic pursuits tend to perform better in sports (Miller & Kerr, 2002). Contrary to the notion of fixed identities, individuals can successfully navigate multiple identities, allowing them to effectively manage the complexities of life (Hickey & Roderick, 2017). This finding underscores the significance of acknowledging and embracing the multiplicity of identities that athletes can cultivate throughout their entire careers, starting from a young age. Rather than solely focusing on the transitional period near retirement, it is essential to foster a holistic approach to athlete development that supports the coexistence of various identities from the outset.

Given the profound psychosocial stressors encountered by elite athletes during their careers, it is challenging to comprehend that we did not foresee the substantial impact on athlete mental health. Moreover, our hesitation to acknowledge the negative influence of sports culture on elite athletes leads us to attribute both the problem and the solution solely to the athlete (Cosh et al., 2015). This approach alone will never fully address the underlying systemic root of the problem. While providing support and interventions to individual athletes is essential, a comprehensive solution must also tackle the broader systemic issues within sports culture.

Athletic culture can enhance retirement preparation by initiating discussions about career-related topics with students from a young age and preparing them for the emotional and social challenges that are commonly encountered during this phase. Normalizing these experiences can foster greater resilience and acceptance, while decreasing pathology and blame. Encouraging ongoing discussions about skill transfer promotes the continuous development of their complete selves, extending beyond the identity of being elite athletes. This approach nurtures their holistic growth, empowering them to see themselves as versatile individuals with valuable attributes that transcend the boundaries of sports.

In the present study, participants readily acknowledged the skills that played a vital role in their athletic success, such as work ethic, dedication, leadership skills, etc. Moreover, many recognized that these same skills could be applied to ensure success in various areas of their lives. However, a distinction arose between two groups of participants: those who believed they were successful in sports because they possessed these skills, and those who believed they had these skills solely because they were athletes. The first group perceived their success in sports as a result of their inherent skills and abilities. They believed that these skills were part of their identity and had contributed to their achievements as athletes. On the other hand, the second group saw their skills as primarily tied to their identity as athletes. They felt that being an athlete had cultivated these skills within them, and they may not have developed them to the same extent had they not pursued a sports career. The participants in the latter group initially struggled with self-awareness, which hindered their ability to effectively transfer these skills to other areas of their lives. As a result, they faced greater challenges in answering the fundamental question of "Who am I now?" during their transition from elite athletics to retirement. For example, Deonte often reflected on the strong work ethic he cultivated while playing football, using it as a reminder that he can overcome difficult moments. He drew from the resilience he developed during his football career, knowing that he has faced far more challenging situations in the past than he is currently encountering. On the other hand, when Tim encountered challenges in retirement, he perceived himself as a failure and found it difficult to draw upon the same persistence and determination that had been instrumental throughout his entire football career.

The current study revealed that many participants did not receive messages that encouraged them to view themselves as multifaceted individuals. For instance, Tim shared his experience of feeling like his coaches did not prioritize seeing him as a human being first, which resulted in a lack of effort to nurture his holistic development. "I wish I would have been taught that I'm a human being first and being an athlete was just what I did. Knowing that would have served me long into my career and into my life afterwards. Not having that connection left me at the mercy of just wherever life would take me, and I found myself settling for mediocrity, I never wanted to do that in sport as an athlete." He expressed that lacking a strong sense of self beyond sports hindered his self-awareness and understanding of how his skills and experiences as an elite athlete could be transferred to new contexts. While he had always pushed himself to grow and excel in sport, he was "not using that same superpower" in his life post sport, being satisfied with just getting by with finding a job to pay the bills. This change in mindset reflects a common challenge faced by many athletes during their transition to life beyond sports. Without a clear sense of purpose and direction, they may lose sight of their innate drive to succeed and struggle to apply their athletic skills and work ethic to other aspects of life.

When considering the role of sports in nurturing well-rounded and responsible citizens, Dannie shared her apprehensions. “I get so nervous because I don’t know if it is being done right. There is that pressure that I don’t think really should be there.” Dannie’s comment reflects concerns about how the current approach to sports might be exerting unnecessary pressure on athletes and potentially detracting from the intended goal of developing character and responsibility. The pressure to perform at a high level may overshadow the focus on imparting valuable life skills and positive values to athletes, leading to a need for reevaluation and potential changes in the way sports are conducted and experienced to better achieve these developmental objectives.

By addressing the structural factors that contribute to identity foreclosure, psychosocial stressors, and challenges in retirement, we can create a more supportive and sustainable environment for elite athletes. This involves examining coaching practices, organizational policies, societal expectations, and the overall culture within sports to create positive and holistic change for athletes at all levels. The responsibility of effecting change must extend beyond the individual athlete to all stakeholders involved in sports, including coaches, administrators, governing bodies, media outlets, and even fans. While no single entity can enact change alone, it is essential to acknowledge the role that each stakeholder plays in shaping the sports culture and creating a climate that is fueling psychosocial stressors. Only by acknowledging and addressing the systemic roots can we foster lasting improvements in athletes’ well-being and retirement experiences.

REFLECTIONS FROM THE JOURNEY: ATHLETES’ ADVICE FOR THE NEXT GENERATION

The participants in the current study acknowledged that with the benefit of hindsight, certain aspects of their athletic journeys have become much clearer to them. They have gained valuable insights and wisdom that they wish they had known when they were actively competing. Reflecting on their experiences, they have identified key lessons and advice that could have positively influenced their athletic careers and personal development.

Issa stressed the importance of prioritizing one’s mental health and offered valuable advice to achieve this by recognizing that sports should not be the sole focal point in life. Despite having experienced identity foreclosure herself, she expressed that the price paid for this was considerable. “Don’t take it too seriously, you can work really hard and love it, but not let it hurt your mental health. I was pretty obsessive, everything I did was surrounding hockey . . . it was not a healthy mindset." Her advice serves as a reminder for athletes to find a healthy equilibrium between dedication and mental well-being, ensuring that their athletic pursuits bring joy and fulfillment without compromising their overall mental health.

Erica, fully aware that it is not an easy task amid the pressures of elite competition, highlighted the undeniable reality that sports performance has a limited time frame. She emphasizes that fixating solely on metrics such as wins and losses can detract from recognizing what truly matters—the relationships forged along the journey.

> At the end of the day, it's going to end for everybody. Whether it ends before you get to college or after division 1, or at the Olympics, it is going to end for all of you. What is important is that you make relationships and develop into a good person and care about others. . . . All of your wins and losses, everything you do at this age is irrelevant. . . . When I look back at my years that I played, I'm not thinking oh we won this game 4–2, I look back and say this is my bridesmaid, this is my best friend, and this is a hilarious time we got stuck on a train. These are the girls who went through it with me and I love them.

Erica's insight serves as a poignant reminder that the camaraderie and bonds formed in sports can leave a lasting impact, surpassing the transient nature of competitive outcomes. She also emphasized the essence of sports, which should be the holistic development of the individual, rather than solely focusing on athletic ability. Athletics should encompass personal growth, character development, and the acquisition of life skills that extend far beyond the playing field. While athletic success is commendable, the ultimate achievement in sports as Dannie previously described lies in building resilient, compassionate, and well-rounded individuals. Jermaine has valuable advice to young athletes, urging them to learn the skill of compartmentalizing their athletic identity. By doing so, they can avoid tying their entire self-worth solely to their achievements in sports. "You have to have a social life, a school life, a family life. You have to have other stuff, and your life doesn't have to be centered around sport. When I was in the beginning of my career, I really struggled with that. I put so much into it, but it's like, man, there's way more to life and to college than just playing your sport." He emphasized the importance of keeping in mind that "at the end of the day, it's just a sport." Moreover, he recognized that the most significant takeaways from his sports career were the lifelong relationships he formed with his teammates, even if he couldn't fully grasp their value at the time.

The athletes in the current study acknowledged that fear and identity foreclosure frequently deterred them from engaging in activities outside of sports, a decision they now regret in retirement. Their singular focus on sports prevented them from exploring other opportunities and experiences that could have enriched their lives beyond athletics. They shared hoping that future athletes will recognize the influence of fear on their decision-making and push through it. Deonte advised about the benefit of being multifaceted in one's desires and curiosity during and after one's athletic career. "Don't be afraid to try as many things as you can as far as jobs, as far as extracurriculars. Don't be afraid to jump into as many things as you can because you never know what you're going to find that you actually love. Because life is really a journey. . . . Don't try to limit your experience of life, try to do as many things as you can and meet as many people as you can." This advice, in hindsight, serves as a valuable lesson for him and for other athletes who are approaching similar junctures in their lives, encouraging them to seize opportunities and explore all that life has to offer beyond their athletic careers.

Tim acknowledged that his identity foreclosure during his athletic career hindered him from exploring his other interests and developing his whole self. Now in his forties, he realizes that he has a lot of catching up to do in terms of self-discovery and personal growth.

> I would say go explore and touch all the elements of life that excite you, that turn you on, that you have any sort of inkling towards, music, theater, whatever. Knitting, I don't care. It's whatever has some sort of interest for you because now I have children and I have my oldest son who is really interested in music and he's really good at it. And I'm sitting here, now in my 40s, I wish I would have explored music way back when, I don't know how I would have, where I would have fit it in, but I really wish I had and I'm trying to pick it up now because I want the same experience.

His journey serves as a valuable lesson for both current and future athletes, emphasizing the importance of embracing various interests and aspects of life beyond sports. By fostering a sense of self that extends beyond athletics, athletes can better prepare themselves for a fulfilling and meaningful life after retirement, equipped with the tools to explore new opportunities and pursue a range of passions.

Some participants in the study acknowledged that while their athletic skills could be applied to various aspects of life beyond sports, they faced challenges in knowing when to stop and when to turn them off. In the competitive world of sports, athletes often develop a relentless drive and intense focus on improving their performance. This single-minded determination can be advantageous in the pursuit of athletic excellence but may create difficulties in transitioning to other domains of life. Deonte depicted this well when he talked about how his work ethic keeps him from allowing himself to stop when he is tired. "Even right now, doing real estate, I'm tired as hell, it might be eleven o'clock at night, and someone's calling me looking for an apartment, there's always going to be that one part of my mind that's like, 'I'm tired, I don't want to do this.' But I learned that when you're tired there's always more on top of that you can do. . . . Even when you're tired, there's another level you can take it to." For athletes like Deonte, the mindset of pushing through fatigue and discomfort has been deeply ingrained through their sports training. In the pursuit of excellence, they may have been conditioned to disregard signs of exhaustion or to view taking breaks as a sign of weakness. This mindset, while beneficial in the competitive world of sports, can have adverse effects on an athlete's well-being and overall life balance.

Kurt also acknowledged his struggles with turning off his work ethic echoing the sentiments shared by many elite athletes as they transition into life beyond sports. As an elite athlete, his identity may have been deeply intertwined with his reputation as a hard worker and high achiever, and the need to find balance in retirement. "I'm trying to make sure I work on making sure that it doesn't consume me. I'm a lot better at it now than I was in football." Moving from an all-encompassing athletic career to a more well-rounded life is a gradual process, as revealed by the athletes in the current study. They emphasized the importance of developing self-awareness, a point that Tim stressed when offering advice to aspiring athletes. "Get a strong sense of who you are because you are not an athlete, it's what you do; identify with who you are." Developing a strong sense of self enables aspiring athletes to better prepare for the inevitable challenges and transitions that come with stepping away from sports.

Dannie, emphasizing the significance of cultivating skills to prepare for retirement during an athletic career, advocated for a mindset that involves regular reflection on the journey and its applicability to other areas of life. "Look back on what sports has been in each sector of your life. What is your common theme? How can you carry that theme once you graduate and once you take the field away from it? How can you still have that feeling and change your field? Change your team? I think that has been something that has been really helpful." This ability to continually look for the lessons in sport is one that this participant believes will help athletes who are facing retirement to more easily see the transferability of their skills, passion, and drive.

The participants in the study emphasized the significance of looking at the big picture and not getting too bogged down in the day-to-day pressures of athletic performance to "not take it too seriously" (Issa, Erica). They shared how easy it was to lose sight of what truly mattered amid the intense competition and the pursuit of success. Jess emphasized this message that it is about the experience and the relationships. "Four years is bigger than one game. . . . Wins or losses, it really doesn't matter in the end. It doesn't matter if you think things should go one way or not. They can always turn out the way you don't want, but in the end it's about the people who were there next to you the whole way." Erica highlighted this in her suggestion that there is a need to "take a step back and enjoy it, soak in the moments with your teammates and like win/loss whatever, because big picture it ends, it was a cool awesome chapter in your life that you're lucky to have had." This message was echoed by Jess as she emphasized that it is important to not let major life decisions be made solely around sports performance, especially as it relates to education. This type of emphasis takes away opportunities that young athletes cannot even see that they might need in the future.

Henry's perspective offers a valuable insight into the balance between sacrifice and personal development in elite sport. While he acknowledged the necessity of making sacrifices to excel in sports, he emphasized the importance of maintaining a focus on personal growth and becoming the person one aspires to be. It's about recognizing that being an athlete is just one part of a larger identity that encompasses various roles, relationships, and personal values. "If you want to have a lot of success, you need to be all in and make sacrifices. But there's stuff in your life that's always going to be more important like family and how we treat people. I don't think there's anything wrong with going all in on something because you're going to be able to live with what happens." Henry's perspective emphasizes that it is not about detracting from athletic commitment that creates balance, it is remembering all the other aspects of oneself are also important. In essence, it is about embracing the complexity of being a whole person and integrating all aspects of one's life. This enables athletes to stay dedicated to their sports while also cultivating a sense of balance and fulfillment in other areas of their lives.

Lastly, Issa shared that she believes that there were some strategies for coping that she wishes she had implemented throughout her athletic career and into retirement. Her recommendation for young athletes included, "Appreciate it. Write down what it means to you and write down what you learned. I think if I had really thought about things like that before it ended I would've been in a little bit clearer of a space after. . . . I would've been able to look at it and say look at all the things that it meant to you. I think that would've been helpful." She expressed that using the term "retirement" to describe the end of an athletic career may be a bit misleading. While the competitive aspect of the career may come to an end, if the transition is handled successfully, the athletic journey will always remain a cherished part of one's identity, filled with pride and fond memories.

Bibliography

Alfermann, D. (2000). Causes and consequences of sport career termination. In D. Lavallee & P. Wylleman (Eds.), *Career transitions in sport: International perspective* (pp. 45–58). Morgantown: Fitness Information Technology.

Alfermann, D., Stambulova, N., & Zemaityte, A. (2004). Reactions to sport career termination: A cross-national comparison of German, Lithuanian, and Russian athletes. *Psychology of Sport and Exercise, 5*(1), 61–75. https://doi.org/10.1016/S1469-0292(02)00050-X.

Aoun, S. M., Keegan, O., Roberts, A., & Breen, L. J. (2020). The impact of bereavement support on wellbeing: A comparative study between Australia and Ireland. *Palliative Care and Social Practice*, *14*, 263235242093513. https://doi.org/10.1177/2632352420935132.

Aoun, S. M., Breen, L. J., Howting, D. A., Rumbold, B., McNamara, B., & Hegney, D. (2015). Who needs bereavement support? A population based survey of bereavement risk and support need. *PLOS ONE*, *10*(3), e0121101. https://doi.org/10.1371/journal.pone.0121101.

Arizmendi, B. J., & O'Connor, M.-F. (2015). What is "normal" in grief? *Australian Critical Care*, *28*(2), 58–62. https://doi.org/10.1016/j.aucc.2015.01.005.

Attig, T. (2004). Disenfranchised grief revisited: Discounting hope and love. *Omega: Journal of Death and Dying, 49*(3), 197–215. https://doi.org/10.2190/P4TT-J3BF-KFDR-5JB1.

Averill, J. R. (1968). Grief: Its nature and significance. *Psychological Bulletin, 70*(6, Pt.1), 721–48. https://doi.org/10.1037/h0026824.

Barcza-Renner, K., Shipherd, A., & Basevitch, I. (2020). A qualitative examination of sport retirement in former NCAA division I athletes. *Journal of Athlete Development and Experience*, *2*(1). https://doi.org/10.25035/jade.02.01.01.

Bean, C. N., Fortier, M., Post, C., & Chima, K. (2014). Understanding how organized youth sport may be harming individual players within the family unit: A literature review. *International Journal of Environmental Research and Public Health, 11*(10), 10226–68. https://doi.org/10.3390/ijerph111010226.

Blakelock, D. J., Chen, M. A., & Prescott, T. (2016). Psychological distress in elite adolescent soccer players following deselection. *Journal of Clinical Sport Psychology, 10*(1), 59–77. https://doi.org/10.1123/jcsp.2015-0010.

Bonanno, G. A., & Kaltman, S. (2001). The varieties of grief experience. *Clinical Psychology Review*, *21*(5), 705–34. https://doi.org/10.1016/S0272-7358(00)00062-3.

Borak, D., Costakis, H., & Crawford, L. (2022). Athletic identity and identity foreclosure among student athletes at a NJCAA institution. *Journal of Higher Education Theory and Practice, 22*(7), Article 7. https://doi.org/10.33423/jhetp.v22i7.5286.

Brenner, J. S., LaBotz, M., Sugimoto, D., & Stracciolini, A. (2019). The psychosocial implications of sport specialization in pediatric athletes. *Journal of Athletic Training, 54*(10), 1021–29. https://doi.org/10.4085/1062-6050-394-18.

Brewer, B., & Cornelius, A. (2001). Norms and factorial invariance of the Athletic Identity Measurement Scale. *Academic Athletic Journal, 15*(2), 103–13. https://krex.k-state.edu/handle/2097/43141.

Brewer, B. W., & Pepitas, A. J. (2017). Athletic identity foreclosure. *Current Opinions in Psychology, 16,* 112–18. https://doi.org/10.1016/j.copsyc.2017.05.004.

Brewer, B. W., Van Raalte, J. L., Cornelius, A. E., & Pans, M. (2022). Third-generation quantitative assessment of athletic identity: Clarifying the concept. *International Journal of Sport Psychology, 53*, 434–58. https://doi.org/10.7352/IJSP.2022.53.434.

Brewer, B. W., Van Raalte, J. L., & Linder, D. E. (1993). Athletic identity: Hercules' muscles or achilles heel? *International Journal of Sport Psychology, 24*, 237–54.

Broadwater, A. (2022, July 25). Constantly looking at old pictures of your body? Read this advice. HuffPost. https://www.huffpost.com/entry/body-grief-missing-old-body_l_62d80ed8e4b000da23fa9958.

Brown, C. J., Webb, T. L., Robinson, M. A., & Cotgreave, R. (2018). Athletes' experiences of social support during their transition out of elite sport: An interpretive phenomenological analysis. *Psychology of Sport and Exercise, 36*, 71–80. https://doi.org/10.1016/j.psychsport.2018.01.003.

Buckley, G. L., Hall, L. E., Lassemillante, A.-C. M., Ackerman, K. E., & Belski, R. (2019). Retired athletes and the intersection of food and body: A systematic literature review exploring compensatory behaviours and body change. *Nutrients*, *11*(6), 1395. https://doi.org/10.3390/nu11061395.

Cacciatore, J., Thieleman, K., Fretts, R., & Jackson, L. B. (2021). What is good grief support? Exploring the actors and actions in social support after traumatic grief. *PLoS ONE*, *16*(5), e0252324. https://doi.org/10.1371/journal.pone.0252324.

Cesur-Soysal, G., & Arı, E. (2022). How we disenfranchise grief for self and other: An empirical study. *OMEGA – Journal of Death and Dying*, 1–20. https://doi.org/10.1177/00302228221075203.

Chang, C., Putukian, M., Aerni, G., Diamond, A., Hong, G., Ingram, Y., Reardon, C. L., & Wolanin, A. (2020). Mental health issues and psychological factors in athletes: Detection, management, effect on performance and prevention: American Medical Society for Sports Medicine Position Statement—Executive Summary. *British Journal of Sports Medicine*, *54*(4), 216–20. https://doi.org/10.1136/bjsports-2019-101583.

Coker, M. C., & Riforgiate, S. E. (2023). Organizing emotions throughout disenfranchised grief: Virtual support group sensemaking through emotion discourses. *Sustainability, 15*(10), Article 10. https://doi.org/10.3390/su15108012.

Corr, C. A. (1999). Enhancing the concept of disenfranchised grief. *Omega: Journal of Death and Dying, 38* (1), 1–20. https://doi.org/10.2190/LD26-42A6-1EAV-3MDN.

Costa, B. M., Hall, L., & Stewart, J. (2007). Qualitative exploration of the nature of grief-related beliefs and expectations. *Omega, 55*(1), 27–56. https://doi.org/10.2190/CL20-02G6-607R-8561.

de Subijana, C. L., Galatti, L., Moreno, R., & Chamorro, J. L. (2020). Analysis of the athletic career and retirement depending on the type of sport: A comparison between individual and team sports. *International Journal of Environmental Research and Public Health, 17*(24). https://doi.org/10.3390/ijerph17249265.

Den Elzen, K., Breen, L. J., & Neimeyer, R. A. (2023) Rewriting grief following bereavement and non-death loss: a pilot writing-for-wellbeing study, *British Journal of Guidance & Counselling, 1–19,* https://doi.org/10.1080/03069885.2022.2160967.

Doka, K. J. (2016). *Grief is a journey: Finding your path through loss.* Atria Books.

———. (2008). Disenfranchised grief in historical and cultural perspective. In M. S. Stroebe, R. O. Hansson, H. Schut, & W. Stroebe (Eds.), *Handbook of bereavement research and practice: Advances in theory and intervention.* (pp. 223–40). American Psychological Association. https://doi.org/10.1037/14498-011.

———. (1989). *Disenfranchised Grief: Recognizing Hidden Sorrow.* Lexington Books.

Douglas, K. & Carless, D. (2009). Abandoning the performance narrative: Two women's stories of transition from professional sport. *Journal of Applied Sport Psychology, 21*(2), 213–30. https://doi.org/10.1080/10413200902795109.

Ellemers, N., Spears, R., & Doosje, B. (2002). Self and social identity. *Annual Review of Psychology, 53*(1), 161–86. https://doi.org/10.1146/annurev.psych.53.100901.135228.

Fortunato, V., & Marchant, D. (1999). Forced retirement from elite football in Australia. *Journal of Personal and Interpersonal Loss, 4*(3), 269–80. https://doi.org/10.1080/10811449908409735.

Fowlkes, M. R. (1990). The social regulation of grief. *Sociological Forum, 5*(4), 635–52. https://doi.org/10.1007/BF01115395.

Gitterman, A., & Knight, C. (2019). Non-death loss: Grieving for the loss of familiar place and for precious time and associated opportunities. *Clinical Social Work Journal, 47*. https://doi.org/10.1007/s10615-018-0682-5.

Good, A., Brewer, B., Petitpas, A., Vanraalte, J., & Mahar, M. (1993). Identity foreclosure, athletic identity, and college sport participation. *Academic Athletic Journal, 8*, 1–12.

Gouttebarge, V., Castaldelli-Maia, J. M., Gorczynski, P., Hainline, B., Hitchcock, M. E., Kerkhoffs, G. M., Rice, S. M., & Reardon, C. L. (2019). Occurrence of mental health symptoms and disorders in current and former elite athletes: A systematic review and meta-analysis. *British Journal of Sports Medicine, 53*(11), 700–6. https://doi.org/10.1136/bjsports-2019-100671.

Grove, J. R., Lavallee, D., & Gordon, S. (1997). Coping with retirement from sport: The influence of athletic identity. *Journal of Applied Sport Psychology, 9*(2), 191–203. https://doi.org/10.1080/10413209708406481.

Hall, C. (2014). Bereavement theory: Recent developments in our understanding of grief and bereavement. *Bereavement Care*, *33*, 7–12. https://doi.org/10.1080/02682621.2014.902610.

Harris, D. L., & Winokuer, H. R. (2019). Living losses: Nonfinite loss, ambiguous loss, and chronic sorrow. In *Principles and Practice of Grief Counseling* (pp. 121–37). Springer Publishing Company. https://doi.org/10.1891/9780826173331.0008.

Hickey, C., & Roderick, M. (2017). The presentation of possible selves in everyday life: The management of identity among transitioning professional athletes. *Sociology of Sport Journal, 34*(3), 270–80. https://doi.org/10.1123/ssj.2017-0018.

Houlston, D. R. (1982). The occupational mobility of professional athletes. *International Review of Sport Sociology, 17*(2), 15–28. https://doi.org/10.1177/101269028201700202.

Howarth, R. (2011). Concepts and controversies in grief and loss. *Journal of Mental Health Counseling*, *33*(1), 4–10. https://doi.org/10.17744/mehc.33.1.900m56162888u737.

Jayanthi, N., Pinkham, C., Dugas, L., Patrick, B., & LaBella, C. (2013). Sports specialization in young athletes. *Sports Health*, *5*(3), 251–57. https://doi.org/10.1177/1941738112464626.

Kaul, N. (2017). Involuntary retirement due to injury in elite athletes from competitive sport: A qualitative approach. *Journal of the Indian Academy of Applied Psychology, 43*(2), 305–15. Retrieved from: https://www.researchgate.net/publication/322695870_Involuntary_Retirement_due_to_Injury_in_Elite_Athletes_from_Competit ive_Sport_A_Qualitative_Approach.

Kirby, E., Kenny, K., Broom, A., MacArtney, J., & Good, P. (2018). The meaning and experience of bereavement support: A qualitative interview study of bereaved family caregivers. *Palliative and Supportive Care*, *16*(4), 396–405. https://doi.org/10.1017/S1478951517000475.

Knight, C., & Gitterman, A. (2019). Ambiguous loss and its disenfranchisement: The need for social work intervention. *Families in Society: Journal of Contemporary Social Services*, *100*(2), 164–73. https://doi.org/10.1177/1044389418799937.

Küttel, A., Boyle, E., & Schmid, J. (2017). Factors contributing to the quality of the transition out of elite sports in Swiss, Danish, and Polish athletes. *Psychology of Sport and Exercise*, *29*, 27–39. https://doi.org/10.1016/j.psychsport.2016.11.008.

Lally, P. (2007). Identity and athletic retirement: A prospective study. *Psychology of Sport and Exercise, 8*(1), 85–99. https://doi.org/10.1016/j.psychsport.2006.03.003.

Lavallee, D., Gordon, S., & Grove, J. R. (1997) Retirement from sport and the loss of athletic identity. *Journal of Personal and Interpersonal Loss*, 2(2), 129–47. https://doi.org/10.1080/10811449708414411.

Lavallee, D., & Robinson, H. K. (2007). In pursuit of an identity: A qualitative exploration of retirement from women's artistic gymnastics. *Psychology of Sport and Exercise, 8*(1), 119–41. https://doi.org/10.1016/j.psychsport.2006.05.003.

Lochbaum, M., Cooper, S., & Limp, S. (2022). The Athletic Identity Measurement Scale: A systematic review with meta-analysis from 1993 to 2021. *European Journal of Investigation in Health, Psychology and Education, 12*(9), 1391–1414. MDPI AG. Retrieved from http://dx.doi.org/10.3390/ejihpe12090097.

Mannes, Z. L., Waxenberg, L. B., Cottler, L. B., Perlstein, W. M., Burrell, L. E., Ferguson, E. G., Edwards, M. E., & Ennis, N. (2019). Prevalence and correlates of psychological distress among retired elite athletes: A systematic review. *International Review of Sport and Exercise Psychology, 12*(1), 265–94. https://doi.org/10.1080/1750984X.2018.1469162.

Manthey, C., & Smith, J. (2023). "You need to allow yourself to grieve that loss and that identity." College athletes' transition to life after college sport. *Journal of Athlete Development and Experience, 5*(1). https://doi.org/10.25035/jade.05.01.02.

Marcia, J. E. (1966). Development and validation of ego-identity status. *Journal of Personality and Social Psychology, 3,* 551–58.

Martin, L., Fogarty, G., & Albion, M. (2014). Changes in athletic identity and life satisfaction of elite athletes as a function of retirement status. *Journal of Applied Sport Psychology, 26*(1), 96–110. https://doi.org/10.1080/10413200.2013.798371.

McCall, G. J., & Simmons, J. L. (1978). *Identities and interactions.* Free Press.

McGannon, K. R., Staden, T. G., & McMahon, J. (2022). From superhero to human: A narrative analysis of digital news stories of retirement from the NFL due to injury. *Journal of Applied Sport Psychology, 34*(5), 938–57. https://doi.org/10.1080/10413200.2021.1987351.

McGlinchey, T., Saward, C., Healy, L., & Sarkar, M. (2022). "From everything to nothing in a split second": Elite youth players' experiences of release from professional football academies. *Frontiers in Sports and Active Living, 4,* 941482.https://doi.org/10.3389/fspor.2022.941482.

Menke, D. J., & Germany, M. L. (2019). Reconstructing athletic identity: College athletes and sport retirement. *Journal of Loss & Trauma, 24*(1), 17–30. https://doi-org./10.1080/15325024.2018.1522475.

Miller, L., & Buttell, F. P. (2018). Are NCAA Division I athletes prepared for end-of-athletic-career transition? A literature review. *Journal of Evidence-Informed Social Work, 15*(1), 52–70. https://doi.org/10.1080/23761407.2017.1411305.

Murphy, S. M. (1996). Transitions in competitive sport: Maximizing individual potential. In S. M. Murphy (Ed.), *Sport psychology interventions* (pp. 331–46). Human Kinetics.

Neimeyer R. A., & Jordan J. R. (2002). Disenfranchisement as empathic failure. In Doka K. (Ed.), *Disenfranchised grief* (pp. 97–117). Champaign, IL: Research Press.

Packman, W., Carmack, B. J., Katz, R., Carlos, F., Field, N. P., & Landers, C. (2014). Online survey as empathic bridging for the disenfranchised grief of pet loss. *OMEGA - Journal of Death and Dying, 69*(4), 333–56. https://doi.org/10.2190/OM.69.4.a.

Papa, A., Lancaster, N. G., & Kahler, J. (2014). Commonalities in grief responding across bereavement and non-bereavement losses. *Journal of Affective Disorders*, *161*, 136–43. https://doi.org/10.1016/j.jad.2014.03.018.

Papa, A., & Maitoza, R. (2013). The role of loss in the experience of grief: The case of job loss. *Journal of Loss and Trauma*, 18(2), 152–69. doi:10.1080/15325024.2012.684580.

Papathomas, A., Petrie, T., & Plateau, C. (2017). Changes in body image perceptions upon leaving elite sport: The retired female athlete paradox. *Sport, Exercise, and Performance Psychology, 7,* 30–45. https://doi.org/10.1037/spy0000111.

Park, S., Lavallee, D., & Tod, D. (2013). Athletes' career transition out of sport: A systematic review. *International Review of Sport and Exercise Psychology, 6*(1), 22–53. https://doi.org/10.1080/1750984X.2012.687053.

Parkes, C. M. (1988). Bereavement as a psychosocial transition: Processes of adaptation to change. *Journal of Social Issues*, *44*(3), 53–65. https://doi.org/10.1111/j.1540-4560.1988.tb02076.x.

Peña-Vargas, C., Armaiz-Peña, G., & Castro-Figueroa, E. (2021). A biopsychosocial approach to grief, depression, and the role of emotional regulation. *Behavioral Sciences*, *11*(8), Article 8. https://doi.org/10.3390/bs11080110.

Penman, E. L., Breen, L. J., Hewitt, L. Y., & Prigerson, H. G. (2014). Public attitudes about normal and pathological grief. *Death Studies*, *38*(6–10), 510–16. https://doi.org/10.1080/07481187.2013.873839.

Petitpas, A. J. (1978). Identity foreclosure: A unique challenge. *Personal and Guidance Journal, 56,* 558–61.

Petitpas, A. J., & France, T. (2010). Identity Foreclosure in Sport. In S. J. Hanrahan, & M. B. Andersen (Eds.). *Routledge handbook of applied sport psychology* (pp. 282–91). Routledge.

Petitpas, A., Van Raalte, J. L., & Brewer, B. W. (2013). Development and current status of athlete career assistance programs in the USA. In N. Stambulova & T. Ryba (Eds.), *Athletes' careers across cultures* (pp. 222–34). Routledge.

Ratcliffe, M. J., & Richardson, L. F. (2023). Grief over non-death losses: A phenomenological perspective. *Passion: Journal of the European Philosophical Society for the Study of Emotions*. https://eprints.whiterose.ac.uk/193069/.

Ratcliffe, M., Richardson, L., & Millar, B. (2023). On the appropriateness of grief to its object. *Journal of the American Philosophical Association*, *9*(2), 318–34. https://doi.org/10.1017/apa.2021.55.

Rice, S. M., Purcell, R., De Silva, S., Mawren, D., McGorry, P. D., & Parker, A. G. (2016). The mental health of elite athletes: A narrative systematic review. *Sports Medicine, 46*(9), 1333–53. https://doi.org/10.1007/s40279-016-0492-2.

Robson, P., & Walter, T. (2013). Hierarchies of loss: A critique of disenfranchised grief. *OMEGA - Journal of Death and Dying*, *66*(2), 97–119. https://doi.org/10.2190/OM.66.2.a.

Schmid, J., Conzelmann, A., Engel, R., Kuettel, A., & Schmid, M. J. (2023). Retirement from elite sport and self-esteem: A longitudinal study over 12 years. *Frontiers in Psychology, 14*. https://www.frontiersin.org/articles/10.3389/fpsyg.2023.1176573.

Silver, M. P. (2021). Adaptation to athletic retirement and perceptions about aging: A qualitative study of retired Olympic athletes. *Journal of Aging and Physical Activity*, *29*(5), 828–42. https://doi.org/10.1123/japa.2020-0270.

Smith, P. H., & Delgado, H. (2020). Working with non-death losses in counseling: An overview of grief needs and approaches. *Adultspan Journal*, *19*(2), 118–27. https://doi.org/10.1002/adsp.12100.

Sothern, N. A., & O'Gorman, J. (2021). Exploring the mental health and wellbeing of professional academy footballers in England. *Soccer & Society*, *22*(6), 641–54. https://doi.org/10.1080/14660970.2021.1952693.

Stets, J. E., & Burke, P. J. (2014). Self-esteem and identities. *Sociological Perspectives, 57*(4), 409–33. https://doi.org/10.1177/0731121414536141.

Stryker, S. (2008). From Mead to a structural symbolic interactionism and beyond. *Annual Review of Sociology, 34*(1), 15–31. https://doi.org/10.1146/annurev.soc.34.040507.134649.

———. (2000). Identity competition: Key to differential social movement participation? In S. Stryker, T. Owens, & R. White (Eds.), *Self, identity, and social movements* (pp. 21–40). University of Minnesota Press.

———. (2002). *Symbolic interactionism: A social structural version.* Blackburn Press.

———. (1968). Identity salience and role performance: The relevance of symbolic interaction theory for family research. *Journal of Marriage and Family*, *30*(4), 558–64. https://doi.org/10.2307/349494.

Stryker, S., & Burke, P. J. (2000). The past, present, and future of an identity theory. *Social Psychology Quarterly*, *63*, 284–97. https://doi.org/10.2307/2695840.

Torregrosa, M., Ramis, Y., Pallarés, S., Azócar, F., & Selva, C. (2015). Olympic athletes back to retirement: A qualitative longitudinal study. *Psychology of Sport and Exercise*, *21*, 50–56. https://doi.org/10.1016/j.psychsport.2015.03.003.

Vignoles, V. (2017). Identity: Personal AND Social. In Kay Deaux and Mark Snyder (Eds.) *Oxford Handbook of Personality and Social Psychology* (62–82). Oxford University Press.

Weiss, O. (2001). Identity reinforcement in sport: Revisiting the symbolic interactionist legacy. *International Review for the Sociology of Sport, 36*(4), 393–405. https://doi.org/10.1177/101269001036004002.

Wiese – Bjornstal, D. M., & Smith, A. M. (1993). Counseling strategies for enhanced recovery of injured athletes within a team approach. In D. Pargman (Ed.), *Psychological bases of sport injuries* (pp. 149–82). Fitness Information Technology.

Wilkinson, R. J. (2021). A literature review exploring the mental health issues in academy football players following career termination due to deselection or injury and how counselling could support future players. *Counselling & Psychotherapy Research, 21*(4), 859–68. https://doi.org/10.1002/capr.12417.

Wippert, P.-M., & Wippert, J. (2010). The effects of involuntary athletic career termination on psychological distress. *Journal of Clinical Sport Psychology, 4*, 133–49. https://doi.org/10.1123/jcsp.4.2.133.

———. (2008). Perceived stress and prevalence of traumatic stress symptoms following athletic career termination. *Journal of Clinical Sport Psychology, 2*(1), 1–16. https://doi.org/10.1123/jcsp.2.1.1.

Yehene, E., Manevich, A., & Rubin, S. S. (2021). Caregivers' grief in acquired non-death interpersonal loss (NoDIL): A process-based model with implications for theory, research, and intervention. *Frontiers in Psychology*, *12*. https://www.frontiersin.org/articles/10.3389/fpsyg.2021.676536.

Zisook, S., & Shear, K. (2009). Grief and bereavement: What psychiatrists need to know. *World Psychiatry*, *8*(2), 67–74. https://doi.org/10.1002/j.2051-5545.2009.tb00217.x.

Index

About the Authors

Gary Senecal received his PhD in psychology from the University of West Georgia in 2015. He currently serves as an Assistant Professor of Human Services & Rehabilitation Studies at Assumption University in Worcester, Massachusetts. His research focuses on existential psychology, humanistic psychology, the phenomenological psychology of violence, and the career transitions of individuals who have retired from or been deselected from careers that exposed them to regular violent endeavors (in particular, contact sport athletes and military veterans). His current book, *American and NATO Ally Reintegration: The Trauma of Social Isolation & Cultural Chasms*, compares and contrasts the reintegration experiences of American and NATO ally veterans from the War in Afghanistan. He is a combat veteran of the United States Army and resides in Worcester, Massachusetts, with his family.

Christian Williams is an Assistant Professor in the Department of Human Services and Rehabilitation Studies at Assumption University, where she also serves as the coordinator of the concentration Working with Children and Adolescents in Community Settings. She has a PhD in clinical psychology, an MS in psychology, and an MA in rehabilitation counseling. As a licensed mental health counselor (LMHC) with eighteen years of experience, Christian has worked with individuals, families, and children in the areas of trauma, resilience, grief, and substance abuse. Her research focuses on understanding the experience of adversity, including addiction, peer and social support, disenfranchised grief, self-efficacy, and posttraumatic growth. She draws on her extensive knowledge and experience to explore the intricacies of human behavior and the profound impact of trauma and resilience on individuals and families.